Social issues and the social services

Social issues and the social services

Edited by Malcolm J. Brown

Charles Knight & Co. Ltd.
London
1974

Charles Knight & Co. Ltd.
25 New Street Square, London EC4A 3JA
Sovereign Way, Tonbridge, Kent

ISBN 0 85314 215 7

Made and printed in England by
STAPLES PRINTERS LIMITED
at The Stanhope Press, Rochester, Kent.

Contents

Acknowledgements

The editor and contributors are grateful for many ideas garnered from a wide range of writers. We are grateful, too, for permission from publishers to reprint extracts selected. The publishers and journals concerned are as follows:

Academic & General Publishers; Aldine Publishing Co.; Allen Lane; George Allen & Unwin Ltd.; the Executive Editor of American Psychological Association; George Bell & Sons; Ernest Benn Ltd. (for Williams & Norgate); *Journal of the British Association of Social Workers*; Brown University Press; Cambridge University Press; Jonathan Cape Ltd.; *Case Conference*; the Director of the Catholic Housing Aid Society; Charles Knight & Co. Ltd.; the University of Chicago Press; *Child Care*; City of Liverpool Planning Department for their publication 'Social malaise: an interim report'; Columbia University Press; Crosby Lockwood Staples Ltd.; the Director of Family Welfare Association; the Greater London Council; the Controller of Her Majesty's Stationery Office; Hutchinson Publishing Group Ltd.; the King Edward's Hospital Fund for London; Local Government Operational Research Unit; Macmillan Journals Ltd.; Manchester University Press; *Municipal and Public Services Journal*; the Institute of Municipal Treasurers and Accountants; the Secretary General of the National Housing and Town Planning Council; *New Society*; Oxford University Press (for the Institute of Race Relations); Pergamon Press Ltd.; *Political Quarterly*; *Political and Economic Planning*; *Race Today*; Random House Inc.; Routledge & Kegan Paul Ltd.; *Public Administration*; *Times Educational Supplement*; the University of Birmingham; Scottish Academic Press; *Public Health Papers* (published by the World Health Organization.); *Case Con.*

Full details of the material quoted will be found in bibliographies at the end of each chapter.

Notes on Contributors

Malcolm J. Brown began his career in social work in the London Probation Service. He worked in Zambia as a social work administrator, and then as a senior lecturer in the University of Zambia. He took his M.S.W. at the University of Pennsylvania, where he spent a year in a child care agency. He then spent a year as United Nations social welfare adviser in Liberia.

He was at the University of Bradford for three years as a lecturer in social work management and social work research. When the Local Authority Social Services Act was implemented he joined the staff of Birmingham University, who were setting up short courses for the newly appointed directors of social services. He is now the Director of Social Work and Post-Experience Courses at the University of Birmingham.

He is the author of some 60 publications on social work. His last book, written with Robert Foren, was *Planning for Service*, London, Charles Knight, 1971.

David Fruin is Senior Lecturer in Research Methods at the National Institute for Social Work Training and is involved in the Institute's action research studies in local authority social service departments. His special interest lies in information systems in the social services. He recently spent five years in the United States, obtaining his Ph.D. in psychology from Johns Hopkins University with a thesis on the assessment of creativity. While in the United States, he participated in a Community Action Agency project and was Director of Research for the Baltimore Job Corps programme. In addition to working for IBM and Burroughs Corporation, he assisted in setting up an experimental village community in Virginia.

W. B. Harbert trained for social work at Hull and Manchester Universities. On qualifying as a psychiatric social worker in 1955, he worked in the Birmingham mental health service where he made a special study of long-stay psychiatric patients, their rehabilitation and after-care.

After a short period in a town clerk's department, where he served as social services co-ordinator and training officer, he became general secretary to the Liverpool Personal Service Society in 1965 and was appointed Director of Social Services for the London Borough of Hackney in December 1970. He served on the Home Office Advisory Council for probation and after-care 1968–72, and is a member of the Finer Committee on one-parent families. Towards the end of 1973, he was appointed Director of Social Services for the new County of Avon.

Arthur Hunt joined the Probation Service in 1951, following studies at Nottingham University and training at Rainer House. Apart from a year at the Tavistock Clinic (1953–4), he served in the Nottinghamshire Probation Service until appointed principal probation officer in Southampton in 1959. He has occupied the post of Director of Social Services in Southampton since January 1971, and will be the new director for Hampshire, in 1974.

He served as a member of the Home Office's Probation Advisory and Training Board (1962–5) and the Advisory Council for Probation and After-care (1965–70), and as a member of the Training Sub-Committees of these bodies. His particular interest is in professional social work education. Most of his published work focuses on the potentials of casework practised within the framework of judicial administration.

Robin Huws-Jones, C.B.E. was principal of the National Institute for Social Work Training 1961–72. He graduated from Liverpool University, and was a lecturer in the Social Sciences Department at Liverpool University 1937–9. He was the director of social sciences courses at University College, Swansea 1948–61. In 1964 he was visiting Professor at the University of Minnesota. He worked as a member of the Minister of Health's long-term study group 1965–9, and was on the Committee on Local Authority and Allied Personal Social Services 1965–8. Since 1967 he has been on the North-East Metropolitan Regional Hospital Board; Mr. Huws-Jones has also been a member of the Central Council for Education and Training in Social Work. He is the author of *The Doctor and the Social Services*, London, 1971 and has contributed to journals.

Barbara Kahan read English at Cambridge and Social Studies at the London School of Economics. She became an HMI of factories in the industrial midlands for five years, doing youth club work as a sideline. She was children's officer in Oxfordshire 1951–70, where the local authority appointed the first full-time caseworker on preventive work in 1952, and she pioneered work with young offenders within the local authority services. As a member of the Home Office Advisory Council, and Central Training Council, and as president and executive member of the Association of Children's Officers, she was involved in many national activities involving training, service developments, new legislation and professional organisations. In 1970 she became deputy chief inspector in the children's department of the Home Office and now heads the development group of the new Social Work Service of the Department of Health and Social Security.

Robert Kornreich is a research assistant in the School of Applied Social Studies, University of Bradford. He is carrying out research into the ways in which 'practitioners' view 'consumers' and also teaches sociology and research methods. His personal research is an analysis of the agitation against the Contagious Diseases Acts, 1864–86, the system of state-regulated common prostitution in Britain.

Professor François Lafitte has been head of Birmingham University's Social Administration Department since 1959. Before than he worked for many years on the editorial staff of *The Times* as a specialist in social policy questions. He began his career on the research staff of Political and Economic Planning. He is Chairman of the British Pregnancy Advisory Service and a member of the development corporation in the new town of Redditch. He has written on various aspects of society and social administration.

J. Wallace McCulloch is an experienced social worker whose main area of practice was in the mental health field before he joined the Medical Research Council Unit for the Study of Epidemiological Factors in Psychiatric Illness. During his six years with the M.R.C., he collaborated in a series of researches into the problems of suicidal behaviour.

He is at present a senior lecturer in the School of Applied Social Studies at the University of Bradford. His current research interest is with the direction of a Home Office-sponsored study of the problems of immigrants and the social services. He is author and co-author of many published papers and author of two books, *Psychiatry for Social Workers*, 1969, and *Suicidal Behaviour* 1972, both published by Pergamon, Oxford.

Ken McDermott worked as a schoolmaster in Liverpool, and joined the probation service in 1952. He specialised in marital conciliation, and then prison and Borstal after-care, and became a senior probation officer in 1962. He helped to develop community engagements and was appointed director of the first Home Office Community Development Project in the Scotland Road area of Liverpool in 1969. He became Deputy Director of Social Services in Birkenhead in 1971.

Adrian Sinfield is Senior Lecturer in Sociology at the University of Essex. He has also taught at Bryn Mawr Graduate Department of Social Work and Social Research, Pennsylvania and at the Columbia University School of Social Work, New York, 1969–70, and has served as assessor to the Council for Social Work Training. He has carried out research on the impact of unemployment on men and their families on Tyneside, 1963–4, and in Syracuse, New York State, 1964–5. He has acted as consultant on the long-term unemployed to the Organisation for Economic Co-operation and Development, Paris, and as consultant on industrial social welfare to the United Nations. His publications include, *The Long-term Unemployed*, OECD, Paris 1968 and *Which Way for Social Work?* Fabian Society, London 1970.

Maurice G. Speed has spent all his working life in the service of local government, holding appointments of county welfare officer in Devon and director of social work for Midlothian, East Lothian and Peebles before joining Cheshire in November 1970. He is a past president of the Association of Directors of Social Services and a member of the Central Council for Education and Training in Social Work. Although practical rather than academic by nature, he accepted an invitation to contribute to this book in the belief that the solution to social problems may emerge more easily if some social administrators are prepared to put their views to public judgment. With the help of a Fellowship from the Council of Europe, he visited Sweden in 1965 to study the social services in that country. He has recently been made a member of the new Personal Social Services Council.

Kenneth M. Spencer read geography at the University of Liverpool where he obtained both his B.A. and M.A. degrees. He was a research assistant at the School of Architecture in the University of Liverpool 1965–7. In 1967 he moved to the newly established Centre for Urban and Regional Studies at Birmingham University as a research associate and later senior research associate. His research interests in housing were developed at the Centre. In 1969 he moved to his present post as lecturer in the Institute of Local Government Studies in the University of Birmingham. He was one of the British delegates to the United Nations Seminar on Socially Deprived Families in 1970. His publications include, 'Housing and socially deprived families' in R. Holman (ed.) *Socially deprived families in Britain*, London, Bedford Square Press, 1970, *Aspects of Administration in a Large Local Authority*, with B. N. Downie, J. R. Long and P. K. Rider, which is research study number 7 of the Royal Commission on Local Government in England, London, HMSO 1968; and he has contributed to various journals.

Introduction

Malcolm J. Brown

Times of radical change inevitably carry with them seeds of frustration and disappointment. People, it seems, are unable accurately to evaluate the consequences of any major development, but insist upon anticipating Utopia, where usually only the potential for relatively minor improvements exists. If there has been excessive criticism of the current situation, the resultant frustrations and disappointments with the new position are likely to be all the greater. This deficiency is by no means exclusive to the enthusiastic layman but is a condition also experienced by the 'experts' in the forefront of change.

Writers of official reports, not unnaturally, are reluctant to see their recommendations 'plop' into the pool of oblivion, but would rather leave their mark upon the history of mankind. To be highly critical of the present (as a justification for the need for change); to be over-optimistic about the future (as an incentive for following their particular recommendations); and to urge speedy transformation from one state to the other (in order that the writers might quickly see the fruits of their efforts), are characteristic of many reports. The Seebohm Report (1968) was no exception.

The Seebohm Committee, appointed 'to review the organisation and responsibilities of the local authority personal social services in England and Wales, and to consider what changes are desirable to secure an effective family service', in the course of its enquiries into the personal social services found:

inadequacies in the amount of provision;
inadequacies in the range of provision;

inadequacies in the qualities of provision;
poor co-ordination of services;
difficult access to services; and
insufficient adaptability.

These defects represented a damning indictment indeed, yet one that could be levied at almost any public service—depending upon the evaluation criteria. The Committee itself did not conduct any research, but relied heavily upon the 'evidence of others'. As Dr. Kershaw (1968) complains, 'the more one studies the report, the more it is evident that it consists largely of the giving of opinions on opinions and that it states only one side of a case which needs prolonged and multi-lateral discussion'. The Committee wanted services that would:

(1) meet needs on the basis of the total requirements of the individual family rather than on the basis of a limited set of symptoms;
(2) provide a clear and comprehensive pattern of responsibility and accountability over the whole field;
(3) attract more resources;
(4) use resources more effectively;
(5) generate adequate recruitment and training of the staff skills which are, or may become, necessary;
(6) meet needs which are at present being neglected;
(7) adapt to changing conditions;
(8) provide a better organisation for collecting and disseminating information relevant to the development of the social services;
(9) be more accessible and comprehensible to those who need to use them;

and made recommendations that it considered most appropriate for attaining them. The underlying philosophy of the Seebohm recommendations represented a departure from the position obtaining in 1968—in so far as service given was an accurate reflection of basic principles. The recommendations encapsulated the 'Seebohm Spirit':

'This new department will, we believe, reach far beyond the discovery and rescue of social casualties; it will enable the greatest possible number of individuals to act reciprocally, giving and receiving service for the well-being of the whole community'.

True to our model, the need for change was seen as being urgent, 'and we (the Committee members) urge the Government to introduce the legislation at the earliest possible date'.

The Bill, and the largely unchanged Act, came as a great disappointment to those who had caught the 'Seebohm spirit'. The Act envisaged that no extra staff or money would be required for its implementation, and did little more than transfer powers and duties from the constituent sections of the local authority to the new unified department. The earlier Scottish Act (HMSO 1968) had laid upon local government the duty to promote the social welfare of the community; much to the annoyance of many social workers and social work supporters, the Act for England and Wales contained no such provision.

The main reason for this is not hard to discover. Social workers and their supporters generated great pressures for early implementation of the report. Seebohm Committee members actively toured the country explaining their proposals and gathering support for their implementation. A 'Seebohm Implementation Group' was brought into being for the purpose of pressurising Government into action. The negative reactions of many members of the medical professions and some members of the magistracy to a number of the Seebohm proposals made the cries of social workers all the more vociferous. During the period of delay some authorities developed plans which placed the personal social services under the control of the medical officer of health.

The overwhelming fear of perpetual doctor domination spurred social workers' efforts to gain instant Seebohm implementations to the maximum. As Thomas (1973) states, 'the pressure succeeded: ministers were persuaded that neither the situation painted in the report nor the uncertainty which it had created were tolerable'. Once the government decided to act, it acted quickly. A consequence of this was that there was insufficient time to enact new powers. A number of important issues, including determining the central government department which was to have responsibility for the personal social services, and the promotion of social welfare, were ignored.

Of itself, the Local Authority Social Services Act, 1970, while implementing the majority of the specific Seebohm recommendations, is little more than one step (albeit a significant one) in the process of rationalisation of the social services. It has brought together the services previously operating in three separate departments and it has placed them under one committee and one director. The repercussions of such a step, however, have been quite dramatic in many areas of the country. The crux of the change centres around the fact that greatly heightened status has been given to the chief officers of the social services, and consequently to the social services themselves. Prior to the implementation of the Act, children's officers, principal social welfare officers, chief mental welfare officers and the like, enjoyed but low status within the authority in relation to say, the chief education officer and the medical officer of health. The unification of the social services rocketed the director up among the big spenders, 'The role maketh the man' and gave the director a new perception of himself, of his department and of his relationships with his committee and his chief officer colleagues. The lessening or elimination of the director's subservience to other chief officers, together with a greater realisation on the part of the newly formed committees of the immense social welfare needs of the community (helped, undoubtedly, by the great publicity given by and to the Seebohm Committee) meant that the department would take its full and rightful place within the local authority. Social services had arrived.

Not that this state was achieved overnight. The process of getting directors into posts was a somewhat unsightly one. For over a year, local authorities in England and Wales were advertising for directors and other senior staff. There was no overall planning or co-ordination for the filling of these appointments and interested personnel often spent many hours in completing forms and attending interviews. One ultimately successful director had completed 42 applications ('The making of a director', 1970) and it is reasonable to suppose that some of the unsuccessful applicants completed many more.* The psychological strains of the prolonged competitive situation; of deciding whether to take one

* This topic is covered very fully by Jef Smith in his chapter 'Top jobs in the Social Services', *The Year Book of Social Policy in Britain, 1971*. Ed. K. Jones, Routledge and Kegan Paul, London, 1972.

directorship offered, or wait for the chance of a bigger one, but risk getting nothing; of prolonged uncertainties as local authorities delayed making their selection, and the frustrating round of related activities, did not bring out the highest qualities of human behaviour.

In times of large-scale opportunities for marked personal advancement, pre-occupation with 'self' is fully understandable. In the event, however, the client, the raison d'être for the new service, slipped somewhat down the priority list. One can only hope that central government will have learnt some lessons for further large-scale change, and that the quality and quantity of future personal social services will have justified the extensive and prolonged setback which was, and still is, being suffered.

While complete information is difficult to collect and collate, there is this general acceptance that there has been a marked deterioration in services which have not yet returned to a pre-unification level. While the 'battle of the bosses' must account for some of this deterioration, it is by no means the only factor. However much change might be welcome, even fought for; when it actually gives evidence of its coming it frequently generates much anxiety. Certainly social workers were to face many changes* and their awareness of, and familiarity with, the concept of anxiety did little to allay their own anxious feelings in the face of so many changes affecting themselves. And anxiety is energy consuming. The newness of the situation itself creates further problems. The absence of priorities, of policies, of procedures, or the lack of familiarity with them, makes for frustration and inefficiency; and a maintenance of standards, in the short term, would have been little short of miraculous.

The most overwhelming anxiety without doubt centred upon the concept of genericism in social work practice. The common base of social work had been one of the main pillars of the case for unification of the personal social services but once it seemed

* The possibilities have been spelled out by Foren and Brown as: changes of role and title; changes of function; changes of caseload; changes of geographical area; changes of 'work-scene' (base); changes of colleagues (membership of new team); changes of leader; changes of clientele; changes of agency policies; changes of agency procedures; changes of professional orientation; and changes of organisational size. *Planning for Service*, Charles Knight, London, 1971.

certain that social workers would need to enlarge their repertoire of knowledge and skills, many got cold feet. Child-care officers dreaded the possibilities of being called to a raving lunatic running amuck in the middle of the night, and mental welfare officers felt most inadequate when it came to deciding whether to take a child into care. While a minority of generically trained officers genuinely welcomed the challenge of a wider caseload and the opportunity of working with families regardless of the variety of problems contained within them, for many workers the dream of unification was becoming something of a nightmare. It needs to be remembered of course that many social workers had not wanted unification but had been less vocal in expressing their fears, doubts and reservations than had been its enthusiastic supporters.

'Going generic' was being seen as something of a milestone by some directors. A few forced through the mixed caseload with little regard for the feelings or abilities of workers. Most went about it steadily however with sympathy for their older and unqualified staff. Even given a great desire to be an 'across the board' worker, an understanding director and sufficient training, consultation and advice, the requirements of such a role stretched the individual to the utmost. With heavy caseloads and little time for stretching, it is still questionable as to how far the average worker can mix his caseload while still offering a quality service.

While those at the lower end of the department hierarchy could do little more than wait and wonder (and worry) about how things were going to turn out, at the top end, once appointments had been made, there was an initial pre-occupation, if not obsession, with organisational structure. While there was no shortage of suggestions as to the forms of structure that might be developed (usually coming from those, who had neither to work for nor to work within them), almost without exception, directors followed the traditional bureaucratic or pyramid model. Excepting the smallest authorities, service was conceived of as being given through the area team and geographic areas of the local authority were placed under the control of an area officer. Nationally, these varied in number from two to fifteen. Within the headquarter's team, the work was carried out by the director with between one to five assistant directors; together with their supporting staff. Each assistant director was to carry functional responsibilities.

Terminology varied but a typical department would have an assistant director for fieldwork, one for residential services, one for planning, research and training and one for finance and administration. A little over half of the directors chose (or had the choice made for them) to function without a deputy. The new structures required (or were made to require) increased personnel and usually, directors were able to persuade committees to seek and obtain the necessary budgetary increases.* Far more senior appointments were made within the department than had been the case prior to unification—the great majority being made from existing staff. This has meant a diminution in the number of face-to-face workers in some instances. While provision has been made for greater numbers of social workers, promotions have, in some departments, only reduced them. The problem has not primarily been one of finance, but availability of trained staff. The more popular areas of the country have fared well. The least popular have not. What with promotions and trained staff leaving for more senior appointments elsewhere, some authorities have less than a third of their trained social workers left at the service-giving level. Whether to risk losing even more trained workers through over-loading them, or whether to recruit substantial numbers of untrained workers with a resultant low level of service to the clientele, is a problem still facing a number of directors.

An increase in the number of senior personnel, while at least temporarily denuding the field, does have the greatest advantage of allowing some time to be given to the consideration of wider issues than those of the individual client—important though he undoubtedly is. One of the main characteristics of the pre-Seebohm era was the belief that anything other than that which had immediate relevance for the client was somehow improper. As a result nearly all grades of professional staff carried caseloads, many children's officers for example were spending more time working with clients than in fulfilling other children's officer functions. While there was a nice human touch to this approach, its cost in relation to neglected alternative functions was very high.

With all resources being thrown into the front-line, all too

* Expenditure on local authority personnel Social Services rose from £267 million in 1969/70 to £401 million in 1970/71.

little, if any, time was given to such vital tasks as ascertaining the overall needs of the community and of attempting to understand fully the problems that existed; of making underlying philosophies explicit; of determining the objectives of the department, of deciding upon priorities (as demands always exceed resources); of thrashing out comprehensive policies; of developing procedures; and of evaluating the services given in a systematic way as a means of constantly improving the impact of the department upon the community which it has been set up to serve. Where these elements are lacking, decisions are made in the absence of adequate information and are often of an ad hoc nature dealing with the specific and being unrelated to wider problems and issues. Where there is no concept of priorities, the most demanding individuals tend to get the most service and the reticent get none. Efforts are often fragmentary, and are hit and miss in quality. In the absence of adequate evaluative criteria, inefficiency and ineffectiveness can be perpetuated year after year. In this situation the shop window becomes more important than the goods upon the shelves.

Perhaps the most encouraging thing following unification is that these matters are now being actively pursued whereas previously they were scarcely ever spoken of. In retrospect it seems quite amazing that this should be the case, none the less, it was so. Departments are still at a very early stage of bringing all things under the microscope and many difficulties are already apparent; but after many years of inactivity, a start has been made. Well over half of the departments in England and Wales have made quite serious effort to study the numbers and needs of chronically sick and disabled people in their areas. Several are spelling out their basic objectives and are doing serious work on determining priorities. About half a dozen are giving considerable time to determining the likely gains of computerising information as a means of aiding the planning processes.

This is most necessary, for Acts of Parliament, which while conferring powers and imposing duties, invariably lack a philosophical base. Further, while listing duties or tasks to be performed, most are deficient in overall objectives and give no direction or guidance as to which particular function or task is more important than another. Central government, being a body sensitive to political pressure, often reflects the popular vogue of the moment.

Its circulars, therefore, in relation to the social services, tend to stress the needs of whichever client group they are making reference to at that particular time, without any reference to the needs of other client groups. Any ordering of priorities, therefore, has to be undertaken in a conscious way at the local level. The alternative to this is to respond to every wind and wave—and get nowhere in particular.

While it is appropriate to determine the needs that exist within a community, this raises great problems not only in conducting mammoth social surveys but in developing acceptable criteria of need. Many requests for help are constrained by previous experience of poor quality or non-existent services and many clients are content with the intolerable. Others, however, may be excessive in their demands. It is hard for authorities to develop adequate guidelines for all circumstances and social workers' concepts and approaches vary enormously. Almost by any standards, however, demands (however defined) exceed resources and some form of priority determination is necessary.

A further encouraging factor of the new unified department is that opportunities are given to the director and his staff to influence the policies of other departments within the local authority. A small number of authorities are taking the idea of corporate management very seriously. Clearly the policies of several departments will have repercussions upon the work of the social services departments and vice versa. It makes sense to attempt to thrash out some overall objectives for the authority and to ensure that respective policies of the departments concerned mesh to form a unified and effective whole. The director should be ever sensitive to the social implications of a proposed policy or decisions and should have had expertise to contribute to the planning and organising of the authority. If his knowledge and skill are appropriate to his new higher status among his chief officer colleagues, then his influence for good can extend well beyond the bounds of his own department. To a lesser extent, all members of the department need to cut across departmental boundaries and share their knowledge and skills in respect of the community. Knowledge in the department should not be limited to that garnered from empirical enquiry.

In addition to obtaining factual information in respect of the characteristics of the area, it is also important that problems should be studied in ways other than the pure summation of needs and numbers. Concepts need to be explored, helpful definitions need to be developed, and issues and arguments need to be analysed and discussed.

It is mainly on the discussion of problems and issues pertinent to the social services that this book concentrates. There is an important opening chapter on the philosophy of social services departments followed by an examination of analysing the needs of a community. The remaining chapters are taken up with analysing social issues together with a short concluding chapter. In all cases people prominent in their field were given the particular theme and asked to address themselves to it. While all subjects have been written on before, the common and probably unique thread throughout the book is that the issues are seen from or in relation to, the social services department, and the implications for it highlighted.

References

Committee on Local Authority and Allied Personal Social Services, (1968) *Report*, (Chairman F. Seebohm), Cmnd. 7303, HMSO, London.

Foren, R., and Brown, M. J., (1971) *Planning for Service*, Charles Knight, London.

Kershaw, J. D., (1968) 'Doctor or social worker?', *British Medical Journal*, August.

'The Making of a director', November (1970) *British Hospital Journal and Social Services Review.*

Smith, J., (1972) 'Top jobs in the social services' *in* Jones, K., ed., *The Year Book of Social Policy in Britain* 1971, Routledge & Kegan Paul, London.

The Social Services (Scotland) Act, 1968, HMSO, London.

Thomas, N. M., (1973) 'The Seebohm Committee: an analysis of its Establishment, functioning and effects' *in* Chapman, R. A., ed., *Commissions in Policy Making*, Allen & Unwin, London.

1 *The philosophy of the social services department*

Barbara Kahan

An organisation which purports to deal with provision of services to human beings must have a philosophy which informs its objectives, operational methods and assumptions. The lack of a clearly formulated philosophy does not imply that none exists, but that it cannot readily be defined and communicated. If it cannot readily be defined and communicated, confusion and misinterpretation by those employed in the organisation and those who use the services are likely to result. A clearly stated philosophy may be positive or negative in its implications for the services it informs; but either way people involved with the organisation will know where they stand. Social services departments will have a philosophy, either by definition or by default. In this opening chapter, a brief attempt is made to examine some of the issues relevant to the formulation of their philosophy. In attempting to do this, it is necessary to draw attention to the brief time which has elapsed since the creation of the social services departments. This may be seen, however, as an advantage since it provides an opportunity to identify in their early stages some crude elements of thinking and feeling which later may become too institutionalised and modified through interaction and familiarity to allow easy identification. Change is very rapid in the present situation, and many developments are taking place as reactions to the stimuli of legislation, demand, resource constraints and the necessity for improvisation. Yet the choice of tactics and strategies adopted by a department will relate inevitably in part to the underlying philosophy which the department, the committee and the local authority hold. It is, therefore, important that that philosophy should have been consciously considered and realistically founded at the outset. The angle at which two lines are drawn in relation to each other may appear small at the point of departure, but widens as the lines grow longer. 'In our beginnings are our ends'—ends and means inevitably condition each other and this is true of objectives and methods in social work.

'The nerve of social work is still a deep concern, sometimes religiously rooted, to *help* people who are in various kinds of difficulties. . . . And certainly "help" nowadays cannot be effectively given merely by good will. Apart from the fact that effective remedies for social distresses may call for political measures, help for people's individual and personal difficulties calls for expert skills, including in our Welfare State the skill of knowing which social agencies can supply the special services needed. Thus the giving of help becomes dependent on acquiring certain kinds of expert knowledge and skill and so is being professionalised.' (Younghusband, 1967.)

Yet, Younghusband argues, the professional ethics which must accompany professionalisation present the social worker with greater difficulty than the doctor whose professional code is designed so that he can properly carry out a generally accepted and recognised purpose. 'His professional ethics are therefore primarily concerned with means.' In social work, 'the end itself is controversial and difficult to state, and any way of stating it is likely to have some ethical notion built into it, either overtly or in a concealed way. It is concealed when the end is described in terms which sound scientifically neutral, but are in fact question-begging.' Social workers 'occupy an uncomfortable but potentially creative position where social science and psychology meet and bear on the practical situations of human life'; but in addition Younghusband claims that moral philosophy, in the sense at least of a considered view of moral judgment, also intersects at the same point (Younghusband, 1967.)

Social work is claimed by some to have its roots in Graeco–Roman–Christian ideas and practice towards those in need, the poor, strangers, relatives, friends, parents, orphans, the sick and old people, and that modern social work stems straight from nineteenth-century stock which in itself grew from those roots.

A different view arrives at two conclusions: 'First, commonly accepted views which summarise the history of social work can be taken only as indicating a range of unanswered questions. Second, social work is very much a product of our time, and will find at best only parallels with other times and other societies. Modern social work can only be understood within the context of modern society: we can ask useful questions about the ways in which "social problems" were defined in medieval times or in the ancient world, but we cannot assume that we are thereby enquiring into the roots of modern social work. In an important sense there is no medieval or ancient social work.' (Timms 1970.) Whether this view of social work is fully accepted or not, it is clear that in the sense in which we now know it social work is a modern development of industrial societies and social work is a modern profession. Social work, in fact, is still so modern and young that whether it can be held to be a profession or not is a question on which there is less than total agreement, particularly outside the ranks of social workers. One concept of a profession suggests that it consists in 'the threefold composite of social values ... first, the value placed upon systematic knowledge and the intellect: knowing. Second, the value placed upon technical skill and trained capacity: doing. And third, the value placed upon putting this conjoint knowledge and skill to work in the service of others: helping. It is these three values as fused into the concept of a profession that enlists the respect of men.' (Merton 1960.) These three components can be seen in the definition of a social worker given by social workers themselves in 1953: 'One who, by education, vocation and training, has fitted himself for professional employment in agencies working for the happiness and stability of the individual in the community.' (Association of Social Workers 1953a.)

The Seebohm Committee was given the task of reviewing organisational problems in the personal social services, problems which had been causing frustration and growing concern over most of the post-war period. Starting from a point where specialisation was used as an instrument of growth and development of services for client groups, the different rates of growth, different philosophies and different professional attitudes and standards over twenty years had resulted in a national situation of anomalies, overlapping, unevenness and deficiencies which left many client needs unmet and undefined, was wasteful of resources and lacking in operational strength because of fragmentation. The Committee's brief was to consider what changes in organisation and responsibilities of local authority services were necessary 'to secure an effective family service' (Committee on Local Authority and Allied Personal Social Services 1969.) The Committee took a more philosophical view than their bare terms of reference implied and in presenting their report hastened in its opening words to state their philosophy: 'We recommend a new local authority department, providing a community based and family oriented service, which will be available to all. This new department will, we believe, reach far beyond the discovery and rescue of social casualties; it will enable the greatest possible number of individuals to act reciprocally, giving and receiving service for the well-being of the whole community.' (Committee on Local Authority and Allied Personal Social Services 1969.) Although there is an evangelical ring about this credo, the Committee took pains to spell out their awareness of some of the problems inherent in implementing it. They envisaged 'a service with a clear and comprehensive responsibility for meeting social need,' but one which contained 'safeguards against neglect and the abuse of power' amongst which safeguards there would be not only more effective management, decentralisation, elected members, and the effects of use by a broader cross-section of the population but also 'further development of professional responsibility among the staff'. They saw a link between post-war rates of development in various personal social services and the extent to which they had been able to attract trained staff. They observed that those which had attracted the larger proportion of trained staff appeared to have been influenced 'by a growing sense of professionalism among social workers'.

Yet in spite of their confidence in professional responsibility it is clear in their report that the Committee were not always happy about some of the implications of professionalism among social workers. Doctors were criticised because they had been 'slow in coming to terms with the new social work "helping profession" . . . growing so rapidly alongside them,' and had neither made adequate use of social workers and social services, nor understood or valued them; but some social workers were thought to be over-preoccupied with 'psychodynamics, often forbiddingly expressed, which may not be what a harassed family doctor or the situation, self-evidently, requires'. One is reminded of Eileen Younghusband's tacit plea for a proper sense of proportion in the focus placed by social workers on methodology in practice, arguing that for social workers to claim professional status on the grounds of being 'a specialist in human relationships, an individual trained and disciplined in human adjustments' (Association of Social Workers 1953b) is too grandiose; she gently suggests 'the wealth of human experience which may be acquired in casework is best geared to some particular social service, so that the help people may be given in working out their personal and emotional troubles can grow out of some specific service or information which the caseworker is able to supply. In many instances the particular service or information is all that is required.'

From the foregoing certain points emerge which can be summarised as follows: social work as we know it springs from modern society, i.e. it is a product of industrialised, urban life, politically and materially competitive and technologically advanced, yet it also springs from 'a deep concern, sometimes religiously rooted, to help people in various difficulties'. It calls for a professional approach based on systematic knowledge and skill to work in the service of others. The service in which this professional approach would operate should have a clear and comprehensive responsibility to meet social need, should be oriented to the family, based in the community, and involved in reciprocal giving and receiving in a manner unprecedented in the past, and aimed at the well-being of the whole community.

Social services departments in the event were created by an Act of Parliament (Local Authority Social Services Act, 1970) which gave no new powers to local authorities but rearranged legislation concerning services which were already their responsibility to provide, thus forming a different organisational pattern.*

Nevertheless in spite of the fact that the legislation was not innovatory but only a 'machinery' bill, a wind of change in attitude and method has been blowing since the new social services

* Certain services within the general definition of social work, remain outside this reorganisation, though some are located in local government. Although certain additional legislation added to the responsibilities of social services departments since 1970 this did not include powers equivalent to those in the Scottish legislation which enable local authorities to promote general welfare.

departments were established. Generalists have taken the place of specialists in many departments, management structures based on theoretical concepts have been created, community-based 'area plans' have been developed in some local authorities, volunteers, community work, surveys of need, research and development all feature large in discussions and organisations.

Many established patterns have been changed or ceased to exist and traditional approaches and practices are being questioned, often quite fundamentally. One of the most outstanding features of the first two years of social services departments was the recognition of massive need, much of it as yet undefined in detail and undetected individually.

Inevitably reactions within and outside the departments included excitement, wider aspirations and long-term goals, but also some bewilderment, frustration and resentment in the short term. Public expectation was high and whilst allowances are made for early teething difficulties, it will be necessary for the departments to have a clear and positive philosophy from which their objectives can stem and be translated into practical terms if these expectations are to be fulfilled.

The attempt to formulate a philosophy immediately gives rise to a number of questions. The objective of the Seebohm Committee, already quoted above (page 14), appears positive and far-reaching in its implications, but one sociologist (Glastonbury 1971) has argued that much of the thinking and detail of the report could be held to be a series of reactions to negative situations of insufficient services, too little co-ordination, narrow viewpoints and watertight operational patterns. In these circumstances, is a new approach based on general principles possible, or will the outcome be merely the updating of the previous model? In either case, has social work reached a stage where there are sufficient broad areas of agreement about causes of need, dimensions of need, standards of services to meet it, and quality of operational performance to ensure a recognisable approach, or a recognisable social service philosophy in each individual department? A social worker has recently put the same point as follows: 'There never was a new department with new aims and objectives. The department was an amalgam of previous departments, which had within them groups of workers of all grades with intensely strong professional loyalties. They had their own attitudes to their work, their own approach to problems and the "new" department's whole working life is strongly influenced by the separate histories of the departments which are now its components.' (Foster 1972.)

Because social work deals with human situations and personalities which are in some respects all individually different, it has often been accepted, sometimes asserted, that a systematic approach is difficult and much reliance has consequently been placed on individualistic working methods. The worker uses his own personality as part of his professional equipment, and training has often concentrated on developing skills and increasing his awareness of his own reactions and involvement in his work rather than teaching agreed methodology or standards of practice. Such an approach places a heavy responsibility on individual workers, and even when professional training has been undertaken and high quality professional consultation and supervision are available to the worker, in the ultimate the service to the public is frequently dependent on individual quality, attitudes and judgment. The situation is further weighted by the fact that many social and personal problems which social workers face raise questions of values, moral, social and personal, on which decisions and judgments have to be made either positively or negatively. Some of the questions have formerly been tacitly answered by traditional attitudes embodied in previous decisions, previous practice, financial and other constraints which have been inherited as a pattern of service delivery by individual workers, and, if questioned at all, have been so largely in an ad hoc rather than a radical manner. In addition individuals have inevitably held and still hold their own unconscious value systems which are largely inexplicit and which influence their judgment in the absence of an explicit and defined departmental value system.

One of the basic questions which falls within this area concerns the quality of life which is acceptable for those whom the social services departments aim to help. What quality of life is the minimum acceptable before intervention by society is justified? Does this vary according to age, sex, condition, income or lack of it, state of health, physical, mental or emotional, acceptability or non-acceptability of the individual or group to society? Can the minimum be defined in relation to special groups, e.g. children, the elderly, the handicapped? How is the minimum decided; by concensus of professionals, by public opinion, by court action, by administrative necessity or political constraint? Some of the problems faced by social workers are not basically personal human problems, but are caused by the way in which society as a whole expresses attitudes and organises itself, or by political pressures or a combination of these and other general factors. Can the problems be defined without bringing social service attitudes into conflict with political and organisational elements of the social system?

Problems involving immigrants, drugs, young offenders, the homeless are examples in which different value systems can meet, and, if clearly defined, produce great difficulty in decision-making for social service workers. It can be argued that the proper course of action would be to provide as good a personal service as possible within 'the system' and leave the wider issues of conflicting values and their consequences to political elements. The medical model on which many aspirations of social work have been based might be cited, but not all social workers accept this argument and their inability to do so leads to the question whether a professional philosophy can be worked out and maintained in the political context of social services departments.

Social workers are inevitably political animals themselves. Their private value systems, their personal needs and views create a degree of ambivalence which is one of the components in the development of personal philosophies, particularly in the absence of a professional or departmental philosophy. An element in the Seebohm philosophy which could bring this ambivalence into sharper focus is the greater emphasis likely to be necessary in future on client and community participation and consumer reaction coupled with the clients' rights movement.

Motivation for involvement in social service activity will be tested in an unprecedented way and personal needs for power, patronage and appreciation will emerge as well as more client-centred motives. Harsh questions about tolerance thresholds of society and individual workers may have to be answered. How long can the chronically dependent expect to be met with dependable response? Is gratitude still an unspoken criterion in rationing of resources? How high a standard of care is possible? How far are individual workers prepared to allow personal autonomy to be limited by an overall philosophy and departmental approach in achieving high standards? On the client's side many other questions are emerging: What entitlement to services exists outside of insurance-based benefits such as unemployment and sickness pay? How far is the client's assessment of his need merely a point of departure or the diagnosis on which help is based? Must he take whatever he is offered or accept refusal which may in his opinion be based on an incomplete understanding of his problems —or an unwillingness to be convinced by them? If the medical model is examined it can readily be seen how different the situations of the doctor and the social worker are. If a patient goes to his doctor complaining of a condition for which he considers he requires help and which is readily recognisable after examination, treatment is likely to be provided or promised, according to the nature and degree of seriousness of the condition. Although relatively minor conditions which need hospital treatment may be put on a waiting list, acute conditions are likely to receive immediate treatment and palliatives of some kind are likely to be given for any morbid condition, however slight, if the patient complains. If the condition is not readily recognisable, the doctor may ask for specialist help and/or investigation, or prescribe observation or minor treatment during an interim period. Most doctors would be unwilling to ignore the continued complaints of a patient who said there was something wrong, even though they might attach less importance to the patient's general condition than the patient does. The Hippocratic oath as restated in modern terms by the World Medical Association, 1947, 'I solemnly pledge myself to consecrate my life to the service of humanity' forms the tacit background of medical practice and in addition there are a number of disciplinary bodies which can comment on or sanction the professional behaviour of a doctor in the performance of his work. The training of the least well-qualified medical practitioner involves six or more years of full-time study and supervised practice and the assumption is that patients need help or they would not ask for it. Although of recent years there has been much comment on the lack of physical cause for many patient demands on doctors, especially general practitioners, the suggestion is not essentially that the patient does not need help but that he needs a different sort of help, for example, help which is psychogenically based. Leaving aside the question of inadequate resources, a term which in itself requires careful examination, and frequent reappraisal, is there a parallel in the social work situation to the visit by a patient to the doctor? A client goes to the social services and complains of a condition for which he considers he requires help. If the condition is readily recognisable, e.g. inability to pay a debt, need for children to be cared for during family crises or illness, homelessness, need for a home help, bedding, furniture, can the client be certain of receiving help, or at least a promise of help as soon as it can be marshalled? Will the urgency of the situation be judged on the client's terms or become part of a time pattern the shape and length of which he has no way of measuring or influencing? Will the cost of remedy (the prescription) be geared to his need/condition—or to a financial plan which is made without his participation or knowledge and which imposes a level of care or help geared to itself—not to him?

If he cannot be sure of receiving help what happens next? What is the minimum level of professional skill to which he will be exposed in the decision-making (the diagnosis)? If his condition is less readily diagnosed is he likely to be referred to a specialist for help and/or investigation? What will happen in between? Will temporary help be given to help the client (the patient) to keep going? Will there be some 'official' recognition that he has a need condition that requires help—or at least investigation?

The answers to some of these questions must be less than satisfactory from the client's viewpoint in many situations in the social services at present. Many practitioners through no fault of their own have no professional training. Those who have would be amongst the first to recognise that its length and content often leave much to be desired. As yet an accepted pattern of consultant specialists does not exist and even general consultation is often much less readily available than either individual workers or departmental heads would wish. Is there a standard by which professional behaviour can be judged and whose judgment would lead to comment or sanction of such behaviour if it were open to criticism?

It is perhaps a little unfair to make medical comparisons of a kind which inevitably reflect harshly on the youthful inadequacy of current social work practice and its professional resources, and it has to be accepted that use of resources by doctors is governed by patterns of funding and organisation which, though not providing all they would like on their patients' behalf, leaves them freer than social workers to make decisions in relation to the use of resources in helping individuals.

Nevertheless since the ultimate reality of the social services departments must be related to the people for whom they exist, a recognition of the importance of the perceptions of those people of what is being offered to them ought to be part of the philosophy of the departments. There must also be recognition of the need to answer questions which reflect consumer expectations. Decisions have to be made about quality of service in the process of deciding on resource needs. For example, the difference between a group-caring situation for children (a residential home) based on an implicit containment concept only and a situation based on an explicit attempt to provide as adequately as possible for the children's individual emotional needs could be the proportionate difference, expressed in statistical and resource terms of one:two.

Similarly the decision to deal with a family or individual problem by intensive support in a domiciliary setting when formerly it might have been institutionalised implies a real difference in resource application of many kinds and not merely an expressed aspiration. In trying to achieve a recognisable approach, a recognisable philosophy put into practical terms, will it be possible for social services departments to allow the degree of individual and group autonomy which modern management delegation theory recommends and professional training has often implied? How far can social workers be individually undirected, particularly if there is no publicly known social work equivalent to the Hippocratic oath? Will it be necessary for even experienced workers to be involved in monitoring which goes further than accepted supervision methods have so far envisaged? How far can departments achieve results of the kind their clients want through warm, unchallenging inter-professional relationships, or will they find the need for tougher, more challenging situations between different levels of responsibility?

Some of these problems are likely to involve considerations of commitment to the task and will inevitably lead to further questions about what is the task? The setting in which the service is based may need to be adapted to the task, with consequent implications for individual commitment. For example, is it reasonable, although based on traditional local government patterns of administration, for social services departments to be closed from Friday early evening to Monday morning with only an emergency on-call service available? Should social services be geared to client demand which for many situations is round the clock, seven days a week, and often with a high concentration of demands at weekends?

There is much discussion in the current professional press about many of the issues this chapter raises, and a philosophical, seeking tone can often be heard. An article entitled 'Equality' quotes Richard Titmuss in his introduction to the 1951 edition of R. H. Tawney's essay 'Equality' first published in 1931. Tawney, Richard Titmuss said, was 'not writing of it [equality] in the naïve sense of equality of talent or merit or personality. His concern was with fundamental equalities before the law; the removal of collectively imposed social and economic inequalities; the equalising of opportunities for all to secure certain goods and services; the education of all children to make them capable of freedom and more capable of fulfilling their personal differences; the enlargement of personal liberties through the discovery of each individual of his own and his neighbour's endowment. . . . The supreme consideration was every man's uniqueness "without regard to the vulgar irrelevances of class and income".' The article using this quotation goes on to consider how such an ideal can become practical and concludes 'To give any sort of useful guidance to individuals, the concept of equality can only operate at the simplest concrete level on the one hand, and as an attitude on the other which guides individuals to look at others as equals—whoever they are—foreigners, the opposite sex, the highly educated or the ESN, the sophisticated or children. To have such an attitude is also an ideal like that of Tawney's, but one which can gradually be worked towards because at least it lies in one's own hands'.

Can one go further than this writer and ask whether social services, instead of being a means of meeting various degrees of individual need are not also a levelling up process which a civilised society owes to those who are born or fall into a disadvantaged position vis-à-vis the rest? Can the social services build up the political impetus required to obtain resources in a competitive financial situation without a philosophical/religious conviction of their role to support their endeavours? How far could they retain this in the middle of the established system?

Some social work attitudes suggest that if social workers appear like their clients in dress and hairstyles they will be enabled to make a readier contact and establish easier relationships with those clients. Others believe that the anxious, help-seeking people who need their services are more likely to find a conventional, bureaucratic appearance combined with adequate knowledge, skill and good will more reassuring. Another current writer puts the dilemma boldly: 'children often perceive, with almost clairvoyant insight, the ambiguity of our situation. I have frequently been told by kids, and I'm sure that you have too, "You are only interested in me because you are paid to be!" And I daresay you too have been set back on your heels by the staggering truth of this assertion. Living with ambiguity and contradiction is difficult, but in our trade utterly necessary.' (Pithers 1972.) Conflict of attitudes between social workers and employers in the political setting of social services is another aspect of this ambiguity which pervades the current scene. An anonymous contribution to the organ of the British Association of Social Workers written by a 'senior social worker' (*B.A.S.W. News* 1972) describes the interaction between professional staff, lay members, professional staff of another department (the council's legal department), the social worker's professional organisation, independent legal advisers acting for the client and for the council, a foster home and a court all concerned with what the writer calls 'one of the most fundamental (issues) of our profession, the right of a child to know her own mother'. In the case discussed in this article the politicians appeared to take a different view of human values from the professionals. The social work view expressed favoured continuing as far as practicable the implementation of a professional responsibility to the clients, mother and child, whilst avoiding 'the kind of direct confrontation which is a threat to the Authority and which could result in an irretrievable situation on both sides'. The reason given for this is that the social workers' 'only concern was for the mother and child'. A converse view was taken in an article describing area teams at work and their problems of generic, specialist and community methods in situations of rising unemployment, workless teenagers, rising prices, high heating and light bills and limited capital provisions. 'Network analysis and personal role conflicts notwithstanding, the profession as a whole is, through the team concept, likely to find itself pushed more and more into the political arena on behalf of its growing army of clients.' (Ball 1972.)

A further problem must be mentioned in the context of a philosophy for social services departments. Traditionally social work was underprivileged within the professional world and individual social workers either had private means or found themselves in practical sympathy with many of their clients because they faced at least some of the same economic constraints. The last few years have brought a drastic change in this situation and social work has not only 'arrived' in terms of power groups within the professions and local government but many individuals within it are now amongst the affluent in the professional manpower group.

The change has not only been drastic but rapid, and has provided unprecedented opportunities for advancement. Fluidity of manpower and consequent instability of services have resulted and with the further changes involved in the reform of local government many individuals in the social services are subjected to pressures of a kind quite different from those which arose from meeting need with inadequate resources. Motivations inevitably are now more complex and career prospects and considerations very much clearer. The problem of giving reality to terms such as continuity of concern, commitment, client-centred casework, has not been diminished by the comparative affluence and mobility of the social worker.

The undoubted strength given to the cause of social work by bigger budgets, larger departments and chief officers of equal status with other chief officers in local government, will need to be supported by acceptance of the importance of client-centred value systems, professional self-discipline to ensure high standards of service delivery and self-imposed and externally developed methods of monitoring and objective scrutiny to avoid the pitfalls of unself-critical assessments of achievement.

Many social workers, in spite of the achievement of changes they fought for and in spite of, or perhaps because of, their success in convincing the public of their value, claim to feel confused and depressed in the current situation. Such rapid and widespread change is difficult to absorb at the same time as the task, because of the new light shed on it, visibly and daily grows in dimensions. All this at a time when social work thinking itself is changing rapidly too. 'At a time when he feels perhaps more closely identified with his client than before—for instance in the struggle against poverty—the social worker finds himself part of a huge amorphous machine which is easily confused with the Establishment. At a time when he needs to be particularly reflective and objective about what he is doing, the changing pressures around him make this especially difficult.' (Courtis 1972.)

The writer, a social worker in a London borough, suggests that it is perhaps an advantage that time will not wait for concepts and attitudes appropriate to the new departments to develop. 'The social workers are going to have to batter out some sort of philosophy to get them through the next week or month or year. They are going to have to embark on a "radical re-think" of almost every aspect of their work.' (Courtis 1972.)

This is a short-term view, but in the long term something more deliberate is likely to be necessary. Social services departments stand at the junction of a number of different processes, some politically determined, some relating to historical and social changes in the settings in which they operate, and others relating to research, the growth of professionalism, organisational patterns and the accidents of individual and group influences. The increasing blurring of definitions between those who give and those who receive services in conjunction with the attempt at reconciling these diverse processes are likely to make social services departments a microcosm of the macrocosmic situation in the society in which they serve. Unless they are to reflect, as a result of ad hoc reactions and decision-making, the confusion and conflicting standards of the macrocosm, they will need to anchor themselves firmly in a coherent philosophy. If they are able to do so they may provide one of the models which help to promote and maintain a healthy society.

References

Association of Social Workers (1953a) *Notes on the Ethics of Social Work*, A.S.W., London.

Association of Social Workers (1953b) *Notes on Social Work*, A.S.W., London.

Ball, D. (1972) 'Teams at Work', *New Soc.*, 9 March.

BASW News (1972) 'Conflict', *BASW News*, 6 April, 18.

Committee on Local Authority and Allied Personal Social Services (1968), *Report* (Chairman: F. Seebohm), Cmnd. 3703, HMSO, London.

Courtis, J. (1972) 'Transition', *Soc. Wk. Today*, 3, 9.

Foster, G. (1972) 'Equality', *Child in Care*, May.

Glastonbury, B. (1971) *Local Authority Social Service Departments—Expectations* (unpublished), Southampton University, Southampton.

Social issues and the social services

Local Authority Social Services Act (1970), HMSO, London.
Merton, R. (1960) 'Some thoughts on the professions in American Society', (Brown University Paper 37), Brown University, Providence, USA.
Pithers, D. S. (1972) 'Purpose of education', *Child in Care*, May.
Timms, N. (1970) *Social Work: an outline for the intending student*, Routledge and Kegan Paul, London.
Younghusband, E. (1967) *Social Work and Social Values*, Allen and Unwin, London.

2 *Analyses of need*

David Fruin

> 'Of the wealth of my material I have no doubt. I am indeed embarrassed by its mass and by my resolution to make use of no fact to which I cannot give a quantitative value.' (Booth 1889.)
>
> 'By Statistical is meant . . . an inquiry into the state of a country for the purpose of ascertaining the quantum of happiness enjoyed by its inhabitants and the means of its future improvement.' (Sir John Sinclair, Bart 1798.)

Analyses of need are undertakings firmly embedded in the context of subjective value judgments about the desires and demands of individual human beings. I say this in order to affirm that however much in this chapter and in our day-to-day activities we may talk in a dispassionate way about the needs of groups of people, fundamentally we are concerned with individuals, and the judgments we make about them reflect our own attitudes on matters of human and social concern. Any analysis, no matter how scientific and objective it may appear, implies a framework of value judgments. For even if we concentrate on what we consider to be the bare essentials for remaining alive, we must still solve the problem of value judgments about whose existence should be maintained, at what cost and who should make the decisions.

Why analyse needs?

If we are to undertake effective planning for the social services, the logical starting point is one which examines the needs of the community and then plans the services to suit the needs, recognising, however, that planning authorities are unable to start afresh but must work within the restrictions placed upon them by the capital and staff resources already committed. The margin for changes in direction and for the establishment of new programmes is always heavily circumscribed.

Nevertheless, despite these restrictions, the analysis of needs is the planning starting-point and should logically precede other management planning activities. At the same time, not all analyses of needs are undertaken for such purposes. Six reasons for undertaking analyses of needs can be considered:

(1) Ethical reasons: analyses of need are not all undertaken merely because it is a professional duty. Early investigators such as Booth and Rowntree clearly conceived their activities within a moral framework.

(2) To increase our understanding of why needs occur within a sociological, psychological or economic framework of knowledge. In such cases often there may be no immediate application of benefit to those in need.

(3) For aggregation at a policy and management level. Thus, 'everyone' may know which are areas of greatest need in a particular city, but if central government must decide which are the neediest areas nationwide then some degree of analysis and aggregation must take place, unless one awards, for example, urban aid grants to the most clamorous applicants.

(4) Political reasons: Recently, certain analyses of needs, i.e. finding the chronically sick and disabled, have in some cases been undertaken more for political and public relations reasons rather than as part of a determined effort to find those in need of services.

(5) For monitoring, evaluation and planning purposes. Warren (1971) presents a typical view, reproduced in Figure 2·1, of the relationship of the analysis of needs to the management of service provision generally.

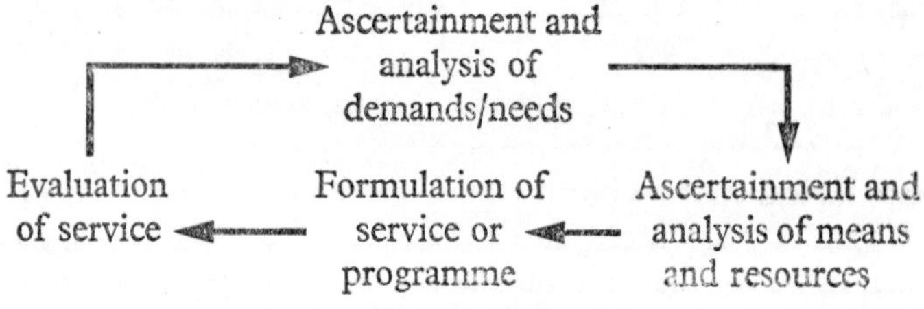

FIGURE 2·1

(6) To make decision-making explicit. The more explicit the bases on which decisions are taken, the greater the likelihood that anomalous and inappropriate decisions come to light.

Today, with a seemingly ever-increasing tendency towards larger local government units and with central government playing a much greater role in the distribution of social services, it is essential to ensure that policies are well-formulated, since errors also can be of a much greater magnitude. In earlier times when each Poor Law Union could set its own standards, broad systematic policies were of less importance, since they could be more readily tailored on a piecemeal basis to suit local conditions and anomalies impinged on comparatively fewer people. The same is true in the American setting. 'When activities designed to meet community needs, such as child care or recreation, were of relatively small scope, planning frequently depended upon ad hoc decisions made by small groups of decision-makers who tended to be protected from public scrutiny. And while their processes of planning were frequently faulty, the consequences of their shortcomings were not so severe as became the case when federal legislation in the 1960s concerned with delinquency, poverty, education, housing and unemployment stimulated the development of large-scale ameliorative programmes in thousands of communities across the land.' (Herman and Munk 1967.)

The concept of need

Given the primacy of need as a basic concept in the social services field, it is of value to recognise the different ways in which the term is used. Bradshaw (1972) has developed a taxonomy of social need and has distinguished four definitions. The first is that of *normative needs* defined in accordance with some agreed standard. The second is that of the *felt needs* of individuals who may either be limited in their felt needs because of ignorance of service availability or they might ask for more than what others consider is deserved. Thirdly, *expressed needs* or demands, play an important part in determining the standard of service provision, although demand, particularly as manifest in waiting list lengths and the like, may be but poorly correlated with normative or felt needs. At the same time it is a truism to state that those people least likely to be capable of making demands upon policy-makers, decision-takers and service-providers are very often the same people who stand in greatest need. Certainly, the statistical returns which local authorities make for central government are more geared to recording services rendered rather than documenting shortfalls. Fourthly, *comparative needs* refer to the imputed needs of a group not in receipt of services but similar in relevant characteristics to another group already receiving services. Thus, much attention is being focused by the Department of Health and Social Security currently as to how to ensure that those estimated on a financial basis, to be in economic need can be made aware of their entitlement to the Family Income Supplement—a clear example of those 'in need' making insufficient demands.

Apart from the broader conceptual problems involved with terminology, Greve, Page and Greve (1971) make clear the arguments, with respect to homelessness, for 'greater clarity and agreement in definition and practice by local authority departments and, indeed, for more explicit guidance from central government' in order to help unravel the basis for decisions on the allocation of social resources. In a legislative context, needs are rarely precisely defined; the National Assistance Act, 1948 places a duty on local authorities to provide residential accommodation for those in need of care and attention not otherwise available, but there is no further elaboration as to eligibility. Yet this is not necessarily a bad thing. Jean Packman (1968) in *Child Care: needs and numbers* draws attention to the lack of clear definitions of needs, specifically within the legislative framework of the Children's Acts, but she stresses that it is appropriate that the definitions of need 'should change and develop as the community's standard of living rises and as understanding and skill develop'.

Her view emphasises the changing and value-orientated bases of human and social needs, and when an attempt must be made to predict future needs rather than assess contemporary ones then the task is magnified in difficulty. A Ministry of Housing and Local Government report (Committee on Public Participation in Planning, 1969) on social provision in new and expanding communities, although perhaps over-stressing the accuracy of predicted traffic estimates, points out that 'whereas road traffic engineers can call upon statistical techniques to show the extent of future need there is no similar technique yet available to produce accurate forecasts of future social needs' (p. 41).

In the area of welfare needs where the recipients of provided benefits have tended to come from the lower end of the social and economic scales, the assessment of needs has been made for the most part by the service providers who, not surprisingly, have a built-in bias to keep themselves in employment by finding that they are needed. Thus, little attention has been focused on the *preferences* of the recipients. Whereas architects, even for local authority housing, have been paying increased attention not only to user needs, but also to user preferences, providers of welfare services have undertaken little consumer research to discover their clients' preferences. Perhaps the welfare model has been too similar to that of the health services, where the doctor/provider can speak with a stronger authority as to what will satisfy the patient's health needs.

A review of user studies on houses and people by Hole and Attenburrow (1966) makes clear that while there is a body of technical information to be gained from a laboratory-type setting, there are also 'other aspects of human requirements in which the user himself has the voice of authority'. Surely social and human needs form one such aspect.

Indications of the growing awareness of deficiencies in this area of consumer involvement, together with possible answers, may be seen in the consumer surveys which have been carried out by the National Institute for Social Work and by the University of Southampton to discover what clients and potential users of social services think about such services and about social workers. In a similar vein, the publication of the Skeffington Report (Ministry of Housing and Local Government 1969), and current attempts to involve in the local authority planning process those affected by planning decisions, may be seen in the same light.

In social service departments and their earlier constituent departments few empirical studies have been made of the process and routes by which people become recognised as being in need and hence attain the status of client. For example, the mechanism of the intake and reception process has been little studied, a notable exception being the study by Hall (1971) of the reception process in a children's department. This study clearly shows the important role which low-ranking staff members, the receptionists, play in implicitly formulating the organisation's definition of need.

As Hall comments 'few students of (social administration) have made any systematic attempt to study the process involved in the administration of the social services' (p. 42).

Approaches to analysis: idiographic and nomothetic methods

There can be said to be two ways of acquiring knowledge in a scientific manner: the case method and the statistical method. The psychologist Allport has delineated the distinction between the two by pointing out that behaviour can be studied either in terms of general principles, universal variables and a large number of cases or by focusing on the individual case. He calls the first the nomothetic approach and the second the idiographic method. 'Psychology will become *more* scientific, i.e. better able to make predictions when it has learned to evaluate single trends in all their intrinsic complexity' (Allport 1960). The same is true of the study of human and social needs generally. An analysis of the two approaches with reference to studies of public administration has been made by Riggs (1962), but within the social services the idiographic-nomothetic distinction is exemplified in practice by the respective roles of fieldworker, who must give and deny services to the individual case, and administrator who sets the bounds within which field staff must work.

Both the idiographic and the nomothetic methods may be equally effective in advancing knowledge or in bringing about changes as a result of new or increased knowledge. Thus, on the idiographic side, legislative changes in the child-care field were hastened in 1945 by the investigation into the case of the death of Dennis O'Neill, a boy boarded out in a foster home. Similarly, the film presentation by Robertson of 'A Two-year-old Goes to Hospital' did much to produce changes in the hospitalisation of children. On the nomothetic side, in fields such as medicine, often only long-term carefully controlled epidemiological studies can clarify which of two or more treatments is the most effective or can unravel complex patterns of disease vectors. Similarly, the controversy over the effects of maternal deprivation (Wootton 1966) cannot be settled by consideration of an isolated case.

The nomothetic-statistical method, by using data derived from many cases, often seems to make for more substantial conclusions. Yet to be able to summarise information from many data sources requires not only a more selective but also a more quantitative approach, if we wish to move from a verbal precis of case histories to some form of numeric average.

Thus, although the Appendices to the 1909 Poor Law Commission are replete with a mass and morass of information, including lists of individual beneficiaries and assessments of their moral character, in such detail as to surprise the present-day respecters of confidentiality, the value of all this information is diminished by the lack of systematisation. While it is the individual who has needs and while it is to individuals that services are given, policy and planning decisions must usually be taken about groups of individuals.

In the present review, I shall therefore concentrate on the statistical method, recognising none the less the importance of many idiographic studies in determining policy changes. This emphasis reflects not only my own statistical bias but also the fact that most studies of analysis of needs have also used as a basic tool the statistical method.

This century has seen a considerable development of techniques facilitating the use of the statistical method which can aid the analysis of large masses of data. In particular, the elaboration of factor analysis and other multivariate tools coupled with increasing availability of computers for high-speed processing and manipulation of data means that large numbers of cases *per se* no longer form a hindrance to comprehension. Despite these advances the need for clear understanding of the basic data is in no sense diminished since complex analysis must be founded on a secure empirical footing—a necessity which has secured recognition in the system analyst's GIGO maxim, Garbage In, Garbage Out.

On the other hand the statistical approach has been hindered by the lack of appropriate data. Without exception, all investigators of social needs have bemoaned the insufficiency, the unreliability and the invalidity of much of the data from case records to national statistical returns.

Numbers and data

The most powerful—in a statistical and mathematical sense—techniques of numeric data analysis can be applied to numbers which indicate ratio measurements, i.e. where the numbers allocated to attributes of people or things have a rational zero point and hence the property of being able to reflect ideas such as 'twice as big' or 'three times as many', and thus satisfy the assumptions of what most people think of as the ordinary number system. However, such numbers are rare in social and psychological data (Doreain 1970, p. 35). It is common enough to be able to make statements of the form 'Area A has twice as many people as Area B', or 'Mr. X's salary is three times as great as Mr. Y's'. But we lack procedures which allow numbers to be allocated so that we can say in a reliable and valid way that 'Area A is twice as poor as Area B', or that 'Mr. X is three times as happy as Mr. Y'.

Relaxing the mathematical demands, the next lower scale of measurement, the interval scale, requires that equal differences between numbers represent equal differences in the underlying quality being measured. Such scales, as exemplified by the Centigrade or Fahrenheit scales of temperature measurement, are difficult to construct in the spheres of interest to social scientists and arguments even continue as to whether I.Q. scores can be considered to be located on an interval scale.

Relaxing the mathematical demands still further, the next scale of measurement, the ordinal scale, only requires that numbers allocated reflect the ordered position of the numbered objects. The Registrar General's five categories of social class represent an ordinal scale. Ordering political candidates on a ballot paper yields an ordinal scale of political preference. Scales are frequently used to gain data in personality tests or questionnaires as exemplified by a typical five-point ordinal scale:

(1) Strongly agree
(2) Agree
(3) Indifferent
(4) Disagree
(5) Strongly disagree.

Again, with increasing frequency, social services departments engage in exercises involved in listing activities and programmes in order of priority. But such orderings say nothing in themselves about the relative differences in importance between adjacent items.

Finally, at the simplest nominal level of measurement, numbers act as no more than names or labels, for example, in identifying diagnostic categories. Thus the numbers in the list:

(1) Affective
(2) Schizophrenic
(3) Organic
(4) Personality/Neurotic disorder

carry no further information other than being abbreviated labels and hence can readily be interchanged. Group 2 is not necessarily 'worse' or 'better' than either Group 1 or Group 3.

The frequent inability to assign numbers which satisfy the requirements of higher order measurement scales often limits the types of data analysis which can be performed; these problems are discussed by Craig and Driver (1972). Significantly, while the numbers associated with sums of money satisfy the ratio scale requirements, many of the concepts which we might be tempted to value in monetary terms have so far (and for the foreseeable future) yielded at best only ordinal scales. Further, while scales of height or weight have a high degree of interpersonal consensus, scales of preferences for leisure activities or groups of objects such as Brent geese or Norman church towers lack universal consensus. Thus, applying cost-benefit analysis techniques which use ratio scales of monetary values to the siting of airports may demand more of the measurement scales concerned with human values than the data allow. Schwarz (1971) writes: 'There are simply too may complex mediations between a monetary accountancy procedure and human needs', while the preface writer to the *United Nations International Social Development Review*, No. 2, remarks that 'the definition and realisation of human rights, including those of unborn generations, hardly lend themselves to precise quantitative calculation, least of all in monetary terms'. Despite these inherent difficulties in scaling, a number of attempts are under way to construct 'social indicators' which can be used to evaluate programmes, compare areas and aid in the determination of the effects of alternative policies. Thus, the U.N. Research Institute for Social Development has been studying cross-national indicators of development with particular reference to correspondence analysis, i.e. determining what level of life expectation is normally found, or what percentage of the 5-19 year-old population is normally enrolled in school in countries at say the £200 per capita national income level. Included in the list of core indicators are social and demographic indicators such as average number of persons per room, telephones per 100,000 population and proportional mortality ratio, etc. These indicators can then be used on a comparative basis to indicate lagging sectors or to examine the balance between the social and economic development of a country.

In the United States, the Department of Health, Education and Welfare recently published *Toward a Social Report* (1969), a document which attempts to outline ways for improving that nation's ability to chart its social progress by the development of social indicators in the statutorily-required Economic Report. It is in fact a rather disappointing document achieving only an uneasy balance between academic social science and the realities of a political and administrative department, a balance which has been criticised by Tauber (1970). As a report it lacks any substantive recommendations as to how social statistics might regularly be collected so that policy-makers could respond appropriately.

Closer at home, the Central Statistical Office has also begun work on social indicators whose aim, to use the words of a recent advertisement recruiting social statisticians, is 'to identify the fundamental aspects of living as far as the normal individual is concerned, then to isolate these aspects and define them quantitatively, to present at any given time a balanced picture of the state of society in relation to the social policies being pursued.' It is also of interest that the Department of the Environment currently intends to require that urban local authorities report each year to the Department on their needs and progress in housing, recreational facilities, public works and communications, an endeavour which if it is to be useful will necessitate that each authority report in a quantitatively similar manner. And in Scotland a review has been initiated by the Social Work Services Group, which requires each authority to assess and report on their needs over the whole of the social work field. In the 60-page document which each authority must return, two sections in particular ask for information about the detection and contacting of persons in need of social services, and about the present arrangements for assessing needs for various categories of people.

If we focus on one aspect of the broad field of social indicators, the health field, superficially at least, one would imagine that the task of constructing health indicators is an easier task than constructing indicators of direct relevance to the new social services departments. Documentary evidence and statistical data has been collected for a longer period of time and there is a stronger tradition too of a numerate approach amongst the practitioners. Nevertheless even in the health field there are considerable difficulties to be faced.

Grogono and Woodgate (1971) for example, describe a health index ranging from 0 to 1, tested on 27 patients, while Culyer, Williams and Lavers (1971) outline a broad, programmatic approach for developing a calculus of health and make reference to a proposed indicator of ill-health. In both articles the authors include in their respective indices the concept of pain and for both proposed indices the authors intend that the indices shall be measured on a ratio scale. Thus, Grogono and Woodgate imply that '·5' on their index is one half of '1·0' on the same index so that a patient with one month of good health (1·0) and one month in poor health (say ·5) is equivalent to a patient with two months at ·75. But this equating of patients and numbers is only meaningful if the scale is a ratio scale. This restriction applies equally to Culyer's index where it is intended that, for example, 'state eight is four times as bad as state two'. In both papers the authors, by the omission of references to, for example, the construction of scales of pain (Stevens, Carton & Schickman 1958) seem to minimise the technical difficulties which other investigators have already discovered, even when constructing scales with objective referents, such as the strength of electric shock for some aspects of pain. In addition the judgment of pain is not simply a professional judgment; social and cultural values have their influence (Susser & Watson 1971, p. 58). Not that the problem of differences between individual judgments cannot be handled: models and data analysis techniques now exist to cope with areas where there is not a high degree of interpersonal agreement on judgments (Tucker & Messick 1963), but these are unable to settle the value questions about whose judgment we should place most reliance upon.

Data collection and analysis techniques

Data Collection When collecting quantified information about people it is essential that it satisfy certain criteria if it is to be gathered and analysed effectively. The criteria can be conveniently summarised thus:

(1) Collectable. If, for example, interviewers feel too embarrassed to ask certain questions such as 'Can you cut your own toenails?' then such items should be deleted from a questionnaire.

(2) Confidential. Where personal information is being collected unless the information is otherwise publicly available, the limits of confidentiality must be clearly established and such rules maintained.

(3) Correct. An apparently obvious requirement but study of case files often shows up information recorded there which is very low in reliability.

(4) Complete. Unless one can obtain a sufficiently complete coverage for all units surveyed, then usually incomplete items rarely prove their worth. Thus, Alderson (1965) has shown even for death certificates that 13% were in error, due to the absence of known information.

(5) Comparable. Often data collected at considerable expense proves to be sufficiently lacking in comparability with similar studies so that much of potential value is lost. (Vide Stacey's *Comparability in Social Research*, 1969.)

(6) Consistent. If one changes one's data collection devices too frequently, then the value of much data which lies in its comparability is lost.

(7) Concise. An over-abundance of data can as readily inundate as it can inform.

The types of data collected cannot be considered independently of the way in which it is gathered nor without regard to the purposes for which it is being assembled. It is therefore useful at this point to note the distinction between the two broad types of group for whom data is collected—the territorial, where the criterion for membership is based on geographical location, and the affinity group, used in the air travel sense to indicate groups whose membership criteria is determined primarily by the similarity of personal attributes. Examples of territorial groups might be all those people living in Enumeration District Number 7 of Census District Number 2718, or all people living within walking distance of a social service area office, or all Glaswegians. Examples of affinity groups might be all blind people, the under-fives, old people attending day centres, and the like. Of course, different groups of policy-makers are interested in particular combinations of territorial and affinity groups. Thus while the central government may be interested in all deaf people, the social services department of Hertfordshire will be especially interested in the deaf people in Hertfordshire.

The distinction between territorially oriented and affinity group oriented studies not only matches the two questions which Holman (1970) poses—where are the deprived and who are the socially deprived?—but also accords with an analysis of poverty concepts used in a Social Science Research Council review of research on poverty (1968). Six categories of concepts are seen as current in thinking about poverty. The first three are described as crisis poverty, the hardships such as follow bereavement, injury, illness, unemployment or other disasters; long-term dependencies i.e. mental or physical handicaps which may be congenital or caused perhaps by non-recovery from crises; and life-cycle poverty as first identified by Rowntree. These three concepts correlate with studies of affinity groups. In addition, the concepts of depressed-area poverty afflicting regions which lag economically, and down-town poverty, or 'twilight zones', would be revealed by studies of territorially defined groups. Finally the SSRC review points to the 'culture of poverty', a term used to describe the combination of the previously defined concepts which may interact to produce a particular value system. This final concept accentuates the impossibility of comprehending social and personal needs from the viewpoint of either a single conceptual basis or a grouping approach alone. But the distinction between a territorial approach and affinity group studies will be used below when describing some of the investigations of analysis of needs already undertaken.

Data sources What are the data sources for gaining data suitable for providing information for the analysis of needs? There is much regularly published material relating to territorial groups with the Population Census being of prime importance. Currently undertaken every five years, alternately with complete coverage and with a 10% sample, it must form the basic material for every local planner. Its value has increased in recent years by the advent of computerised methods to speed up the processing and by the increased availability of information for enumeration districts.

Most of these districts range in population size from 500 to 1,000 and they are small enough to ensure a sufficient degree of homogeneity of inhabitants and large enough to ensure anonymity of any individual's responses. In addition the 1971 Census saw the inclusion of a geocode for the place of enumeration of every household. Geocodes are National Grid geographic co-ordinate references which permit the aggregation of individual data into units of any desired size. The availability of data for enumeration districts, with the added refinement of geocoding, therefore permits data to be obtained for small areal units which may be indicative of that area's needs: data about the degree of over-crowding or the provision of amenities such as baths and lavatories or the population composition.

Other regularly produced material from the Office of Population Censuses and Surveys (OPCS) includes the reports of the Family Expenditure Survey and the General Household Survey both of which are in continuous operation. However, both surveys are of more direct interest to national rather than local planners since they are not published with sufficient areal disaggregation to provide material relating to individual local authorities. Other material collected and published regularly by central bodies includes the reports by the Home Office, the Department of Health and Social Security, the Department of the Environment and other government agencies as well as summaries such as those of the Institute of Municipal Treasurers and Accountants which compare local authorities' provisions and costs relating to social service activities. Often from these published statistics material can be culled which allows for some inferences to be made about different areas' needs and services.

Other central sources include information held by the Inland Revenue on incomes, by DHSS on social security benefits and by the Department of Employment and Productivity on unemployment, but these sources suffer, perhaps fortunately, from problems of confidentiality and from difficulties of non-comparability with other statistics owing to the lack of co-terminous boundaries with other administrative areas.

At the local level a host of other data has been used in studying and inferring needs of areas—rating and valuation lists, truancy figures, suicide distribution, numbers of evictions, rent tribunal cases, etc. All suffer from the lack of comparability between different areas because of varying definitions and different administrative policies. These difficulties are well documented in the Southwark working paper on methods of analysing need (1970).

At present the SSRC and the Royal Statistical Society are sponsoring the publication of a series of volumes on the sources and nature of the statistics of the United Kingdom, and the topic of social services statistics will be covered by chapters on the personal social services, social security, the health services and the voluntary services. Because of the comparative lack of standard and regularly published material which relates directly to the analysis of needs, often recourse must be made to specially commissioned investigations. In fact it is scarcely likely that one could ever rely solely on annual returns for assessing needs, since as new needs are recognised and action taken to respond to them, there must inevitably be time-lag before new reporting procedures can be assimilated into routine statistical reports. A predominant role in gathering new information is played by the survey, and considerable expertise has been developed in the undertaking and analysis of surveys, ranging from statistical sampling theory to interviewing skills (Moser & Kalton 1971).

Although in other areas of scientific investigation, a major technique for acquiring information is the use of the experimental method, this is not a technique which has gained wide currency in the social services field. Two of the few exceptions are the study by Goldberg, Mortimer & Williams (1970) to determine the effectiveness with elderly clients of trained versus professionally untrained workers, and the study by Reid & Shyne (1969) to compare the relative effectiveness of planned short-term casework with open-ended long-term casework.

Data analysis Once data has been collected a major problem is the meaningful compression of it. The standard and generally well-known procedures of tabulating results and calculating measures of central tendency, such as the mean, median and the mode, are of course used. But the more esoteric, to the layman, data manipulations such as factor analysis and principal components analysis, and even graphic presentation, are frequently so devoid of intuitive meaning to those taking decisions that simpler and more readily comprehensible methods must be used in their place. The statistician is thus not encouraged to retreat to a lofty tower of statistical nicety. In this respect the cluster analysis techniques as used in the Local Government Operational Research Unit (LGORU) studies of old people (Brotherton, Gwynne & Thursfield 1971; LGORU 1972) are to be preferred to the principal components analysis used in part of the Liverpool study of social malaise (Amos 1970). However, there is an increasing willingness on the part of social service providers to accept that numeracy is a skill which has some place even in the social worker's world.

Where data relate to different geographic areas a very parsimonious procedure is to map it. From Mayhew (1851) to the present day, analysts interested in social phenomena have used mapping techniques to draw attention to regional variations. On a smaller scale, Booth (1889-91) especially used such methods to delineate those areas of London which manifested the greatest poverty. Certainly with both the advent of computer mapping programmes for Census geocoded data and the integral requirement for maps as part of local authority development plans, we can expect the role of maps to increase as an aid to decision-taking. A more unusual social cartographic exercise has been carried out by Hope (1969) who mapped the social space of Edinburgh, so that wards similar on social indices appeared in close proximity in the form of representation used. On the other hand, a knowledge of physical proximity and location alone is insufficient for mapping individuals' perceptions of the world about them. This is reflected in the considerable growth of geographical studies relating to individuals' perception of their environment (Downs 1970; Goodey 1971).

The territorial approach: social area analyses of needs

The redistribution of national income occurs in many ways but there are two forms of particular relevance to the present theme: it is allocated to individuals, in terms of wages, benefits and allowances; and it is allocated to areas through various channels such as development incentive grants, urban aid grants, rate support grants, etc. The rate support grant, to local authorities, for example, is composed of three elements—needs, domestic and resources. The needs element, not being simply geared to geographic size nor overall population, reflects a philosophy of redistribution according to needs rather than, say, contributions. It is therefore of interest to see what the Treasury, other government departments and local authorities agree upon as to the major determinants of the needs of local authorities. The factors which enter the calculation for determining the needs element, apart from gross population, include the number of young and old people, high and low density, road mileage, declining population and whether or not the local authority is in the metropolitan district.

The recent years have seen an explicit governmental acceptance that these last factors alone are in themselves incapable of summarising the full variations between authorities—there is also available other quantitative material which is indicative of presumptive differential needs and which can inform administrative decisions on the allocation of resources. Thus the priority approach of positive discrimination, developed through Educational Priority Areas, Community Development Projects and the Urban Programmes generally is indicative of a greater concern with adjusting input resources to an area's individual needs.

The social area analysis which is here implied has a strong historic record in this century, with a line of development from Booth's studies in England, through the human ecology approach to urban studies of Park, Burgess & McKenzie of the Chicago school, to the work of Shevky & Bell (1955). The American authors especially have used the methods of multivariate data analysis to illuminate theories of urban growth and urban social structure. In Britain, the ecological approach has been used, for example, by Morris (1957) in the field of criminal studies, while Moser & Scott (1961) were the first to apply the technique of component analysis to the study of British towns.

With specific reference to analysing variations in needs and resources between local authorities in the health and welfare fields, the studies undertaken by Davies and his colleagues deserve particular attention. (Davies 1968; Davies, Barton, McMillan & Williamson 1971). Of especial interest is his concept of territorial justice formulated thus: 'there should be a perfect positive correlation between indices of standards and the index measuring the relative needs of each area for the service, the relative inequality of the standards indices being the same as that of the index of relative needs.' (Davies 1968, p. 55). That Davies is able to show that the figures do not fulfil the criteria specified, thereby implying territorial injustice, can cause no surprise, but the data collected in support of these investigations do provide material to influence future policy.

It is of interest to examine the various indicators which different investigations have used in attempting to delineate an area's needs. Davies, in constructing his Social Conditions Index for his study of the relative needs of authorities for old people's services used eight variables:

(1) Proportion of households living at more than $1\frac{1}{2}$ persons per room.
(2) Proportion of households in undivided dwellings with 5 amenities or 4.
(3) Infant mortality rate.
(4) Average expectation of life at 1 year.
(5) Mortality rate from bronchitis.
(6) Proportion of occupied and retired males in social classes IV and V.
(7) Proportion of the labour force in Standard Industrial Groups I-XVI.
(8) Net product of a penny rate per thousand population.

The Plowden Report (Central Advisory Council for Education 1967), with an educational focus, suggested eight area indicators:

(1) Social class composition, based on occupation.
(2) Family size.
(3) Supplements in cash and kind from the state—free school meals, social security benefits, etc.
(4) Overcrowding and sharing.
(5) Poor attendance at school and truancy.
(6) Proportion of retarded, disturbed or handicapped pupils.
(7) Incomplete families.
(8) Children unable to speak English.

The study by Craig & Driver (1972) at the Office of Population Censuses and Surveys made a preliminary examination of the problems of using census data to identify and quantify adverse social conditions in small areas. The indicators which these investigators selected for forming into an aggregate index were:

(1) Children aged 0-14 as a percentage of total population.

(2) Males 65 or over and females 60 or over as a percentage of total population.

(3) Males in Social Classes IV and V as a percentage of all males classified by social class.

(4) Households with no hot-water tap as a percentage of all households.

(5) Households living at more than 1·5 persons per room as a percentage of all households.

The Liverpool study of social malaise (Amos 1970) where the units of analysis were wards and 330 enumeration districts, looked at indicators of social malaise based on 36 measures relating to crime, employment instability, ill-health, as well as the number of people identified as in receipt of service from social support agencies. The social malaise data was then examined in the light of 6 locally obtained housing stress measures and 58 items derived from Census material. In all 33,000 separate statistics entered into the initial analysis.

In such studies as these, and in the absence of a court of appeal that can decide which of the many variables is, *a priori*, the most important, there is the very real problem of data compression. Davies used principal component analysis which summarises the original variables by obtaining from them, if the original variables are inter-related, a smaller number of derived variables or principal components which can adequately account for the original pattern of variation. In his analysis, Davies found, for the study of old people's needs, that the first such principal component accounted for over half the variation in the data, and it was this he used as his Social Conditions Index.

An example of a simpler procedure, but one which does not take into account the inter-relationships between the original variables, has been used by the Inner London Education Authority (ILEA) to compile its own index of educational priority schools. Extending the Plowden criteria, some ten measures were used:

(1) Social class, based on occupation.

(2) Housing stress, derived from Census density estimates.

(3) Large families; the percentage of families of 4 or more children.

(4) Poverty as indicated by free meal take-up.
(5) The number of immigrants in the school.
(6) The percentage of pupils in the lowest 25% at 11+.
(7) Teacher stress as indicated by the number of short absences.
(8) Pupil turnover.
(9) Parental interest assessed from the percentage of parents attending the child's first medical.
(10) Floor space per child to indicate building adequacy.

Each of these ten measures was given equal weight in the composite index, which contrasts with principal components analysis in which, for example, two highly interrelated variables together contribute less than two variables independent of one another. The ILEA procedure (ILEA 1971a), using individual primary school catchment areas as the unit of analysis, was to scale each measure by allocating 0 or 100 to the most extreme observations, with the few extremes in each direction undifferentiatedly receiving equally 0 or 100; then to allocate the values 1 to 99 proportionately to the remaining observations; and finally to calculate each school's index by summing the ten 0-100 scores. Each of the 650 schools could then be ranked from 1 to 650. This ordered list was used administratively in a number of ways (ILEA 1971b). For example, the first 152 sites (a number of schools share sites) were allocated sums of money to be spent at the head's discretion; the first 60 sites were selected by the Department of Education and Science for the teachers in them to receive extra allowances; and the first 50 sites were allocated extra non-teaching staff.

In a similar manner, the Birmingham Education Committee (1968) used seven factors to aid in decisions about resource allocation. Using the data for enumeration districts, seven maps, one for each factor, were compiled with each below-average district shaded for each factor. When the seven maps were superimposed, to produce a *sieve map*, districts below average on all factors appeared as true black spots. Statistically, this procedure is equivalent, in terms of equal weighting of factors, to that of the ILEA.

A further example of need indicators informing policy decisions at a local level is the study (Deacon & Cannan 1970) carried out to decide on the number and location of social service department area team offices in Islington. Maps were used to plot the distribution of social priority areas defined as high on a housing stress index or low in terms of socio-economic occupational status. Then a range of from three to twelve possible office locations was explored and evaluated in terms of accessibility, both by the total population and by the population of social priority area inhabitants, and in terms of the expected size of social work teams needed. An interesting attempt was also made to relate within one area the current caseloads of each pre-Seebohm department to the indices of housing stress and socio-economic status. However, the authors of the report noted that 'we were forced to the conclusion that where a positive correlation between caseload density and measures of housing stress or socio-economic status *was* demonstrated, this indicated the degree to which existing social work was meeting the need it aimed to meet. Where no positive correlation was demonstrated this was taken to reflect the existence of barriers to the use of social work services for those most in need'. (Deacon 1970, p. 47.) They also report that juvenile delinquency rates were not significantly correlated with the housing index but rather with the measure of socio-economic status. This finding accords with that of Morris: 'the physical characteristics are of little relevance save as an indirect determinant of the social status of an area', (p. 130), and that of Amos: 'unfit housing . . . may not always be particularly relevant to social problems' (p. 4).

At a national level, the Urban Programme has from its inception made explicit use of indicators in channelling funds. Thus, the initial allocation of resources, intended to extend nursery education, went only to projects in areas with a either high degree of overcrowding, (more than 2% of households with a density greater than 1½ persons per room), or with at least 6% of immigrants on the school roll. But as Smith & Smith (1971) comment, more recently 'the trend is to support projects that attempt new ways of working in poverty areas. . . . Instead of a topping-up operation, the emphasis is now on developing new approaches' (p. 1277). Consequently, social need indicators are less used as strict criteria but are considered in conjunction with other factors, such as novelty of ideas and local support, in aiding allocation decisions. Similarly, the action-research oriented Community Development Projects, established by the Home Office, are also located in response to the combination of the priority of an area's social needs and the support likely to be obtained from local social service agencies.

Some problems The value of the particular indicators chosen depends not only on the wisdom of the investigator in picking appropriate indicators in the first place, but also on factors such as their reliability and the degree to which they reflect artefactual constraints in their collection.

Thus in the Liverpool study the correlations for the numbers of children's cases and the numbers of houses disinfested for two successive years were comparatively low, indicating that not too much reliance should be placed on any one year's figures. Often there are problems of obtaining all data for a comparable time period. Census data can become rapidly out of date in areas of redevelopment (Craig 1972). And there are always problems to be encountered when trying to obtain data from different administrative sources.

Some benefits Apart from the explicit value of social area analysis in aiding policy decisions, working with many departments has other advantages. An understanding of the multifactorial basis of needs indicators emphasises the consequent necessity for a multi-faceted approach to deal with social issues. By the active involvement of many departments and agencies in providing material for such needs studies, the groundwork is laid for an inter-departmental and corporate approach at both the national and local level. The Urban Programme, co-ordinated by the Home Office, involves also the Department of Health and Social Security, the Department of Education and Science, the Department of the Environment and the Department of Employment and statutory bodies, borough departments and voluntary agencies and, apart from its substantive findings, encouraged the development of a more rational and evaluative approach to the social problems of the area. Indeed, a significant by-product of such inter-departmental co-operation at a local level can be the changed awareness of social servants, particularly social workers, about their role in social planning. The Town and Country Planning Act, 1968 made clear that the planning of the physical environment could not be isolated from its social consequences and the Skeffington Report demonstrated the opportunities for greater community involvement in the planning process. Social workers can contribute in major ways: they can assist directly by virtue of their professional knowledge base and thereby participate in planning to alleviate the needs of the people they serve; and, in terms of community development, they can stimulate others to play a more active part in shaping their own futures.

The affinity group approach

Since other chapters of this book are dealing with the problems of a variety of groups and their particular needs, I shall confine the present review of affinity group approaches to focusing upon some methodological topics.

Despite the emphasis so far on areas even within formally designated areas of need, different people require different forms of service—adding resources to schools in educational priority areas does little to benefit the elderly, just as the construction of an old people's home does not have much effect upon school children.

Therefore groups of similar individuals must be identified in such a way that policies about the provision of services for them can be planned and a first stage in any study of affinity groups must be to obtain a numerical estimate of prevalence.

Frequently, groups already of administrative interest can be identified from standard sources such as Census material, Registrar General's returns or hospital statistics. But to attach other items of information to the identified numbers often proves impossible since the data presentation is incompatible with the researcher's requirements. One then has the choice of either establishing new methods of data recording, perhaps by developing improved record linkage systems, or one must undertake ad hoc inquiries, usually in the form of a special survey. This latter method is usually the more suitable since to record on a regular basis all the information that one might possibly require would be a costly and cumbersome procedure.

Three broad approaches of estimating the needs of affinity groups can be discerned:

(1) the use of waiting lists and other indicators of present demand;

(2) the application of data from previous surveys, undertaken elsewhere; and
(3) specific field surveys of the needs of local groups.

Two recent studies can be used to exemplify these different approaches to the development of policies towards serving the needs of particular groups—the LGORU studies (1972) and the PA International Management Consultants' evaluation of future social services expenditure for Leicester (1972).

The LGORU study focused on the needs of the elderly and on the administrative problems of making decisions about the relative needs of different groups. The report begins by noting that while the administrator may be 'as deeply concerned as the fieldworker in providing the right help at the right time, he cannot assimilate details of hundreds of case histories'. (p. 1). The problem becomes one of developing procedures to yield a comparatively small number of groups which fieldworkers and administrators can use on a joint basis for assessing the extent of needs and priorities. In the first study the project team was able to draw upon questionnaire data already gathered by Harris & Clausen (1968) on a random sample of some 900 elderly people living in Sheffield. The questionnaire data covered three broad areas—the personal characteristics of the individuals, the availability of helping friends and relatives and the conditions in which they lived. Items included age, sex, marital state, income, housing tenure, as well as data on health and household amenities, etc. Altogether some 48 items were obtainable for these living in private accommodation and 23 for those in residential accommodation. With the computer assistance of a cluster analysis programme each individual was then compared with every other individual on each of the items, and for each pair of individuals a similarity score was calculated which served as the basis for the formation of groups containing similar individuals. For those in private accommodation, 20 groups with an average membership size of 42 seemed sufficient to reflect the similarity and differences of the individuals sampled; for the people in residential accommodation, 5 groups, with an average of 10 people in each, seemed adequate.

With the method tested, the project team felt confident enough to repeat the procedure in the environment of the Manchester Social Service Department. This time, and using only cases known to the department, 16 groups appeared to be needed in order to provide the best data compression without placing overly dissimilar cases in the same group. Then the most representative case for each group was examined by the appropriate social worker and other senior workers, and the needs of each individual case were decided upon by specifying the desirable standard of care in terms of the 11 services of early or regular social work visits, visits by social work assistants, home helps, meals-on-wheels, aids, sheltered housing, residential placement, short-term care, day centres and holidays. The report states that 'It is not suggested that each case in a group should receive the same care. On the contrary, the social worker dealing with each case will be in a position to determine the proper care for each individual. For members of the same group this could require more resources or less than those suggested for the representative case. . . . What we are relying on is that these variations in the way each case in a group is treated will tend to balance out.' (LGORU 1972, p. 32.)

By scaling up from the levels of service proposed for the 363 sampled cases, estimates were obtained for the total resources, both staff and facilities, which the department would need to provide for all cases in contact. In addition the report suggests that the 16 cases can be used as reference cases for determining future standards of care, to plot individuals' progress from one case type to another, and as instructional material for departmental training. Further work is under way to extend the system to include physically handicapped and mentally disordered clients, where some 20 reference cases may be needed, children's cases where possible 25 will suffice, and family casework where an as yet unknown number will be needed. Although the Manchester report suffers from considering only those making demands on the department and not including those with similar characteristics in the general community, it does allow estimates to be made of the improvements necessary to achieve a prescribed level of care for those already known. At the same time, the grouping procedure aids resource allocation decisions by providing quantitative estimates of the numbers who would be affected by increased expenditure on particular services.

The Leicester investigation had a much tighter time schedule and a broader brief—to evaluate the future social services expenditure within three months. There was, therefore, greater emphasis upon using present demands as an indicator of future needs. For example, the figure for the expected demand for residential places (33·59 per 1,000 population 65 and over) is derived by adding to the numbers presently in homes, an adjusted number of those on the waiting list together with a turnover margin and an emergency reserve. As the report says 'the above results take no account of . . . persons at risk whose names are not even on the waiting list'. For sheltered housing, on the other hand, the estimates were calculated by applying figures obtained on the basis of a previous national survey (Townsend & Wedderburn 1965) and another more localised survey (Cumberland County Council 1966). As might be expected, whereas the shortfall for residential places in 1976 is predicted to be some 7%, that for sheltered housing is some 66%. Thus the estimates based on administrative criteria, such as waiting lists, contrast with those based on studies of the assessed needs of individuals in the community, but not necessarily in contact with the social services. Within the Leicester study itself estimates of needs derived from a field survey of the physically handicapped as opposed to known clients, imply for 1976 a proportionate increase of some 140% in the general class of registrations.

Having exemplified the use of these three approaches to estimating needs some of their advantages and disadvantages can now be considered. The demand approach, unless administrative channels are very open, will probably underestimate 'true' need, but may nevertheless still provide some conservative estimate of current service shortfalls. The application of findings from surveys of other areas can only be successful if one believes that the new area is comparable in significant detail to the surveyed area, but if this is the case the procedure can save considerable time and effort. For example, an over-reliance on national figures, such as those from the national survey (Harris 1971) to estimate local incidence of handicapped people would be hazardous since even the regional figures presented probably mask much local variation.

Thus for many topics only local field surveys can reveal local need, and if these are undertaken in an appropriate manner, then irrespective of their substantive findings they can lead to incidental and immediate changes in the social and administrative environment. For example, the survey into the development of services for the elderly in Essex (Essex County Council 1970) and the survey of the chronically sick and disabled in the Isle of Wight (Brown, Thomas & Smith 1972) both comment on such factors as the post-survey continuation of volunteer involvement; improved understanding amongst both statutory and voluntary agencies of the benefits of joint working arrangements; and the establishment of contact services 'at risk' groups. Such forms of action research are developments to be welcomed. Even the apparent academic exercise of gathering data about people and places indicative of need yields immediate benefits since investigators will need to make personal contact with other departments and with other agencies in their search for relevant material. And these inter-organisational contacts will be of value in the development of multi-factorial strategies for multi-factorial problems.

Conclusions

Although social area analysis can help in pinpointing needy areas, and although the study of particular affinity groups can clarify their needs, the choice of the actual services and programmes which these needy areas and individuals should receive remains a crucial problem. This is especially so when the concern is not only with providing services for people now in need but also attempting to develop strategies to prevent people becoming in need at a future date, i.e. focusing on both causes and effects. The social sciences have yet to reach such a state of knowledge that recipes for prevention and cures can be offered with a high degree of empirical confidence. Questions about the best place for intervention in a complex of social processes remain to be answered: Moynihan (1970) has described the American experience of over-optimistic reliance upon one theory of the causation of juvenile delinquency, the 'opportunity' theory of Cloward & Ohlin (1960) which despite its minority acceptance by criminologists, formed the basis for the federal programme 'Mobilization for Youth'. The lack of the programme's success attributed to it by both academics and politicians probably reflects the inadequacy of any one single approach in making a dramatic impact on basic problems of society. Halsey, studying the effectiveness of the English educational priority area projects has also stressed that a strictly educational approach to community problems will be insufficient to resolve an area's difficulties. In the medical field, too, the increasing number of community health centres, belated though many of them are, also reflects a growing awareness that medical matters cannot be considered in isolation from their social setting.

Until recently social workers have worked in a compartmentalised fashion despite their traditional fostering of close contact at ground level with a variety of other agencies. Nevertheless they have had little impact in influencing policies at higher levels. Now, with the strength of greater unity and larger departments as power bases, the hope must be that social workers will use this power not just for their own professionalism but to participate in an authoritative way in planning to remedy the needs of their clients.

References

Alderson, M. R. (1966) 'The accuracy of the certification of death and the classification of the underlying cause of death from the death certificate'. M.D. thesis, University of London, London.

Allport, G. W. (1940) 'The psychologist's frame of reference', *Psychol. B.* 37, 1.

Amos, F. J. C. (1970) *Social Malaise in Liverpool.* Liverpool Corporation, Liverpool.

Birmingham Education Committee (1968) *Report of the Education Committee on School Building in Educational Priority Areas.* BEC, Birmingham.

Booth, C., ed. (1889-91) *Labour and Life of the People.* Williams and Norgate, London.

Bradshaw, J. (1972) 'The concept of social need', *New Soc.*, 30 March, 640.

Brotherton, J., Gwynne, D. & Thursfield, P. (1971) *Planning Welfare Services for the Elderly*, Report C.108, Local Government Operational Research Unit, London.

Brown, M. J., Thomas, N. M. & Smith, A. (1972) *Report on the Survey of Chronically Sick and Disabled Persons Resident on the Isle of Wight.* Institute of Local Government Studies, University of Birmingham, Birmingham.

Central Advisory Council for Education (1967) *Children and their Primary Schools.* HMSO, London.

Cloward, R. A. & Ohlin, L. E. (1960) *Delinquency and Opportunity: a theory of delinquent gangs.* Free Press, New York.

Committee on Public Participation in Planning (1969) *People and Planning* (Chairman: A. M. Skeffington). HMSO, London.

Craig, J. & Driver, A. (1972) 'The identification and comparison of small areas of adverse social conditions', *Appl. Statist.*, 21, 25.

Culyer, A. J., Laver, R. J. & Williams, A. (1971) 'Social indicators: health', *in Social Trends No.* 2, ed. M. Nissel. Central Statistical Office. HMSO, London.

Cumberland County Council (1966) *The Needs of the Aged in Cumberland: report of the Second Working Party*. Cumberland C.C.
Davies, B. P. (1968) *Social Needs and Resources in Local Services*. Michael Joseph, London.
Davies, B. P., Barton, A. J., McMillan, I. S. & Williamson, V. K. (1971) *Variations in Services for the Aged* (Occasional Papers on Social Administration, No. 40). Bell and Sons, London.
Deacon, B. & Cannan, C. (1970) 'Social priority areas and Seebohm', *Soc. Wk. Today*, 1, 44.
Doreian, P. (1970) *Mathematics and the Study of Social Relations*. Weidenfeld and Nicolson, London.
Downs, R. M. (1970) *Geographic Space Perception: past approaches and future prospects. Progress in Geography: international review of current research*. Edward Arnold, London.
Essex County Council (1970) *Development of Services for the Elderly*. Essex C.C.
Goldberg, E. M., Mortimer A. & Williams, B. T. (1970) *Helping the Aged: a field experiment in social work*. Allen and Unwin, London.
Goodey, B. (1971) *Perception of the Environment*. Centre for Urban and Regional Studies, University of Birmingham, Birmingham.
Greve, J., Page, D. & Greve, S. (1971) *Homelessness in London*. Scottish Academic Press, Edinburgh.
Grogono, A. W. & Woodgate, D. J. (1971) 'Index for measuring health', *The Lancet*, 7732, 1024.
Hall, A. S. (1971) 'Client reception in a social service agency', *Publ. Admin.*, 49, 25.
Harris, A. I. & Clauser, R. (1968) *Social Welfare for the Elderly*. HMSO, London.
Harris, A. I., Cox, E. & Smith, C. R. W. (1971) *Handicapped and Impaired in Great Britain, Part* 1. HMSO, London.
Herman, M. & Munk, M. (1969) *Decision-making in Poverty Programs*. Columbia University Press, New York.
Hole, W. V. & Attenburrow, J. J. (1966) *Houses and People*. HMSO, London.
Holman, R. (1970) 'Combating social deprivation', *in Socially Deprived Families in Britain*, ed. R. Holman. Bedford Square Press, London.
Hope, K. (1969) 'A guide to social investment', *Appl. Soc. Stud.*, 1, 21.
Inner London Education Authority (1971a) *ILEA Index of Educational Priority Areas*. (R.S. 501/71), ILEA London.
Inner London Education Authority (1971b) *Resources Allocated to Primary Schools with Special Difficulties* (R.S. 505/71), ILEA, London.
Local Government Operational Research Unit (1972) *Manchester's Old People* (Report No. C120). LGORU, London.
Mayhew, H. (1851) *London Labour and the London Poor*, vols. 1 and 2. London Labour, London.
Morris, T. (1957) *The Criminal Area*. Routledge and Kegan Paul, London.
Moser, C. A. & Kalton, G. (1971) *Survey Methods in Social Investigation*, 2nd ed. Heinemann, London.

Moser, C. A. & Scott, W. (1961) *British Towns: a statistical study of their social and economic differences.* Oliver and Boyd, Edinburgh.

Moynihan, D. P. (1970) *Maximum Feasible Misunderstanding.* Free Press, New York.

P.A. International Management Consultants Ltd (1972) *An Evaluation of Future Social Services Expenditure on Behalf of the City of Leicester.* P.A. International Management Consultants Ltd., London.

Packman, J. (1968) *Child Care: needs and numbers.* Allen and Unwin, London.

Reid, W. J. & Shyne, A. W. (1969) *Brief and Extended Casework.* Columbia University Press, New York.

Riggs, F. W. (1962) *Convergences in the Study of Comparative Public Administration and Local Government.* University of Florida, Gainesville.

Schwartz, J. (1971) 'Human Needs and Monetary Accountancy Planning Methods: a discussion of cost-benefit analysis in transport planning', *Quart. B. GLC Intelligence unit,* 15, 19.

Shevky, E. & Bell, W. (1955) *Social Area Analysis.* Stanford University Press, Stanford.

Smith, T. & Smith, G. (1971) 'Urban First Aid', *New Soc.,* 30 December, 1277.

Social Science Research Council (1968) *Research on Poverty.* Heinemann, London.

Southwark Community Project, National Institute for Social Work Training and Planning Division, London Borough of Southwark (1970) 'Working paper on methods of analysing need'. LBS, London.

Stacey, M., ed. (1969) *Comparability in Social Research.* Heinemann, London.

Stevens, S. S., Carton, A. S. & Slickman, G. M. (1958) 'A scale of apparent intensity of electric shock', *J. Exp. Psychol.,* 56, 328.

Susser, M. W. & Watson, W. (1971) *Sociology in Medicine.* Oxford University Press, London.

Tauber, K. E. (1970) 'Toward a social report: a review article', *Human Resources,* 5, 354.

Townsend, P. & Wedderburn, D. (1965) *The Aged in the Welfare State.* Bell, London.

Tucker, L. R. & Messick, S. J. (1963) 'An individual difference model for multi-dimensional scaling', *Psychometrika,* 28, 333.

United States Department of Health, Education and Welfare (1969) *Toward a Social Report.* U.S. Government Printing Office, Washington.

Warren, M. D. (1971) 'Evaluation of services', *in Management and the Health Services,* ed. A. Gatherer & M. D. Warren. Pergamon Press, Oxford.

Wootton, B. (1966) 'A social scientist's approach to maternal deprivation', *in Deprivation of Maternal Care.* Public Health Papers, no. 14, W.H.O. Geneva.

3 *Poverty and the social services department*

Adrian Sinfield

Workers in the social services departments are constantly being confronted by the problems of poverty: yet the planning of the new departments has shown scant attention to its persistence. Indeed, the Seebohm report scarcely mentions the word and certainly gave the problem no priority. In view of this neglect of the positive contribution that the personal social services department can make, this chapter discusses some of the ways in which the power and resources of the new department can be used as one important part of society's fight against poverty (see note 1).

In the day-to-day practice of most departments there has been more recognition of the rediscovery of poverty over the last decade, reflected in the shift away from reinterpreting poverty in terms of such treatment categories as 'problem families' to regarding it as one of the major obstacles to its work. The department does its job *despite* all the poverty and misery that persists. The next move is more difficult to make. The recognition of poverty as a central challenge which is to be given high priority by the department entails a reassessment of policy and planning priorities on the basis of our knowledge of poverty and its causes. For, in a modern industrial society, poverty means exclusion, the lack of resources and opportunity to participate in the rising living standards of the rest of the community.

The efforts of the new department alone will not of course be in any way sufficient to avoid poverty: it can only be part, although a crucial part, of the many ways in which the whole society organises to fight poverty. In fact, the scale and extent of changes needed to end poverty may often appear so vast that we feel rendered impotent, and there is a great danger that workers in the social services department may become cynical of their own role, accepting the critics' labels of 'social tranquillisers', 'agents of social control' or 'patchers up' as inescapable. It becomes all too 'tempting for social workers to believe there is nothing social work departments, let alone individual social workers, can do to alleviate the more general problem' (Cheetham 1972, p. 58; Case-Con 1972, pp. 3-4).

The nature of poverty

But analysis of the nature and extent of poverty in the still unequal and class-bound society of Britain today shows the crucial part that may be played by the social services department. Poverty is not simply a shortage of income but a lack of resources which include the whole range of services and benefits provided by central and local government or to which they are able to give access. These are part of what Charles Reich has called 'the new property' and form part of the common wealth of society.

The value of many resources, especially services, in maintaining or raising living standards is not shown by calculations of poverty based on government surveys of household incomes and expenditure. These tell us nothing about the need for or the provision of services, let alone their nature and quality. We cannot discover from such sources the extent to which poverty of income is combined with poverty of the social services—education, health, housing and personal social services, as well as social security payments. Equally they are silent about the extent of poverty in the community as a whole that may impoverish all residents by the lack of facilities and the dereliction of the neighbourhood. Finally, estimates based on household surveys understate the dimensions of poverty in yet another way. The homeless and those living in hostels, cheap hotels and institutions are the uncounted poor, many particularly dependent on the resources of the social services.

The danger of the available statistic therefore is that we tend to forget the limitations with which it was originally surrounded. *The Poor and the Poorest* was aimed to show the minimal extent of poverty, not its full dimensions (see the qualifications, for example, on pp. 7 and 63, Abel-Smith & Townsend 1965).

But not only was the income collected in the Ministry of Labour surveys a very limited indicator of the poverty of resources and standards of living. The principal definition of poverty used—'the level of living of National Assistance Board applicants'—was a restricted one (the basic scale rate plus 40% and the actual rent paid, Abel-Smith 1965, p. 16). Certainly this measure falls short of Townsend's own definition of the poor as those 'individuals and families whose financial resources and/or whose other resources including their educational and occupational skills, the condition of their environment at home and at work and their material possessions, fall seriously below those commanded by the average person or family . . . in the community in which they live, whether the community is a local, national or international one' (Townsend 1964, p. 8; and 1962, p. 225).

Such a relative and dynamic definition underlines the way in which poverty is linked to issues of inequality, stratification and the systems distributing resources throughout society. The range of resources included and the meaning given to 'seriously below' reflects of course judgments about what constitutes meaningful membership of society. But even by conventional and limited measures of poverty, using a lower cut-off point than *The Poor and the Poorest*, poverty remains a major problem. 'A significant minority of the population (between 4% and 9%) have incomes which are below . . . the "national minimum" defined by the government through the supplementary benefits scales' (Atkinson 1970, p. 96). Since 1969 the sharp increase in unemployment with the far greater number out of work for long periods, and the inflationary rise in prices, especially in housing and food, have pushed more into poverty than increased benefits and new programmes have helped to escape.

Poverty and participation

Many studies have emphasised the ways in which limited or reduced resources restrict people's ability to take part in the range of activities that are taken for granted by the rest of society (especially Townsend & Wedderburn 1965b; Townsend 1970b; Land 1969; Marsden 1969; Sainsbury 1971; and for a brief review of the research, Sinfield 1968). These have revealed the harsh constraints upon the lives of older people when wages have ceased (Townsend & Wedderburn 1965b, p. 137). The burden of recurrent as well as long-term unemployment may be particularly heavy, depleting the social capital and resources of many families with each successive spell out of work (Sinfield 1970, p. 235).

Persistently low wages or income can bring chronic poverty: a small drop in real income or even prolonged low income can create acute problems. Amongst the old the greatest poverty and deprivation is found amongst those longest dependent on a state pension who have long since exhausted any savings or resources (Wedderburn 1965). Their poverty forces such choices as repairing their last pair of walking shoes or buying a birthday present for a grandchild, and the restricted expenditure limits their participation in, and integration with, the rest of society. This withdrawal is frequently put down to the biological handicaps of ageing. In fact it is remarkable how easily as a society we regard such events as 'natural' and thus inevitable. (See Land 1969, for similar budget-juggling by large families in poverty and Marsden 1969, for fatherless families.)

Poverty can increase social isolation especially among those who lack a family nearby to maintain their contacts with the rest of society. Social isolation and poverty are particularly likely to occur together among single and widowed women, especially those over 70 (Tunstall 1966, p. 12). The ageing man out of work and with no family cannot afford to eat or drink out and loses contact with the informal network which is the best source of job information (Sinfield 1970, p. 230).

For the isolated, social services can play an important role in substituting for the family; they can also make a major contribution in supplementing the family's resources, especially when these are limited. The combination of low incomes and the absence of the necessary supportive services was vital in one of the very few studies of social work clients to take poverty into account (Wilson 1962, p. 49).

In very many families inadequate resources are spread more thinly, with the result that poverty is simply shared among the family, restricting the opportunities and resources of all members. Indeed the persistence of poverty was disguised by the efforts of many families in providing services, resources and often accommodation for older or disabled relatives. As one survey of the retired pointed out, 'if this report does not present a more alarmist picture of the real hardship caused by poverty for the old, it is very largely because of the help which they receive in one form or another from their family and friends' (Cole & Utting 1962, p. 103, see also Isaacs 1972). The poorest old people for example were very much more likely to share house with children or other relatives than those with higher incomes (Townsend 1965b, p. 198).

These surveys have shown little empirical support for those who are concerned about the 'misuse' of social services and their 'undermining of family responsibilities'. Most elderly recipients of social services tended to be the infirm or the incapacitated with no family or with none in reach. At the same time there was still considerable unmet need. 'Substantially more old people than are receiving different services feel a need, and otherwise seem to qualify, for them.' (Townsend 1965b, p. 135 and Isaacs 1972; similarly, see Sainsbury 1971, on the disabled.)

Poverty of the community

In many areas people live amid a poverty of surroundings and opportunities that reflects 'generations of public and social neglect, a neglect which meshes in with the "private" distress caused by housing and money worries' (Silburn 1971, p. 135). This is a cumulative aggregation of poverty that can be found in the overcrowded and inadequately-serviced slums of generally prosperous cities (see on Nottingham, Coates & Silburn 1970). It also appears in isolated towns with jobs declining in quantity and reward where the younger, more skilled, workers are compelled to move away for work. The 'D' villages of the north-east provide a particularly vivid example of the social costs left upon the remaining inhabitants as the mines have closed down (see also Gregory 1965, on a case-study of environmental pollution).

In both types of area, houses marked for eventual demolition are not maintained, let alone redecorated. Schools designated last year to be rebuilt in 1984 (as one I know) may receive few grants for basic upkeep and suffer a constant mobility of the qualified staff.

The causes of poverty

The increasing amount of research in the last decade has shown more clearly that the basic causes of poverty are to be found in the social, economic and political institutions of society and in the systems which distribute and redistribute resources and opportunities amongst the members of a society (Townsend 1970b). The greater extent of poverty among the old in Britain than in Denmark reflects public decisions institutionalised in the market and in the social division of welfare which results in greater inequality after work than during the working life (Shanas 1968, p. 384).

In this way poverty is linked with inequality in the vertical stratification between the classes of non-manual and manual work and in the horizontal division between those in work and the retired, between the healthy and the sick, and between the able-bodied and the disabled. This concentration on the allocation of resources to different groups across and among classes underlines the need for more effective income maintenance and a greater provision and variety of services.

By contrast, focus on the personal characteristics, psychological attributes or life-styles of the poor as causes of their situation may indicate a concern not so much with the fact of poverty as the behaviour of the poor, with the implication that it is the behaviour and not the poverty that is unacceptable to the rest of society (for Critique Herzog 1967, and Valentine 1968).

Priorities for policy

Analysis of the nature of poverty in a still unequal society underlines the basic importance of services and benefits as part of the resources which preserve or promote standards of living. At the same time the standard of these services must be maintained so that they do not impoverish the recipients. Policies to improve access to services and reduce social isolation will help to ensure that more needs are met and more promptly. Closer contact with the community will increase awareness of the range and extent of unmet needs and community poverty and enable better identification of both persisting and emerging patterns of need. With this knowledge the workers in the social services departments can play a vital part in improving public awareness of both the nature and extent of poverty and the scale of resources and range of programmes needed to tackle it.

These are objectives for the local social services department as a whole. Yet there is remarkably little written about internal organisation and co-ordination. The literature is generally confined to the social worker and his relations with clients; but the success of the department after the Seebohm re-organisation is now even more dependent on efficient and effective interaction between all workers and all divisions. The home help service can, for example, not only meet needs identified by other staff but ensure that their clients do not lack other services that are available. The research division can identify needs and indicate their extent and also monitor the services aimed to meet the needs; in addition it can act as an early warning system to identify new social costs, or even prevent them.

The planner and fixer

The identification of these objectives for the department underlines the key role of the social worker as a 'planner, organising a whole range of services' (Brill 1972, p. 95). With inadequate resources, often conflicting departmental policies and a variety of bureaucratic protocol and ritual at many levels of government, the value of the social worker as 'a social lubricant' cannot be overemphasised (Brill 1972, p. 96). Acting 'to manipulate, persuade and cajole agencies on behalf of clients, at a purely practical level', he is 'a fixer', skilled at obtaining informal decisions and shortcutting laid-down procedures and 'proper channels' (Palmer 1971, p. 2038 and vividly illustrated by his flow-charts).

The resources of the poor can be considerably increased, by giving priority to ensuring that people receive all the services, benefits, rebates etc. available to them through the social services department and other local and central government departments. Although this can be a very time-consuming process, workers can play a particularly important role as intermediaries with the local social security office which is by far the most important source of means-tested financial aid.

The total value of benefits can be considerable, even for those in work. 'A woman living alone earning £11 per week can pick up nearly £8 in benefits and a farm worker with four children earning £18 can claim nearly £11 worth of benefits' (Bradshaw & Wakeman 1972; see also Bull 1972). Reductions in charges for local services can make a significant difference to resources although they vary greatly from area to area. The charge for domestic help ranged from nothing to £5 a week for the same size family with the same income in 1966 (Reddin 1968, p. 12). Departments need to consider the effects of such means-tests in restricting access and reducing the benefit of services to those with limited resources.

By encouraging people to apply, and if necessary helping them to do so, workers increase the rate of take-up which varies considerably even for benefits provided on a standard scale by the central government. For example, families in working poverty living in the south-west or Wales appear much more likely to be receiving Family Income Supplement than poor families living in the south-east (writer's calculations based on Table 105, p. 331, Health and Social Security, Department of, 1972a). This may be partly due to a greater awareness of the programme in areas where there is a higher incidence of low pay.

The dangers of rationing

Yet, operating from area offices of a now comprehensive department with a much greater amount of resources available, social workers are coming to see their own role as 'a rationing agent' more clearly (Brill 1972, pp. 82-3, and Rees 1972). There is the danger that 'forced to act as protectors and guardians of inadequate social services', their use of 'professional skills that enable them to handle dissatisfied clients with tact and understanding may reduce public pressure for the improvement of social services' (George & Wilding 1972, p. 154). In this way professional expertise becomes subverted to damping down demand rather than meeting needs and assuring rights. Similarly, concern over 'dependency' may help to rationalise the limited resources and inhibit appreciation of the full extent of need, particularly among the poorest families.

Expenditure on financial assistance by 24 children's departments in the north-west in 1966 varied between £18 per thousand children and £0.70 (Heywood & Allen 1971, p. 5). Although most of the families were said to be in poverty, the adequacy of the expenditure was given very little discussion, even where one county's social workers spent only *one-fifth* of the department's estimated allocation for financial help (Heywood 1971, p. 65, emphasis added; see also Handler 1968).

Providers of many services and benefits have tended to see themselves as guardians of resources against a potential flood of applicants and have generally resisted any form of publicity. Today advertising in the local press, radio and television, by exhibitions and especially by billposting is still too rare. There is considerable ambivalence about advertising, and some remarkable inconsistencies. The availability of rate rebates has been given much more publicity in many areas than free school meals or educational maintenance allowances, meals-on-wheels or home-helps. The quality of the information made public also needs to be improved.

By contrast to the provider's picture of the demanding client, consumers describe in detail and with considerable feeling their reluctance to apply, their delays and the use of every other resort first (see especially Mayer & Timms 1970, pp. 103-5). Some only apply long after they might first have done so, and very many never apply or arrive at all (Sinfield 1970, pp. 232-3; Marsden 1969). Many therefore receive no help and remain in poverty, while others depend on a family's resources which have to be stretched even more thinly to cope. Those most likely to need a service may also be those least likely to know of it. In 1967 only half the elderly housewives interviewed in a government survey knew that they might be eligible for the home help service (Hunt 1970, p. 26).

The need for better contact

Many departments, but by no means all, have tried to improve contact with the public by placing social workers in places, such as schools and general practices, especially convenient to certain groups and by the use of sites in central shopping areas rather than remote offices upstairs in the town hall. Better use can be made of home helps, deliverers of meals-on-wheels and others inside and outside the department who are already in contact with high risk groups such as the elderly or handicapped.

Many members of the community with no formal attachment to the social services department, such as teachers, doctors, clergy and police, are well placed to act as intermediaries, but there is generally little systematic attempt to improve or build on this. The greater dependence of the separate departments in the past on referrals, and their failure to ensure that these worked effectively, contributed to the extent of unmet needs (on doctors' ignorance of many health and welfare services or their failure to recognise patients' need for them, see Sumner & Smith 1969, pp. 182-3).

Accessibility to the public depends not only on easy and quick access to an area office but also to someone who can answer queries. The crucial role of 'the gatekeeper' is still not well enough appreciated. The receptionist and telephone operator (often the same person in a position well planned for neither duty) helps both to control the demands made on any agency and to determine the ways in which they are met (Deutscher 1968, and Hall 1971).

Easier access and better information alone are not of course sufficient as a strategy against poverty 'but their absence means that existing services are not used by the very people who need them most. And this . . . is a two-way process because, if services are not requested by those who need them, those who provide them will never learn the extent of unmet need' (Cheetham 1972, p. 60). The lack of contact becomes a dangerously insidious self-reinforcing process, fostering complacency among those who have the services to give and alienation among those without them. The apparent inadequacy of supply restricts public demand, and inefficiency masks unmet need.

Abolition of patch-repair welfare

More time and resources also need to be devoted to improving the standard of services as well as improving their availability and coverage. 'All too often it can be fairly said that the impression gained of social care provisions—homes, luncheon clubs, day centres and the like—is one of meanness: makeshift premises, dreary decor and cutprice equipment with staff working against the odds to create the necessary homely or stimulating environment' (Brown 1972, p. 75; and Townsend 1965a, of old people's homes).

Services can be so poverty-stricken that they help to keep families trapped in poverty. Homeless families placed in large blocks of institutional Part III accommodation may find their present address a handicap in finding work, obtaining credit in shops and even in gaining new living quarters (Cartwright 1971). The administration may also make life more difficult for the families. In one borough a shiftworker finishing at 5 a.m. had to walk the streets until the unit opened at 7.30 a.m. Workers who missed the last meal at 5 p.m. were not refunded the charge.

Other local and central government departments tolerate practices which foster the social stigma and isolation that help to preserve poverty (Holman 1970).

One city housing department keeps a block of flats - to quote the housing manager - as a 'punishment block' for families with persistent rent arrears. The use of patch-repair housing for the poor can also promote new categories of deserving and undeserving council tenants.

Terms such as 'temporary' may conceal an official tolerance of long-lasting inadequacy: gradually, inferior services come to be accepted and the deficiency of resources minimised or even forgotten. Over a century ago Florence Nightingale wrote, 'it may seem a strange principle to enunciate as the very first requirement in a hospital that it should do the sick no harm' (quoted in Titmuss 1958, p. 131). Even such a crude measure applied to the social services indicates the extent to which much provision is inadequate.

A standard of adequacy more fitting to services available to all is that they should be of a quality acceptable to the providers for themselves and their families. Such a challenge is in a way shocking. First, it frightens by the expenditure needed to reach such a standard in many areas. Second, it reminds one forcefully of the punitive and deterrent aspects of many social service policies and the residual basis on which many others are still provided for second-class citizens. The shadow cast by the poor laws is a long one.

Poverty and social development

The ways in which the social services department can move towards 'a wider conception of social service, directed to the well-being of the whole community' (Committee on Local Authority and Allied Personal Social Services 1968, paragraph 474) must depend on a wider vision of the department's activities than currently seems to be envisaged in much community development (see, for example, Committee on Local Authority 1968, chapter XVI). Work with neighbourhood groups, the utilisation of local resources and increased citizen participation in providing and planning services are all important advances from previous traditions of individual-oriented and paternalistic social service (Younghusband 1968). Linked with the often spontaneous growth of claimants' unions and other groups, there may be considerable return from the social action which 'can transform a local protest from an emotional spasm into a formidable counter-attack' (Jay 1972, p. 14).

But, if local action is not accompanied by a reallocation of resources from outside the area, poverty may persist and participation lead to disillusionment. It is ironic that some 'radicals' and 'professionals' both finish up advocating a degree of isolationist self-help for the poor that has never been expected or demanded of other groups in society. All the evidence of research into poverty calls attention to the need for resources, and community poverty demands strategies to increase and maintain the resources of an area on a permanent basis (Rein 1970, part III; Holman 1970, and Smith 1971, p. 1280). One particular community resource recognised by very few departments is local industry which often provides a wide range of personal social services for its own staff (United Nations 1971).

The new department offers the opportunity for a new impetus towards the planning of social growth and development on a local and, with co-ordination, a regional basis. This commits workers not only to reactive community work, resisting bad or indifferent plans and policies, but to a more positive approach. It will often involve taking the initiative in proposing priorities for planning, spelling out the need for extra resources and services and actively seeking to stimulate major programmes and changes that protect, preserve and improve the standards of living of the poor.

With successful 'community-based' area offices and an active research division, the new departments provide a better opportunity to discover the range and extent of unmet needs in the area as a whole and the degree to which the local community is impoverished in terms of its resources and facilities. Better understanding of the area and its range of needs in relation to existing resources and services is vital for establishing policy priorities and for convincing local and central government of the need to produce extra resources. A sounder awareness of the scope of the problems may also provoke a more innovative approach to tackling both the symptoms and causes of what the Seebohm committee calls 'social distress'.

An essential part of any form of community planning needs to be some form of co-ordination between those departments which have traditionally recognised and treated the same problems separately, and often in conflicting ways. The housing department for example may exacerbate the problem of homelessness; but good inter-departmental relationships required to meet other objectives have often depended upon a tacit neglect of such policy conflict. Individual workers have been restrained by senior staff from breaking the truce (Glastonbury 1971, pp. 155–6).

There has been less specific recognition of the role of central government departments and even less willingness to intercede. But a local employment service that is weak in protecting the disabled worker and acquiesces in the age discrimination that leaves more and more older men to decay on the dole is creating social problems rather than providing a social service. A co-ordinated policy for the disabled at local level worked out with all local and central government departments could do much to reduce the segregation of the disabled and increase their resources.

In arguing for a leading role to be played by the new department, one has to admit the lack of power of the social services departments at both central and local government level. Children's and welfare departments previously ranked low in the local authority hierarchy. Their committee members were 'not the real powers on the council' and generally lost their battles with the finance committee (Harrison & Norton 1967, p. 335). Now the new departments have to make a powerful case for extra resources both to their local employers and to central government, using the evidence of unmet need obtained not only in the daily work but also by special surveys. This puts a great weight on their ability to persuade those commanding the resources and generally to take a part in making the rest of society aware of the extent of change needed.

Intelligence, education and agitation

In the past social workers were generally expected to be seen but not heard as they went about their work. Now one of the major objectives of the social services department is to report, educate and agitate on the causes of 'social distress', and its abolition and prevention. This is needed to fulfil the Seebohm goal of a department designed to 'reach far beyond the discovery and rescue of social casualties' (Committee on Local Authority and Allied Personal Social Services 1968, paragraph 2). It is this work, shared across the whole department, which above all determines the extent to which the personal social services act just to contain the hardships of poverty or take an active role in social development and increasing social welfare.

This places great weight on the meticulous and relentless documentation of persisting and changing patterns of need as *one* aspect of the department's policy and planning. With local offices responsible for all services in one area and the skills of its research division, the department will become more aware of the inadequacies of resources and the shortcomings of programmes. It will be better able to identify the needs of those who have not previously been the specific responsibility of any department and these will include many of the uncounted poor mentioned above (p. 58).

A later stage from which most of the old departments shied is to bring the need for extra resources and programmes to the attention of the rest of society and to involve the community in the debate over priorities. At present the personal social services tend to lack both power and resources. In 1971 total government expenditure on the personal social services still comprised less than 2¾% of spending on all the social services. (£11,335m. was spent on health, education, social security, housing and the personal social services. The expenditure on the personal social services comprised £309m., 2.72% of the total (Table 49, Central Statistical Office, 1972).)

Extra resources from central government bring greater strength to the department at local level, and standards of service in the worst areas can be promoted by the establishment of minimum requirements and a central government inspectorate. But the attainment of nationally-defined minima, generally slow to change and set with one eye on political feasibility, may be quite inadequate for successfully meeting the variety and extent of needs in many areas. A national advisory service as vigorous as the Hospital Advisory Service may do much more to encourage and support local initiative, as well as goad central government into providing more guidance and resources (see its refreshingly lively annual reports).

There has been reluctance among social workers to push for the extra resources needed by their clients, but Helen Perlman, one of the leaders of case-work in the United States, has stressed, 'a case-worker . . . should repeatedly point to and decry the absence (of resources to meet social needs) when they are lacking, and interpret the need for them to his own agency, his professional organisation, and to other welfare-minded groups in the community' (p. 445). Yet those who believe such initiatives to be a basic part of their work are regarded as exceptional. The majority are still more likely to describe this as something they would like to do if there were time, if their caseload were smaller, if there were any interest from the top or at least no fear of reproof, and if somebody would tell them how.

Agitation and advocacy can of course take many forms. At the centre of it is the public information and lobbyist role of educating and persuading the rest of the community. One advantage of community action by the Islington social workers is that 'the impact of poverty, bad housing and misery is not muffled by the formal structure but is now conveyed directly' (Carter & Barter 1972, p. 5). But for this to be continued on the regular and systematic basis that is necessary to gain momentum for change, such activity needs both institutional and professional support against the many organisational and societal pressures more likely to restrict the power and resources of the department. Over-spending, but not under-spending, is regarded as inefficient administration. 'Real District Auditors ask awkward questions about improper expenditure, not about improper underspending' (Lynes 1971, p. 20).

To be able to carry out this committed role, the workers in the social services departments need the protection and support of their professional associations and the opportunity to draw public attention to problems they face without fear of reproof or dismissal. If the professions push for more resources, better standards of service and wider coverage, individual workers can more easily refuse patch-repair welfare for those they serve. In the past most professions have tended towards a conservative approach to reform. Although debate about the best strategies for social work is increasing as a result of groups like Case-Con, the current re-organisation and the greater awareness of unmet needs, there is little evidence yet of a powerful, co-ordinated and committed pressure for programmes to reduce the economic and social burdens of those they serve.

Training and the social worker

Throughout this chapter I have been arguing for personal social services that play their part in society's fight against poverty. The role of the workers in the social services will be very much influenced by the preparation and training they receive and so this last section concentrates on the content of training for the social services. With only limited space the discussion is confined to the social worker who currently plays a key role; but clearly much of it has relevance for all the workers including home helps, receptionists and non-professional administrators.

The Seebohm report gives virtually no lead at all on the content of training (Committee on Local Authority and Allied Personal

Social Services 1968, chapter XVIII), despite its importance for socialising the worker, reinforcing a professional ideology and basically structuring his perception of what is his proper job. The importance of social work training is emphasised by the fact that in the past social workers were not taught to recognise poverty: in fact many were trained to discount or re-interpret it as a symptom of personal inadequacies. At best many learnt only to treat the 'presenting symptoms' of poverty and were given little understanding of the extent to which stress, anxiety, withdrawal and handicap could all be fostered by economic and social deprivation. There was little attention to the causes of poverty external to the family. Although responsibility for the failure to recognise the persistence of poverty and inequality must be shared with the other social science professions, 'in their pre-occupation with psychological matters, social workers have tended to develop an occupational blindness to economic realities' (Mayer 1970, p. 141 and note 2).

One lesson to be drawn from this is that social workers need more teaching on the nature of society and its problems and not just on social work techniques. Study of power and property in a stratified society needs to be closely linked to analysis of the nature and extent of poverty and inequality (Miller & Roby 1970; Tawney 1913; Townsend 1970b). Knowledge of the pressure of restricted resources at different stages of the family cycle and over a lifetime can make workers more sensitive to the psychological and social impact of poverty (Wynn 1970; Schorr 1968). Altogether, in social work as in the other social science professions, we need to develop an awareness that the revelation of one generation can become the blinkering stereotype of the next (Herzog 1967). One part of this is the constant and suspicious testing of the theories that inform policy and practice, by seeking to ask the questions that we take for granted (Schorr 1969, p. 9).

A sound knowledge of the rights and entitlements of the citizen and a good understanding of the strengths and weaknesses of the social security and social service systems are also essential. Better knowledge of the discretionary element of many benefits would make the trained worker less accepting and more questioning of the practice, as well as the theory, of many services and benefits. The worker who believes (as some I have met) that the Family Income Supplement formally abolished the wage-stop is not likely to appreciate the hardship experienced by a wage-stopped family.

It has not generally been recognised how much the teaching of the history of social policy can influence thinking on possibilities of change, and methods of change, for the future. The history of policy has been too influenced by the perspective of the providers, and study of the vigorous resistance to the New Poor Law of 1834, particularly and persistently successful in parts of the north, might encourage more discussion on such issues as local protest, claimants' unions and citizen involvement today (Edsall 1971).

Finally, any training with as wide a range of topics and material as social work presents problems of integration and the burden of this cannot be left to the students. One important opportunity for integration lies in a more varied fieldwork experience that gives more contact with central and local government departments, some knowledge of the work of the research and development division and some involvement in welfare rights activities (Bull 1969, and Bryant & Bradshaw 1971).

Poverty is a force for human erosion. We now know, more clearly than ever before, the multitude of ways in which it can impoverish the lives of those it touches. In this chapter I have tried to indicate the important part that can be played by the local social services department in helping to reduce and prevent poverty. This is not to deny the other demands made on the department, nor of course to suggest that the personal social services alone can end poverty. Major structural changes in the distribution and redistribution of resources in society are needed, and here just as in the United States, it has often been true that services 'have been used as a substitute for more searching policies to redistribute income, power and resources' (Rein 1970, p. 296).

In seeking to spell out the positive contribution that the social services department can make, I have given emphasis to the essential work of meeting needs at an individual, family and area level; to the particular value of services and benefits for those with least resources; to the danger of acquiescing in patch-repair and second-class services that support and even strengthen existing divisions in society; and to the intelligence and advocate roles of the department in identifying new as well as persisting needs, and helping to make the rest of the community aware of the issues involved and the extent of change needed.

Amid the uncertainties and anxieties that have accompanied much of the current re-organisation, with the impending upheaval of local government territories, with increasing rates of worker mobility and a greater awareness of the inadequacy of resources even to meet existing programmes, the establishment of long-term planning must seem particularly difficult. But it is at just such a period, when sectional thinking and the traditional alignment of interests and groups are weakened, that policies for change may have most success.

Notes

I would like to acknowledge very gratefully the advice, guidance and criticism I have received from Carolyn Burton, Ian Cartwright, Joan Higgins, Dennis Marsden, Dorothy Sinfield and Peter Townsend, and to thank Luise Dobson for typing the successive drafts.

1. Exceptions to this general neglect in Britain are Robert Holman (1970), and Muriel Brown (1972) and many contributors to *Case-Con*. Its fourth edition raises the dilemmas facing social workers in a capitalist society particularly sharply. In the Seebohm report the importance of a secure home in the general prevention of social distress is well emphasised (particularly Committee on Local Authority and Allied Personal Social Services 1968, paragraphs 441–6, and chapter XIII), but the need for a secure income and adequate resources is neglected, apart from the occasional passing reference to low incomes and 'the neglected flotsam and jetsam of society' (paragraph 139).
2. The theoretical rationale of much basic training in social work until recently seems in part to have been an attempt to find alternative explanations for certain forms of behaviour on the assumption that poverty no longer existed. Acceptance of the 'problem family' interpretation of poverty deserves more detailed investigation for the social policy lessons it can provide. To an extent the thesis helped to legitimise an emphasis on individual counselling techniques and the potential value of rehabilitation or resocialisation, given the chronic lack of resources available to those working in the social services.

References

Abel-Smith, B. & Townsend, P. (1965) *The Poor and the Poorest.* Bell, London.

Atkinson, A. B. (1970) *Poverty in Britain and the Reform of Social Security.* Cambridge University Press, Cambridge.

Bottomley, V. (1971) *Families with Low Incomes in London* (Poverty pamphlet). CPAG, London.

Bradshaw, J. & Wakeman, I. (1972) 'The Poverty Trap Updated', *Polit. Quart.*, 43, 959.

Brill, M. (1972) 'The Local Authority social worker', *in The Year Book of Social Policy in Britain 1971*, ed. Kathleen Jones. Routledge and Kegan Paul, London.

Brown, M. (1972) 'Inequality and the personal social services', *in Labour and Inequality*, ed. P. Townsend & N. Bosanquet.

Bryant, R. & Bradshaw, J. (1971) *Welfare Rights and Social Action: the York Experiment* (Poverty pamphlet 6). CPAG, London.

Bull, D. (1970) *Action for Welfare Rights*, Fabian Society, London, reprinted in *The Fifth Social Service*, P. Townsend *et al.*, (1971).

Bull, D., ed. (1971) *Family Poverty.* Duckworth, London.

Bull, D. (1972) 'For Your Client's Benefit', *Soc. Wk. Today*, 3, 10.

Carter, D. & Barter, J. (1972) 'Climbing off the Fence', *Soc. Wk. Today*, 3, 4.

Cartwright, I. (1971) 'Eighteen Families who became Homeless', M.A. thesis, University of Essex, Colchester.

Case-Con (1972) 'Radical social work: what is it and can it survive?', *Case-Con*, April.

Central Statistical Office (1972) *National Income and Expenditure.* HMSO, London.

Cheetham, J. (1972) *Social Work with Immigrants.* Routledge and Kegan Paul, London.

Coates, K. & Silburn, R. (1970) *Poverty: the forgotten Englishmen.* Penguin, Harmondsworth.

Cole, D. & Utting, J. (1962) *The Economic Circumstances of Old People.* Codicote Press, Welwyn.

Committee on Local Authority and Allied Personal Social Services (1968) *Report* (Chairman: F. Seebohm). Cmnd. 3703. HMSO, London.

Davie, R. *et al.*, (1972) *From Birth to Seven.* Longman and National Children's Bureau, London.

Davies, B. (1968) *Social Needs and Resources in Local Services.* Michael Joseph, London.

Deutscher, I. (1968) 'The gatekeeper in public housing', *in Among the People*, edited by I. Deutscher and E. Thompson. Basic Books, New York.

Edsall, N. C. (1971) *The Anti-Poor Law Movement: 1834–1944.* Manchester University Press, Manchester.

Foren, R. & Brown, M. J. (1971) *Planning for Service.* Charles Knight, London.

Social issues and the social services

George, V. & Wilding, P. (1972) *Motherless Families*. Routledge and Kegan Paul, London.

Glastonbury, B. (1971) *Homeless near a Thousand Homes*. Allen and Unwin, London.

Goldberg, E. M. (1970) *Helping the Aged*. Allen and Unwin, London.

Goldthorpe, J. (1969) 'Social inequality and social integration in modern Britain', *Adv. Sci.*, 190.

Gregory, P. (1965) *Polluted Homes*. Bell, London.

Greve, J., Page, D. & Greve, S. (1971) *Homelessness in London*. Scottish Academic Press, Edinburgh.

Hall, A. S. (1971) 'Client reception in a social service agency', *Publ. Admin.*, 49, 25.

Handler, J. F. (1968) 'The coercive children's officer', *New Soc.*, 3 October, 485.

Harrison, M. & Norton, A. (1967) *Local Government in England and Wales: Vol. V of Management of Local Government*. Committee on the Management of Local Government, Ministry of Housing and Local Government. HMSO, London.

Health and Social Security, Department of (1972a) *Families receiving Supplementary Benefit*. HMSO, London.

Health and Social Security, Department of (1972b) *Annual Report 1971*. HMSO, London.

Herzog, E. (1967) *About the Poor: some facts and some fictions*. U.S. Dept. of H.E.W., Children's Bureau, Washington.

Heywood, J. S. & Allen, B. K. (1971) *Financial Help in Social Work*. Manchester University Press, Manchester.

Holman, R. (ed.) (1970) *Socially Deprived Families in Britain*. Bedford Press, London.

Hospital Advisory Service (1971) *Annual Report 1970*. HMSO, London.

Hospital Advisory Service (1972) *Annual Report 1971*. HMSO, London.

Hunt, A. (1970) *The Home Help Service in England and Wales*. HMSO, London.

Isaacs, B. *et al.*, (1972) *Survival of the Unfittest: a study of geriatric patients in Glasgow*. Routledge and Kegan Paul, London.

Jay, A. (1972) *The Householder's Guide to Community Defence against Bureaucratic Aggression*. Jonathan Cape, London.

Land, H. (1969) *Large Families in London*. Bell, London.

Lynes, T. (1971) 'The Failure of Selectivity', *in Family Poverty*, ed. D. Bull. Duckworth, London.

Marsden, D. (1969) *Mothers Alone: fatherless families in poverty*. Allen Lane Press, London, revised ed. Penguin, 1973.

Mayer, J. E. & Timms, N. (1970) *The Client Speaks*. Routledge and Kegan Paul, London.

Miller, S. M. & Roby, P. (1970) *The Future of Inequality*. Basic Books, New York.

Morris, P. (1969) *Put Away*. Routledge and Kegan Paul, London.

National Innovations Centre (1972) *Welfare Rights Stalls*. NIC, London.

Palmer, E. (1971) 'Keeping the Options Open', *Brit. Hospital J. Soc. Service R.*, 45, 2033.
Perlmann, H. H. (1968) 'Can Casework Work?', *Soc. Service R.*, 42, 435.
Philp, A. F. & Timms, N. (1957) *The Problem of the Problem Family.* Family Service Unit, London.
Philp, A. F. (1963) *Family Failure.* Faber, London.
Piven, F. F. & Cloward, R. (1972) *Regulating the Poor.* Tavistock, London.
Reddin, M. (1968) 'Local Authority Means-tested Services', *in Social Services for All*, P. Townsend *et al.* Fabian Society, London.
Rees, A. M. (1972) 'Access to the Personal Health and Welfare Services', *Soc. Econ. Admin.*, 6.
Reich, C. (1964) 'The New Property', *Yale Law J.*, 73, 5.
Rein, M. (1970) *Social Policy: issues of choice and change.* Random House, New York.
Ryan, W. (1971) *Blaming the Victim.* Orbach and Chambers, London.
Sainsbury, S. (1971) *Registered as Disabled.* Bell, London.
Schorr, A. (1968) 'The family cycle and income development', *in Poverty in America*, ed. L. A. Ferman *et al.* University of Michigan, Ann Arbor (revised ed.).
Schorr, A. (1969) *Exploration in Social Policy.* Basic Books, New York.
Shanas, E., Townsend, P., Wedderburn, D., Friis, M., Milhøj, P., & Stehouwer, J. (1968) *Old People in Three Industrial Societies.* Atherton Press, New York.
Silburn, R. (1971) 'The potential and limitations of community action', *in Family Poverty*, ed. D. Bull. Duckworth, London.
Sinfield, A. (1968) 'Poverty Rediscovered', *Race*, 10, 202; reprinted with updated bibliography in *Planning for Change: problems of an urban society*, vol. 3, ed. J. B. Cullingworth. Allen and Unwin, London, 1973.
Sinfield, A. (1969) *Which Way for Social Work?* Fabian Society, London, reprinted in *The Fifth Social Service*, P. Townsend *et al.* Fabian Society, London, 1970.
Sinfield, A. (1970) 'Poor and Out of Work in Shields', *in The Concept of Poverty*, ed. P. Townsend. Heinemann, London.
Smith, T. & Smith, G. (1971) 'Urban First Aid', *New Soc.*, 30 December, 1277.
Sumner, G. & Smith, R. (1969) *Planning Local Authority Services for the Elderly.* Allen and Unwin, London.
Tawney, R. (1913) 'Poverty as an Industrial Problem', *in Memoranda on Problems of Poverty*, vol. 2. Ratan Tata Foundation. William Morris Press, London, 9.
Titmuss, R. M. (1958) *Essays on the 'Welfare State'.* Allen and Unwin, London.
Titmuss, R. M. (1968) *Commitment to Welfare.* Allen and Unwin, London.
Townsend, P. (1962) 'The Meaning of Poverty', *Brit. J. Sociol.*, 13, 210.
Townsend, P. (1964) *The Definition of Poverty* (Second Conference on Handicapped Families) Aide à Toute Détresse, UNESCO, Paris.

Townsend, P. (1965a) *The Last Refuge*. Routledge and Kegan Paul, London.
Townsend, P. & Wedderburn, D. (1965b) *The Aged in the Welfare State*. Bell, London.
Townsend, P. *et al.* (1968) *Social Services for all?* Fabian Society, London.
Townsend, P. *et al.* (1970a) *The Fifth Social Service*. Fabian Society, London.
Townsend, P. (ed.) (1970b) *The Concept of Poverty*. Heinemann, London.
Townsend, P. & Bosanquet, N. (eds.) (1972) *Labour and Inequality*. Fabian Society, London.
Tunstall, J. (1966) *Old and Alone*. Routledge and Kegan Paul, London.
United Nations (1971) *Industrial Social Welfare*. United Nations, New York.
Valentine, C. (1968) *Culture and Poverty*. University of Chicago Press, Chicago.
Veit-Wilson, J. H. (1971) *The Right to Privacy and the Collection of School Dinner Money*. Newcastle-upon-Tyne Polytechnic, Newcastle.
Wedderburn, D. (1965) 'Facts and Theories of the Welfare State', *in The Socialist Register* 1965, ed. J. Saville and R. Milliband. Merlin Press, London.
Wilson, H. (1962) *Delinquency and Child Neglect*. Allen and Unwin, London.
Wilson, H. & Herbert, G. (1972) 'Hazards of environment', *New Soc.*, 8 June, 508.
Wootton, B. (1959) *Social Science and Social Pathology*. Allen and Unwin, London.
Wynn, M. (1970) *Family Policy*. Michael Joseph, London.
Younghusband, E. (1968) *Community Work and Social Change* (Report of Calouste Gulbenkian Study Group). Longmans, Harlow, Essex.

4 *Homes, the homeless and the social services department*

Kenneth M. Spencer

The issue of homelessness is a highly topical and controversial subject area, which from time to time has captured the mind of the public in this country. One might imagine that growing public concern would have led to improved service provision and a reduction in the number of the homeless, but this is not the case. Services have been marginally improved though the number of homeless continues to rise at what many consider to be an alarming rate. A variety of reports in recent years have deliberated over the problems of homelessness and many have made useful recommendations. However, there has been little action on the part of central government, or indeed on the part of many local authorities, to really attempt to get to grips with the problems posed by homelessness. D. V. Donnison (1971a) is highly critical of the lack of action on the findings of government sponsored research reports. One can only hope that new initiatives in this area of social policy are imminent.

In this chapter the material is inevitably highly selective and reflects the viewpoint of the author. For a detailed analysis and fuller discussion of some of the points raised the reader is referred to the References.

Introduction

The objectives of this chapter are to consider homelessness in England and Wales, to relate this to housing market situations and to look at various proposals for improving homeless family services.

It should be pointed out that homeless single persons are dealt with by a separate machinery and that this hiatus between the homeless family and the homeless single person is of considerable significance. Most investigations into homelessness have dealt with family units and little work has considered the problems of homeless single people. Official statistics on homelessness relate to those families in temporary accommodation which is provided under the National Assistance Act, 1948, and the Children and Young Persons Act, 1963. Though the 1948 Act refers to persons, most official attention revolves around families.

In this chapter homeless single persons are also considered. Suffice it at this stage to emphasise the need for far more adequate information on the numbers, characteristics and condition of these single people and the machinery for assisting them. A major study of this group is long overdue.

'Homelessness is a subject on which far more is said than known. We have been surprised at how little is known about it and the inadequacy of the available data. Until there is a better understanding of the nature of the problem policy cannot be soundly based' (Central Housing Advisory Committee 1969, paragraph 328). Similarly the National Housing and Town Planning Council (1970), states in relation to homelessness, 'we repeat, fuller and more accurate information on a local basis is necessary before the needs of the situation can be properly judged'. To a large extent the research results of Greve, Page & Greve (1971) and Glastonbury (1971) have helped immensely to fill the lacunae identified above, but only in specific localities. One hopes that local authorities in other areas will take up the challenge and develop their own studies in order to provide a firmer base for policy decisions aimed at improving the situation.

These two government sponsored studies, in London and South Wales and the West respectively, stemmed from a culmination of several events. A principal factor was the growth of public concern, much of this developing from J. Sandford's documentary play *Cathy Come Home* which was first shown in 1966 on television; the play was, however, written in 1963. There was also the impact of the growing publicity campaigns of Shelter, without doubt one of the most effective charitable campaigners of the last few years. The annual reports of Shelter hardly ever failed to hit the national headlines (Shelter 1968, and Shelter 1969). It voiced the concern of a large body of people and proved to be a rallying point in the fight for a more humane understanding and treatment of homeless persons (Wilson 1970).

The national and local news media were not slow to identify the activities of various squatter groups, particularly in London, and other survey documents which would otherwise have lacked national publicity (Notting Hill Housing Service 1969 and Tower Hamlets Council of Social Service 1967, are examples). This period also witnessed a growing concern with housing issues in general, and more information was being gathered and processed in relation to the national and local housing situations (see for example Spencer 1970).

In 1969 Richard Crossman, then Minister of Health and Social Security, commissioned the two research studies whose findings were published in 1971, though the results had been made available to the Department of Health and Social Security in 1970. It may have been the growing problem of homelessness as reflected in local authority returns to the Department which sparked off these studies.

One must not assume that nothing was being done about the problems of homelessness before 1969. The London County Council, the authority responsible for temporary accommodation before the reorganisation of London local government, commissioned J. Greve to undertake a study of the problem. The results of this study were presented in 1962 (London County Council 1962; see also Greve 1964). The subsequent study of London (Greve *et al.*, 1971) has enabled many useful comparisons to be made, and without doubt the London area is the most highly researched so far as homeless families are concerned.

Local authority replies were called for in response to Ministry of Health Joint Circular (1966), which asked for details about the provision made for homeless families. Replies provided information, as requested, upon measures to prevent homelessness; arrangements for co-ordinating policy, field services and information; the provision of temporary accommodation and plans for its improvement; and arrangements for the rehabilitation of incomplete families. A Ministry of Health Joint Circular (1967) made recommendations that preventive services should be developed, that homeless families should be rehoused promptly, that standards in temporary accommodation should be improved and that the widespread practice of splitting fathers from families moving into temporary accommodation should cease. Many local authorities did take action along some of the lines suggested. Over time some of the worst communal accommodation centres were closed down, and the splitting up of families was generally discontinued (though less rapidly in some authorities than others). The response was very varied with the result that there still remained, as is the case at present, a situation of considerable differences between areas in terms of arrangements for homeless families. In other words, a family's chances of prompt, decent rehousing very much depend upon the policies and pressures in the specific local authority area in which one becomes homeless. The policy still exists in several areas of providing such families with fares to take them to another authority area which is deemed to be 'really' responsible for them. Passages back to Ireland or to other areas are still relatively frequent an occurrence, especially in some of the housing pressure areas. In some instances this may be in the best interests of the family concerned, in others one would suspect it is done in the 'best interests' of the local authority concerned in the case.

A survey was published in 1966 which investigated the circumstances of homeless single persons (National Assistance Board 1966). It is concerned with persons sleeping rough (on the night of 6 December, 1965), persons in lodging houses, persons in reception centres, and homeless persons who had applied for national assistance. This survey contains the most recent national data on homeless single persons.

By 1972 one can say that we now know far more about the circumstances of homeless families and the policies adopted to deal with their problems. What is required is the development of improved policies, because one feature of the London (Greve *et al.* 1971), and the South Wales and the West studies (Glastonbury 1971) which remains most disturbing is that they demonstrate the often desperate state of affairs which exists in many local authorities' provision for homeless families. In areas where the housing shortage and housing conditions in general are a main cause of homelessness then a speedy and urgent effort is required to make a substantial impact upon housing conditions. In some cases it is recognised that this would require extra resources, but the concept of a government effecting positive discrimination in areas of high social deprivation is not new (Holman 1970). It is probable that some of the solutions may be reached through the improvement of preventive and rehabilitation services for both families and single people. J. Sandford's play *Edna, the Inebriate Woman*, has drawn attention to the plight of the single homeless, but 1972 is not 1966 and perhaps the British public has become only too accustomed to seeing suffering and tragedy, in for example Northern Ireland and Vietnam.

The housing market

Homelessness cannot be divorced from the local and regional housing market situation. If the supply of accommodation in an area cannot keep pace with demand the results may, amongst other things, lead to overcrowding and homelessness. For families on incomes which do not allow them the prospect of owning their own home there remain virtually only two alternatives. There is the possibility of obtaining council housing. In housing shortage areas, however, local authorities operate complex and varying housing allocation policies, amongst which the issue of residential qualification often looms large (C.H.A.C. (1969) provides a full discussion of these allocation procedures). In some London boroughs the residence qualification is as high as five years, and this qualification simply means that one becomes eligible for consideration only. The Report of the Committee on Housing in Greater London (1965) demonstrates the uniqueness of the London housing situation which can be regarded as 'in a class by itself' (C.H.A.C. 1969, paragraph 338).

The remaining alternative is the possibility of obtaining privately rented accommodation. In this sector there has been a rapid decline in the amount of accommodation available and this creates problems for those seeking a home in this shrinking market. In 1950, some 45% of dwellings in England and Wales were rented from private landlords, but by 1970 this figure had dropped to 15% (Central Statistical Office 1971, based on table 90). The reduction of privately rented unfurnished accommodation is particularly acute, though in many areas the level of furnished accommodation is remaining fairly steady, or being slightly increased. Furnished accommodation is usually associated with higher rent levels, lack of really adequate security of tenure, small size of the dwelling, a sharing of amenities and overcrowding (Woolf 1967). Also in areas of housing shortage rents, including fair rent levels, tend to be relatively high and competition from groups of people sharing accommodation costs, groups of students and young business people for example, pushes rent levels out of reach of many low income families. The Report of the Committee on the Rent Acts 1971 goes into much detail on these issues, but was widely criticised because of its stand against extending the security of tenure provisions for furnished tenants, though a minority report was in favour of such an extension.

One could conclude that particularly in London and to a lesser extent in Birmingham, the housing shortage of itself is a major cause of homelessness. Elsewhere the proportion of families in temporary accommodation because of such shortages is much smaller, and the reasons for families being rendered homeless revolve around eviction because of rent arrears, marital disputes and the recent arrival of families in an area. In his comparison of two study areas Glastonbury (1971) states, 'The major difference ... is that London is dogged by a chronic and acute housing shortage. In South Wales and the West of England the housing shortage is much less severe, but there is a higher level of social breakdown amongst the families becoming homeless, and a need for improved housing conditions and allocation of the existing supply'. Another body would 'hazard a guess that homelessness may be at its worst in a few large conurbations which are generally attractive to families seeking employment' (N.H.T.P.C. 1970, p. 13).

Table 4.1 presents a crude but useful measure of housing shortages in the various regions of England and Wales (C.S.O. 1971, table 91).

TABLE 4.1

*Dwelling excess or deficiency by regions, December, 1970**

Northern	−16,000	East Anglia	+ 8,000
Yorkshire and Humberside	+ 6,000	South East	−236,000
North West	−41,000	Greater London	−179,000
East Midlands	− 8,000	Outer Metropolitan area / Outer South East	− 57,000
West Midlands	−65,000	Wales	− 1,000
South West	+17,000		
		Total	−336,000

* The excess (+) or deficiency (−) measure is based upon potential households plus 4% for vacancies and second homes.

Many towns contain large areas of poor housing, and bad conditions are also found, though not in such large concentrations, in very many rural areas. Bad housing conditions can lead to ill-health, mental stress, family tensions, and homelessness. Studies have already shown the relationships between poor housing and social deprivation (Spencer 1970).

A recent survey of small local authorities showed that many municipal boroughs and urban district councils 'had little experience of homelessness and some none at all. Similarly the rural district councils in our sample said that they seldom encountered homelessness, but a number referred to evictions from tied accommodation' (C.H.A.C. 1969, paragraph 337).

A further disturbing finding of the London study was the growth in the proportion of households living in shared dwellings, from one-fifth in 1961 to one-quarter in 1966. Many of the inner London boroughs had witnessed substantial increases in the sharing of accommodation, partly due to the 15% decrease over the five-year period of privately rented dwellings in inner London (plus Newham and Haringey) (Greve *et al.* 1971). The Greater London Council has identified a number of housing stress areas with acute housing problems. It is no accident that these areas which suffer from lack of household amenities, bad levels of repair and maintenance, high degrees of overcrowding, much sharing of accommodation, and high levels of furnished tenancies, are the areas where harassment, illegal evictions and other coercive activities are increasing. These are areas which produce large numbers of homeless families.

The homeless

The experience of homelessness can, for many families, be a traumatic experience and frequently leads to an undermining of a family's sense of security. In some cases nervous, psychiatric and other disorders can be exacerbated. In this section five issues are considered: trends and definitions, family characteristics, causes of homelessness, the flow through temporary accommodation, and homeless single persons.

TRENDS AND DEFINITIONS

Table 4.2 presents the basic official data on numbers of homeless families (C.S.O. 1971, table 96). This is, however, but a partial view of the situation as is explained later.

TABLE 4.2

Homeless persons in temporary accommodation

	1966		1969		1970	
	Families	*Persons*	*Families*	*Persons*	*Families*	*Persons*
Greater London	1,594	7,723	2,352	11,296	2,820	12,970
Rest of England and Wales	964	5,308	1,852	10,193	2,106	11,313
Total	2,558	13,031	4,204	21,489	4,926	24,283

The period from 1966 to 1970 saw a substantial increase in the number of families in temporary accommodation. Between 1969 and 1970 there was a 19.8% increase of these families in London and 13.7% in the rest of England and Wales, while the number of such families in 1970 was almost twice the number in 1966. In 1970, over half the families, 57%, were to be found in London.

The Protection from Eviction Act 1964, and the Rent Act 1965, had led, in the years immediately after they entered the statute, to a reduced number of families applying for and being admitted to temporary accommodation. Their impact, however, was exceedingly short-lived. In 1966 and 1967, following the recommendations of the joint circulars, there was a marked increase in the number of men admitted into temporary accommodation with their families.

Of people in the London accommodation in 1970, some 32.5% were children aged 5 and under (41% elsewhere), while 35.8% of the London families had 3–5 children and 7.7% had 6 children or more (52.4% and 14.4% in the rest of England and Wales). These figures partially reflect the smaller average household size in London, but they also show that very young children and large families are found in large proportions in temporary accommodation, especially outside London.

These data, some of which indicate the problem to be a growing one, refer only to families in temporary accommodation provided by local authorities. In no way can one accept that these figures show the actual number of either homeless families or homeless persons. One must be led in the direction of the comment in the London study (Greve *et al.* 1971), that official statistics measure trends in the provision of temporary accommodation rather than trends in the number of homeless families. This may well be less true outside areas of housing pressure. Shelter (1969) has argued that a national figure of three million homeless is more realistic. Their figure included all living in housing conditions which were considered as unsatisfactory.

This raises a most important point: that of definition. The Shelter definition is perhaps too broad, but certainly the official definitions as used by very many local authorities are much too narrow. In some cases children are taken into care because of homelessness or poor housing. The Children and Young Persons Act, 1963 has reduced these cases, but taking into care does continue, sometimes in circumstances which appear questionable. In 1968–9, 15 children were taken into care because of homelessness in Cardiff, 20 in Somerset (Glastonbury 1971, p. 209), while in 1970 in inner London there were 189 such cases and 274 in outer London (Greve *et al.* 1971, p. 163). In national terms, there were 2,192 cases in 1968–9, and 2,693 in 1969–70, which respectively accounted for 4.3% and 5.2% of all child receptions into care (Greve *et al.* 1971, p. 162).

Local authorities operate differing definitions of homelessness. They act as filters of applicants, and only those fitting locally determined conditions proceed into temporary accommodation, but the situation is more complex than this. Families may be accepted into temporary accommodation at one point in time but not at another, often depending upon the level of demand for the accommodation available. Thus, the data on homeless families are themselves open to suspicion on the grounds that there are no standard criteria against which to compare figures from different local authorities.

There is also the issue of the 'hidden' homeless, for example those who are forced into sharing with relatives or friends (often leading to overcrowding and the problem of unauthorised occupants). To many this may be preferable to the prospect of temporary accommodation. Other families are living in intolerable housing conditions, yet others are virtually forced into caravan accommodation, a number which may well be on the increase (Consumer Council 1967). Furthermore, what happens to the majority of families whose applications for temporary accommodation are rejected? We know far too little about the fate of many of these families, who are perhaps unlikely to return to an organisation which they consider to have failed them. This in no way depreciates the value of work of an advisory nature, or the fact that some families may be helped to find alternative, suitable accommodation, perhaps with a housing association or other privately rented housing. There are also families which have to live apart because they cannot find a home of their own. Fatherless families often find themselves in difficulties with finding adequate housing (Ministry of Social Security 1967), especially in those areas where local authorities are not prepared to allocate council tenancies to them (C.H.A.C. 1969).

The wide range of operational definitions of homelessness is no surprise, as the legislation is particularly vague. Section 21 (b) of the National Assistance Act, 1948 simply places an obligation upon a local authority to provide temporary accommodation to persons in urgent need, that need having arisen through circumstances which could not have been reasonably foreseen, or in such other cases as the authority may determine. Definitions of 'urgent' and 'circumstances which could not have been reasonably foreseen', constitute at least two areas in which there appears to be widespread differences of interpretation. The question arises whether a greatly improved statutory definition of homelessness is required, which at the same time does allow that element of flexibility, which can sometimes make the law that little more humane.

The Catholic Housing Aid Society (1968) suggests that 'any family who, because of the physical housing conditions in which they are forced to live, cannot have a normal family life', should be regarded as homeless. Certainly a more realistic national policy, as well as local policies, is needed to make more effective the combating of homelessness. Glastonbury (1971, pp. 185–6) estimates that in Glamorganshire, Gloucestershire, Somerset, Cardiff, Swansea and Bristol, in the period 1963 to 1968 an annual average of 15,000 persons (2,000 families of two or more persons and 3,000 individuals) have been homeless. This compares with about 200 families, or 900 persons, who passed through temporary accommodation in the average year. This lends much weight to the argument that local authority temporary accommodation deals only with the tip of the homelessness iceberg.

THE CHARACTERISTICS OF HOMELESS FAMILIES

Some of the characteristics of homeless families have already been commented upon in relation to Table 4.2, but several other points need to be made. A principal finding of the London study was that homeless families in temporary accommodation in 1969 to 1970 were essentially similar to those families who went through temporary accommodation in the late 1950s and early 1960s, as identified by London County Council (1962) and J. Greve (1964). The main differences were that there were more of them, and that the proportion of Commonwealth immigrants becoming homeless had increased significantly. Many of the characteristics of the London families appear to be general elsewhere; as is indicated by Glastonbury (1971) and Birmingham City Council (1967).

A comparison of these findings shows that families entering temporary accommodation have below average incomes for the areas in which they find themselves. In South Wales and the West nearly two-thirds of the employed male household heads were earning less than £15 a week, in London the comparative figure was about one-third. In addition to the low-paid wage earners, predominantly unskilled or semi-skilled manual workers, there were high proportions of unemployed men and fatherless families who were dependent upon supplementary benefit payments. The two snapshot pictures of the homeless in London indicate that the proportion of unemployed men had risen markedly. Similarly in Birmingham in 1966, 35% of families had been in receipt of national assistance for some time.

Those families on the lowest incomes were usually the fatherless families who comprised one-third of those in London's temporary accommodation in 1968–9. In Glastonbury's study the proportion was 29.5%, while in Birmingham 15% were unmarried mothers.

Young families, in terms of mothers' and children's ages, are particularly vulnerable. At the time of entry to temporary accommodation, Glastonbury shows that 17.5% of mothers were aged under 21, compared with 20% in Birmingham and 9% in London (aged under 20 years in this case and related to applications not admissions). A further 50% in London were aged 20–29, and 45.4% in South Wales and the West were aged 21–30.

Housing standards before admission to temporary accommodation were in general poor, and the sharing of dwellings appears to be an important indicator of potential homelessness. Very many people were in furnished accommodation, and significantly more families become homeless from this kind of accommodation. Most families were previously in privately rented accommodation (87% in London and 62% in South Wales and the West), while the proportions of families from local authority housing were 10% and 28% and the lowest levels were found, as one might expect, amongst the owner-occupiers, 3% and 10%.

Associated with this heavy dependence upon the privately rented furnished accommodation are the relatively high rent levels that families were paying, despite the general picture of below average incomes. London, of course, reflects a picture of higher rent levels than elsewhere (Woolf 1967, and Report of the Committee on the Rent Acts 1971), and some 36% of applicants for London's temporary accommodation were paying over £5 a week, and only 24% were paying under £3. This contrasts markedly with Glastonbury's findings where the respective levels were 4% and 62.5%. In the Birmingham study of 1966 it was found that 47% of families had been paying over £2.50 a week prior to their eviction, usually from furnished accommodation. Thus, low income families are paying quite high rents for furnished accommodation, where security of tenure is tenuous (despite the consolidated Rent Act, 1968).

Increasing proportions of Commonwealth immigrant families are becoming homeless, and the pattern of their circumstances tends to vary from that found amongst the United Kingdom and Eire-born in the following ways (Greve *et al.* 1971, pp. 90–1). Fewer of the male household heads were unemployed, but their earnings were much lower than those of other families entering temporary accommodation, and they also tended to have larger families while the causes of their becoming homeless also varied from the pattern of the rest. A large number of studies have demonstrated that coloured families usually encounter greater difficulties in obtaining accommodation, and when they do so they are often charged higher rents, frequently exorbitant (see for example Report of the Committee on Housing in Greater London 1965; Report of the Committee on the Rent Acts 1971; and Burney 1967).

REASONS FOR BECOMING HOMELESS

Local authorities are required to assess for each family admitted to temporary accommodation the cause of its homelessness. Together with other information this is submitted in their quarterly return (the H41 form) to the Department of Health and Social Security. The identification of the cause of homelessness is not always as simple a matter as might, at first sight, appear. 'Immediate causes, however, often obscure the real reasons why families are in difficulty. There are cases so complex as to defy categorisation, but there are also many more where the so-called immediate cause is quite secondary to the situation which precipitated the trouble' (Greve *et al.* 1971, p. 75). Hence, it can be extremely difficult sometimes to unravel the cause-effect complex, but the London study does demonstrate that the causes of homelessness, measured often in an imprecise manner, have remained basically the same over the 1960s. Domestic friction (marital or with friends or relatives) is an important cause of homelessness in both Glastonbury's and Greve's studies, but it is difficult to compare causes directly as the different studies used different measuring techniques. Because of this the only soundly based comparisons one can draw are that rent arrears was seen as a more important problem in South Wales and the West than in London, but was a major factor in both areas; similarly evictions because of unauthorised occupancy (often sharing someone else's home) was an extremely important cause in London, and fairly important in South Wales and the West. Glastonbury (1971, p. 218) does produce a comparative table of causes, but one feels that this is highly suspect as it is based upon different criteria of measurement.

The pattern of causes amongst coloured immigrants varies from the pattern for London as a whole, as far fewer were evicted for rent arrears by private landlords, but a high proportion were evicted because the landlord had defaulted on his mortgage payments, or because the landlord required the accommodation for his own use. Marital disputes were far less significant as a cause, as were cases of unauthorised occupants, and none had been evicted from local authority housing.

Greve *et al.* (1971, p. 8) found a frequent practice of dividing the homeless into two groups, 'those who were regarded as victims of the housing shortage, homeless through no fault of their own, and those whose housing problems were seen as stemming from their personal failure or deficiencies'. Responsible officers in the London boroughs felt that the housing shortage was the principal reason for most of the cases of homeless families.

It should be remembered that very few people are aware of their legal position in relation to the Rent Acts, that security of tenure in the furnished sector is tenuous, and once a Notice to Quit is served many people appear to make alternative arrangements, often one suspects becoming numbered amongst the 'hidden' homeless. Rent tribunals can only extend security of tenure in furnished accommodation for a limited period, usually for one or two six-month periods. Yet many people are unaware of this, others who are aware may not appeal to the rent tribunal if they feel harassment by the landlord may ensue. On this point very few cases of prosecutions for illegal evictions and harassment have led to large fines or the imprisonment of landlords.

Many local authorities refuse to rehouse families claiming to be homeless until the family can produce a court eviction order, even then many wait until the day the bailiffs arrive before taking action, presumably in the hope that some families may be pressurised into making their own alternative arrangements. The C.H.A.C. (1969, paragraph 341) concludes that local authorities are right in treating each case of homelessness on its merits, and of insisting on court proceedings and the production of eviction orders in certain cases, but where the local authority is satisfied that a tenant is highly likely to be evicted then it should not insist upon court proceedings. One can only hope that more local authorities will heed these words of sound advice.

WHAT HAPPENS TO THE HOMELESS?

On admittance to part III accommodation under the National Assistance Act of 1948, a family's immediate destination may be a highly regimented hostel or reception centre. The stay in this communal establishment is usually quite short, often not longer than seven to ten days. One could argue that the objective should be to cease operating these establishments as soon as possible, and depend upon family accommodation units much more, and indeed this does appear to be a current trend. However, life in the reception centre is often sufficiently uncomfortable to lead a family into trying to make its own alternative arrangements.

The next stage is often one of accommodation in a family unit of temporary accommodation, which might be, for example, in an old block of flats, in which case the whole block may be occupied by homeless families. In other cases accommodation may be provided in older housing within, or on the verge of, clearance areas. Such housing has minimum amenity provision, and may be situated in an area where many other homeless, or 'problem' families may have been housed. In many localities the reception centre stage may be omitted and families move direct into family units of temporary accommodation.

In the county local government system where housing is a lower tier responsibility and social services a county responsibility friction can, and does, arise over homeless families. Glastonbury (1971) shows that there were many disputes between counties and districts; there was a tendency to think of problems as a county responsibility and district councils often appeared to wash their hands of the matter. Attitudes such as this can only be deplored, and it appears in such cases that the interests of the clients tend to be pushed to one side. The problem is basically one of ensuring a mechanism for proper and effective co-ordination.

Families may at some stage spend time in a rehabilitation centre, especially when the family is in need of intensive social work support. Others receive social work assistance in their temporary accommodation, but one should not equate homeless families with families having social problems. Many of them just need decent housing, and no amount of social work will provide that, unless its primary objective is that of getting a decent home as quickly as possible for the family, an objective that will sometimes lead the social worker into conflict with the housing department and with others.

After spending time (some might argue 'serving' is a more appropriate term), in temporary accommodation a family may be rehoused by the housing department. In areas of little housing pressure good standard accommodation may be available for this purpose. In high housing pressure areas the family may well be allocated 'intermediate' or 'half-way' housing, managed by the housing department, which would be poor quality housing, often scheduled for demolition in the near future. The satisfactory tenants may eventually move on to better standard local authority housing, but unsatisfactory tenants, as judged by the housing authority, may be moved from one short life property to another, constantly pursued by the bulldozer.

The actual progress of homeless families from admittance to rehousing varies considerably from authority to authority, and also varies depending upon the individual family's circumstances at admission and during the stay in temporary accommodation. In times of pressure upon temporary accommodation it is essential for authorities to adopt a flexible approach and to ensure that the pipeline stays open and that any blockages, e.g. at the rehousing stage, are speedily eliminated. Because of growing pressure there had been a 15% increase in temporary accommodation available in inner London, and 116% increase in outer London, during 1965–9. Nevertheless, 11 London boroughs had to refuse admission because of lack of accommodation at a time when demand was high (Greve *et al.* 1971, pp. 155–7).

In some areas a family may be rehoused direct into a council tenancy, particularly if their circumstances place them close to the top of the housing waiting list, and particularly if they are in a non-housing pressure area. Many other families spend only a few days in temporary accommodation. This is often the case in situations where marital dispute led to homelessness, as by that time the storm has usually settled enough for the family to be reunited. Length of stay in temporary accommodation does vary geographically, with London being an area where long stays are common. Greve *et al.* (1971, p. 72) show that in 1969 in inner London, 28.2% of families stayed for less than one month, 20% for one to six months, 32% for six to eighteen months, and an alarming proportion of 19.8% for over eighteen months. Large families were often in this latter group because of difficulties in obtaining suitably sized accommodation. The respective figures for outer London were: 24.7, 31.2, 34.3 and 9.8%. By marked contrast, Glastonbury (1971, p. 224) indicates that 57% stayed less than one month, 37% one to six months and only 6% over six months. Besides the large families in inner London those families rendered homeless because of local authority rent arrears were also more likely to remain in temporary accommodation longer.

Because of the decreasing market in privately rented accommodation increasing proportions of homeless families are channelled into council tenancies. This is particularly the case in London and other housing shortage areas, and between 1966 and 1970 the percentage of families so housed rose from 47 to 59 in inner London and 56 to 68 in outer London. Those whose plight had been caused by rent arrears were more likely than any other cause group to be rehoused by the local authority (Greve *et al.* 1971, pp. 73 and 81).

However, many families are required to serve their time in

temporary accommodation and often in intermediate housing before being allocated decent council housing, thus demonstrating that, 'Homelessness cannot be allowed as a short cut to a council house,' (Birmingham City Council 1967, item 19). This identifies the dilemma of many housing authorities: should homelessness automatically lead to swift council rehousing? In many authorities this would be the case, but in shortage areas they would argue that this should not be the situation, for fear of opening the floodgates. One can understand why this public attitude is maintained, but all authorities are aware that homelessness often is a short cut to a council house, and in most cases it is right that this should be so. Particularly in housing pressure areas this outcome is almost inevitable.

HOMELESS SINGLE PERSONS

The most recent comprehensive information about homeless single persons is to be found in the report of N.A.B., 1966, which presents and analyses the findings of a census of such persons held on the night of 6 December 1965. The census of England, Wales and Scotland, indicated that about 13,500 persons, nearly all men, used reception centres or sometimes slept rough. Because of the difficulties of undertaking such a census this is bound to be an underestimate of the size of the real problem, and since 1965 the scale of the problem is likely to have increased rather than decreased. On that night, in the middle of winter, about 1,000 people were sleeping rough and a further 1,262 were enumerated in reception centre accommodation (run by central government), the largest of these being at Camberwell.

There appears to be relatively little activity by central or local government to grapple with this problem; it is a problem which tends to get swept under the carpet, and the services provided by many voluntary organisations are relied upon to an exceptionally high degree. Of the lodging houses and hostels provided by bodies other than local government, the Salvation Army had 62 centres with 7,395 beds for men and 652 for women, while the Church Army had 26 centres with 1,831 beds for men and 252 for women. Most of the lodging houses and hostels (60% of 567) were run on a commercial basis, and many centres stated that they had to turn people away because their accommodation was, from time to time, fully occupied.

The main findings of the N.A.B. (1966) report which relate to individuals are presented in Table 4.3 and the data speak largely for themselves, though the survey was by no means fully comprehensive, for example it does not consider the question of how many elderly people in geriatric beds are there just because there is nowhere else for them to go (Sumner & Smith 1969).

TABLE 4.3

Homeless single persons, National Assistance Board Census, 1965

Key to columns: 1. Those sleeping rough
2. Those in hostels and lodging houses
3. Those in reception centres
4. Homeless single persons applying for national assistance

	1	2	3	4
1 Sometimes slept rough	100	28	70	78
2 Sometimes used reception centres	21	23	100	43
3 Sometimes used hostels and lodging houses	41	100	73	62
4 Were not married	—	67	71	66
5 Were aged over 40	—	80	65	47
6 Had received national assistance in the past	90	—	92	92
7 Had received national assistance in the last month	—	60	—	51
8 Of working age but not working	57	40	—	—
9 Had worked for less than six months in the last year	—	—	60	46
10 Had been in prison	—	28	60	56
11 Had been in prison during the last two months	9	—	—	—
12 Were thought to be physically or mentally handicapped	—	18	21	16
13 Were heavy drinkers or suspected alcoholics	—	—	28	—
14 Felt they needed help or advice	20	22	—	—
15 No close relatives, or out of touch for over one year	62	53	68	50

A large question mark must surely hang over the minimal role played by central and local government in this situation; improvements are urgently needed. Brandon (1969) has written about the problems of these people, and more recently has drawn attention to the virtual withdrawal of the statutory organisations in the last 25 years, citing the example of 250 reception centres in 1948 having been reduced to 17 in 1971 (Brandon 1971), while he is also highly critical of the Seebohm committee's apparent lack of concern about the homeless single person (Report of the Committee on Local Authority and Allied Personal Social Services 1968).

Voluntary organisations such as Christian Action, the Cyrenians, the Salvation and Church Armies and the numerous small localised groups, can only have a limited effect upon the problem. Nor is the situation being aided by the closure of much bed space provision in hostels and lodging houses due to the progress of redevelopment. Brandon (1971) suggests the need for better co-ordination and envisages a three-fold division of responsibility, 'Voluntary societies to operate in the contact field—organising soup runs, night shelters and short-stay projects, where greatest flexibility is needed; central government to specialise in the provision of expensive socio-medical assessment facilities with properly trained and qualified staff (the reception centres may well evolve along these lines); leaving local authorities and voluntary societies to develop the long stay provision so urgently required.'

Basically there is a strong case for a national study to assess the scale of the problem of homeless single persons, to consider the various services provided and, in the light of these findings, to make recommendations for speedy action. Furthermore one must firmly place this issue upon the shoulders of government. The voluntary agencies do not have the resources of finance or manpower to solve these problems by themselves, but it very much appears that this is the direction in which national policy, if it can be so called, is moving.

Implications for the social services

The Seebohm Committee (1968) and the C.H.A.C. (1969) both make recommendations about combating homelessness more effectively. Despite this, the studies of South Wales and the West, and London, indicate that many local authorities had not developed these suggestions into policy. Though it should be pointed out that both studies were undertaken shortly before the implementation of social services reorganisation, and no national data are yet available which indicate policy changes since reorganisation. One suspects that there has been little change and many authorities would do well to consider seriously these recommendations, together with those outlined in Greve *et al.* (1971).

The principal suggestions of the Seebohm Committee (1968) were as follows:

(1) responsibility for homeless families should lie with the housing authority, other than providing for limited overnight accommodation, and social workers should be available to help homeless families requiring assistance;
(2) families should not be split up and privacy should be available to families in communal centres;
(3) recuperative family training units in special residential care centres, into which some homeless families may be temporarily placed, should be the responsibility of the social service department;
(4) an efficient early warning system to enable families in difficulties or potential difficulties to be identified; in the local authority housing sector this would not be difficult, but in the case of the private housing sector three suggestions are made: (a) the establishment of a housing advice service and a development of the knowledge in the local authority about private sector housing, (b) the need for local authorities to take an increased responsibility for rehousing the most vulnerable families so that fewer will depend upon the private sector, (c) courts and rent tribunals should work in close collaboration with local authorities so that assistance and prevention of homelessness might be possible;
(5) the early identification and notification of families at risk should be seen as a corporate responsibility of local government departments, the supplementary benefits commission, voluntary groups and others involved with the homeless;
(6) services amongst neighbouring authorities should be co-ordinated effectively.

Developing this, one could add that local authorities ought to become more sensitive to the needs of the single homeless person and develop new approaches to their assistance. It is essential that homelessness is seen as a corporate responsibility rather than as a housing or social services issue. There are undoubtedly areas of conflict between social services and housing and there is a need for much improved understanding, co-ordination and communication. Other local authority officers are also involved, the public health inspector responsible for enforcing overcrowding legislation, slum identification, housing improvement, the town planners who need to make allowances in their estimates of housing need and in their use of planning control mechanisms, the health visitor, the educationalist and so on. Unless the problem of homelessness is recognised as a corporate responsibility and issues are identified, alternative solutions considered, and rational decisions reached, then progress can only be limited because we will only be dealing with the periphery of the problem (Stewart 1971). An initial starting point within authorities may well be the establishment of an interdisciplinary working group to review policy and make recommendations (including representatives from organisations other than local government).

On considering where responsibility for the homeless should be vested, the evidence points to the housing authority, but at present responsibility usually lies with the social services department. The aims of housing management and social work can lead to conflict or a divergence of opinion. In London the housing officers tended to think more in terms of the deserving and the undeserving homeless compared with welfare and children's officers (only in one London borough was the housing department responsible for homeless services, though since 1957 Birmingham's housing department has held this responsibility). This attitude was still common amongst social workers in some areas. The general view was that homelessness was a housing problem when not caused by family inadequacy, otherwise it was a social services problem (Greve *et al.* 1971, p. 128).

Glastonbury (1971) argues that in areas where housing shortages do not create much of the homelessness, it ought to be the responsibility of the social services department, but in areas such as London and Birmingham, the housing department should be responsible. One's own view is that the responsibility ought to rest firmly with the housing department, which must be made ultimately responsible for the rehousing of difficult tenants as well as those regarded as satisfactory. Brook (1971) argues that every housing department should include housing welfare officers to deal with certain tenancy problems such as rent arrears, but problems requiring intensive case work or specialised skills should be referred to social service departments, and full co-operation should be established. Indeed, the need may be more for a specialised group of social workers in the social services department who can be called upon to undertake, amongst other things, contact with rent arrears cases, as certain solutions are more readily available in that department, for example rent guarantees, lump sum payments. With responsibility vested in the housing department the problem of housing quota allocations to the social service department for homeless families would be overcome. While some of these suggestions may be costly, this may be cheaper in the long run than allowing homelessness to develop (Institute of Municipal Treasurers and Accountants 1968).

Housing departments are being pushed in the direction of not only managing a local authority stock of dwellings, but also of assessing housing need, of reviewing the state of housing, and of providing advisory services, all of which relate to all forms of housing tenure (Donnison 1971b). In the light of these trends it would also appear logical for homelessness to be dealt with by the housing authority. To date only a few authorities have established housing advice centres, but one has only to consider the work of the Shelter Housing Advice Centre to realise the great potentiality of service which can be provided by such bodies (see for example Greve *et al.* 1971, chapter 11).

One must also recognise the important roles played by various voluntary bodies and charitable associations, and the roles played by central government in its provision of reception centres for homeless single persons, as well as the work of the supplementary benefits commission. Thus the problem of homelessness is the concern of a multitude of institutions, large and small, statutory and voluntary, rich and poor, nationwide and localised, all of which need to be co-ordinated into effectiveness in firstly, combating homelessness by preventive means, for example rent guarantees (an often under-utilised mechanism), lump sum payments, social work assistance, day nursery provision, home help, legal assistance, and secondly, in dealing expeditiously and humanely with those who are deprived of a home. It could perhaps be argued that the very fact of such a large number of organisations being involved is itself a hindrance to the provision of better services.

Housing departments in housing pressure areas can often be placed in a position where it may be in the best interests of a family for it to remain as unauthorised occupants in a council dwelling for a short period, rather than for the department to pursue a policy of threatened eviction of both tenants and unauthorised occupants when such occupants are discovered. Similarly, in relation to public health campaigns to extirpate overcrowding, the result of pursuing an active policy may well lead to homelessness on a scale hitherto unseen in most local authority areas. The use of unfit dwellings between their closure and demolition has provided another major issue. Many squatters' groups were formed, especially in inner London, and families moved into the condemned properties. Many local authorities reached sensible agreement, and through local housing associations were able to utilise these properties until just a few weeks before demolition, thereafter the families were housed either by the housing association, or in some cases by the local authority.

These three examples simply demonstrate the point that the law of the land must sometimes be viewed flexibly, that issues must be considered on their merits and an effort must be made to determine what is in the best interests of a family at a particular point in time. It is on occasions such as this that public opinion may well develop into a powerful force in the situation.

In relation to that department responsible for administering homeless services, there are several other points which should be made. Departments should take a close and serious look at their policies of returning homeless families to their previous local authorities; this may well help to ease pressure on local temporary accommodation, but is it always in the best interests of the family and good social work practice to return families in this way? In the past a policy of concentration of temporary accommodation units has been followed in many authorities; as a result homeless families are herded together, in a few streets, or in a few blocks of old flats. Such a policy can lead to more problems than it solves, for example an address in a homeless family block could lead to stigmatisation in the work situation, in the job hunting process, in the school situation, in the credit-worthiness world of retailing and so on. Some authorities are beginning to disperse their homeless families, others would like to do so but are hindered by the remaining life span of old blocks of temporary accommodation. Concentration often leads to local residents accusing the local authority of using their neighbourhood as a dumping ground for problem families (which in the public mind is often synonymous with homeless families). There is also the question of whether specialist caseworkers are required for dealing with homeless families. One's own view is that specialists with housing and legal knowledge are needed, but that such social workers might not concern themselves with homeless families all their time. Nevertheless, this does suggest that a core group with appropriate knowledge and skills is definitely required. Finally, there is a need for a monitoring system for homeless families, a system which will enable decision makers to maintain a close watch on the flow of homeless families through the various stages, and which will identify any bottleneck developments, thus enabling managers to take speedy action to relieve pressure at that particular point. This can be particularly crucial in housing pressure areas when temporary accommodation is stretched to capacity to meet the demands placed upon it. One such bottleneck in London's case is the number of large families remaining in temporary accommodation for a relatively long time because large family accommodation is at a premium in the metropolis.

Local government reorganisation is seen by many social workers as an opportunity lost, in so far as relationships between housing and social services departments are concerned. Social services will remain a county function and housing remain a district function, a fact which many social workers believe will ensure difficulty over efforts of co-ordination and co-operation (in the metropolitan counties both functions are to be vested at the district level). However, if housing authorities are made responsible for homeless family services the situation may not present the difficulties currently envisaged. Indeed, the scale of county district organisation in the reorganised local government system is to be such that for many county services, e.g. social services, a decentralised pattern of administration would be appropriate. If this were based largely upon the district divisions the maintenance of close contact between social workers and housing managers would become a greater possibility. The separation of the local authority health function into an area health authority will mean that in the future close ties will need to be developed between the two bodies, particularly as midwives and health visitors are quite likely to be people in contact with potentially homeless families, and an adequate notification system will need to be established.

The Housing Finance Act 1972, is also likely to have an impact upon the problem of homelessness. Politically this is highly emotive, but it will assist many, though not all, low income families with their housing costs. Housing allowances are to be paid to private tenants, as well as rent rebates to local authority tenants. The same criteria are used for both groups, but only tenants in unfurnished accommodation are eligible for rent allowances. Yet it is clear from the studies undertaken that large proportions of homeless families come from furnished accommodation, where they are often paying a high percentage of their income in rent. There seems extremely slender justification for excluding tenants in furnished accommodation from eligibility for rent allowances (Nevitt 1971, Page 1971, and Housing Centre Trust 1971). There are signs, however, that by 1973 furnished tenancies may well be included within the rent allowance scheme.* It should be pointed out that the rebate and allowance schemes are more generous than the majority of existing rebate schemes for local authority tenants, but at the same time the fair rent system will affect greater numbers of households and will be associated with increased rent payments for the great majority of people (Parker 1972). This proposal may be viewed as one of several contributory influences leading to spiralling house prices, and to pushing home ownership further out of the reach of many who previously saw themselves on its doorstep. The housing trends in this country may well lead to a situation in the 1970s when homelessness will become an even bigger problem than it has been in the 1960s, partly because our definitions may change, but partly because of internal pressures within local housing market situations. Improved policies and services will be needed if this challenge is to be met, policies which will need to overlap central and local government departmental boundaries.

In conclusion two points need to be emphasised. One is the tremendous variation in the standard of service provision for homeless families, and some authorities which are lagging behind need a considerable effort to rectify the situation. Indeed, the London study indicates that in some boroughs there was a feeling that the total amount of temporary accommodation equalled the need to be met, and policies stemmed from this. The remedy rests

* Editors note: The Furnished Lettings (Rent allowances) Act, 1973, provides allowances for many furnished tenancies.

with local government in the first instance, and with parliament and new legislation in the second instance. In this context it is worth noting that a joint working party was established with members from the London Boroughs Association and the Department of Health and Social Security to discuss and present their findings on the problems of homelessness in London (Department of Health and Social Security, London Boroughs Association 1971 and 1972). Finally, the plight of homeless single persons necessitates much more attention by local and central government, and one can only press for the Department of Health and Social Security to recognise the urgent need for a review of services for this group of people, with the objective of providing greatly improved mechanisms and facilities for their assistance.

References

Birmingham City Council (1967) *Housing Management Committee Report*, February. B.C.C., Birmingham.

Brandon, D. (1969) 'Homeless single persons', *Brit. J. Psych. Soc. Wk.*, 10, 80.

Brandon, D. (1971) 'Homelessness', *Soc. Wk. Today*, 2, 3.

Brook, W. (1971) 'Presidential address to the Institute of Housing Managers', *Local Gov. Chronicle*, 5 November.

Burney, E. (1967) *Housing on Trial*. Oxford University Press, London.

Catholic Housing Aid Society (1968) *A survey of the Catholic Housing Aid Society*. Catholic Housing Aid Society, London.

Central Housing Advisory Committee (1969) *Council Housing Purposes, Procedures and Priorities*. HMSO, London.

Central Statistical Office (1971) *Social Trends*, no. 2. HMSO, London.

Children and Young Persons Act (1963) HMSO, London.

Committee on Housing in Greater London (1965) *Report* (Chairman: Sir Milner Holland), Cmnd. 2605. HMSO, London.

Committee on Local Authority and Allied Personal Social Services (1968) *Report* (Chairman: F. Seebohm), Cmnd. 3703. HMSO, London.

Committee on the Rent Acts (1971) *Report* (Chairman: H. E. Francis), Cmnd. 4609. HMSO, London.

Consumer Council (1967) *Living in a Caravan*. HMSO, London.

Department of Health and Social Security, & London Boroughs Association (1971) *First Report of the Joint Working Party on Homelessness in London*. HMSO, London.

Department of Health and Social Security, & London Boroughs Association (1972) *Final Report of the Joint Working Party on Homelessness in London*. HMSO, London.

Donnison, D. V. (1971a) 'No more reports', *New Soc.*, 27 May.

Donnison, D. V. (1971b) 'A housing service', *New Soc.*, 11 November.

Glastonbury, B. (1971) *Homeless near a Thousand Homes.* Allen and Unwin, London.
Greve, J. (1964) *London's Homeless.* Condicote Press.
Greve, J., Page, D. & Greve, S. (1971) *Homelessness in London.* Scottish Academic Press, Edinburgh.
Holman, R. (1970) 'Combating social deprivation', *in Socially Deprived Families in Britain,* ed. R. Holman. Bedford Square Press, London.
Housing Centre Trust (1971) 'The inclusion of furnished lettings in the rent allowance scheme', *Housing R.*, 20, 154.
Housing Finance Act (1972) HMSO, London.
Institute of Municipal Treasurers and Accountants (1968) 'Homeless families', and 'Eviction from council housing', *in Cost benefit analysis in local government.* IMTA, London.
London County Council (1962) *Report of the research team to the Committee of Inquiry into homelessness* (General Purposes Committee Report no. 3). LCC, London.
Ministry of Social Security (1967) *Circumstances of Families.* HMSO, London.
Ministry of Health (1966) *Joint Circular* 20. HMSO, London.
Ministry of Health (1967) *Joint Circular* 19. HMSO, London.
National Assistance Act (1948) HMSO, London.
National Assistance Board (1966) *Homeless Single Persons.* HMSO, London.
National Housing and Town Planning Council (1970) *Homelessness* (Housing study group report). NHTPC, London.
Nevitt, A. A. (1971) 'A fair deal for housing?' *Polit. Quart.*, 42, 428.
Notting Hill Housing Service (1969) *The Notting Hill Survey.* NHHS, London.
Page, D. (1971) 'Rent allowance injustice', *Munic. J.*, 79, 1537.
Parker, R. A. (1972) *The Housing Finance Bill and Council Tenants.* Child Poverty Action Group, London.
Protection from Eviction Act (1964) HMSO, London.
Rent Act (1965) HMSO, London.
Shelter (1968) *Notice to Quit.* Shelter, London.
Shelter (1969) *Face the Facts.* Shelter, London.
Spencer, K. (1970) 'Housing and socially deprived families', *in Socially Deprived Families in Britain,* ed. R. Holman. Bedford Square Press, London.
Stewart, J. D. (1971) *Management in Local Government: a viewpoint.* Charles Knight, London.
Sumner, G. & Smith, R. (1969) *Planning Local Authority Services for the Elderly.* Allen and Unwin, London.
Tower Hamlets Council of Social Service (1967) *People without Roots.* THCSS, London.
Wilson, D. (1970) *I Know it Was the Place's Fault.* Oliphants, London.
Woolf, M. (1967) *The Housing Survey in England and Wales,* 1964. HMSO, London

5 *Delinquency and the social services department*

Arthur Hunt

Although national variations in the patterns of offending behaviour are clearly evident, the contemporary global picture is of increasing incidence in criminality and delinquency, of a relationship between these phenomena and changes in economic and social structures, and diversity in theories of causation. Suggested solutions to the problems of prophylaxis, treatment and control are equally varied but there can be no doubt that the advent of a comprehensive social service organisation has presented this country with unique opportunities to develop composite approaches to a major functional disorder of urbanised and industrialised society. Levels of crime and delinquency are important indicators of a social malaise which should be the vital concern, not only of the remedialist and teacher, but also of the politicians and the planners of the physical environment. It is with the interplay of social and physical environment, defective nurturing behaviour and the discrete use of treatment and control that this discussion is primarily concerned.

In spite of significant experiments in systems of data collection, statistical presentation and operational research, lack of precision in the quantification of offending behaviour remains. For this reason, all strategic considerations need to be qualified by the general statement that many more offences are committed than are reported, detected or recorded, with the corollary that as the sensitivity and responsiveness of the social services department increases, so this 'dark figure' of crime and delinquency will be presented as an additional dimension to the formally identified behaviours. The processes, both informal and formal, which determine the collective characteristics of offenders subjected to judicial procedures have been extensively described by such authors as Walker (1965), Trasler (1962) and Avison (1966), and from these it is possible to draw certain clear inferences of significance to those planning and implementing programmes of treatment, care and protection. The filtering effects of social positioning and prosecution practice greatly increase the chance of conviction of the most compulsive, socially inadequate, psychologically disturbed and socially disadvantaged offenders. It is not surprising to find, therefore, that services traditionally concerned with the treatment of offenders have been occupied with problems of the deteriorating urban environment, with marginal employability in a period of unprecedented technological advance, with the pathogenic family and with the criminogenic sub-culture.

These are problems which, increasingly, will face the social services departments of the future and the solutions are most likely to be found in approaches which expand understanding of the normal as well as the deviant and social pathology as well as the unique maladaptations of the individual. For example, the research of Andenaes (1968) provides a significant indication of the chance elements operating in the identification of offending behaviour and McDavid and McCandless (1962) have emphasised the value of a conceptual distinction drawn between asocial or delinquent behaviour on the one hand and anti-social or criminal behaviour on the other. Andenaes has described a recent study in which 4,000 soldiers from Oslo were interviewed. 45% of them admitted to at least one theft from stores and 12% to burglaries. It was apparent that this 18-year-old group admitted to delinquencies going back to childhood or adolescence, but Andenaes emphasises that even in the case of adults, it is difficult to draw a sharp dividing line between the law-abiding citizen and the law breaker and that the essential considerations must be the seriousness of the crime, the frequency at which it is being committed and the period over which such crimes have taken place.

McDavid and McCandless have argued that the central connotation of the term 'delinquency' focuses on 'failure of duty', whereas with crime the clear connotation centres on gross violation or 'aggravated offence against morality'. Semantics apart, this definition is helpful because it supports the contention that there is a clear difference in behaviour which stems from normal motivational bases, but which derives from inability to control or inhibit socially unacceptable acts, from that in which there is a directly abnormal motivation to commit such acts. The many typologies and offender classifications appearing in the professional literature of the past three decades appear, in the main, to acknowledge situational, non-deviant delinquency as a distinctive phenomenon presenting major implications for the educational services, and the necessity to base diagnosis and treatment more on personal characteristics and the quality of the social environment than on the behaviour of the offender in one criminal incident. In emphasising the importance of this latter consideration Davies (1969) quotes Woddis's statement that 'almost any clinical type of mental disorder may be associated with any type of crime' and Wootton's comment on several studies of different offences: 'each of these inquiries . . . illustrates the multiplicity of circumstances which give rise to outwardly similar forms of behaviour'.

Both the Seebohm Report (Committee on Local Authority and Allied Personal Social Services 1968) and the White Paper 'Children in Trouble' (1968) envisaged a much greater contribution from local authority personal services to the solution of problems located on a normality/abnormality continuum of this kind and, particularly, those problems where the disordered family situation was overlaid by the complex effects of defective housing, limited educational opportunity and acute social disadvantage. The majority of recidivists in penal establishments of all types have suffered handicaps in all or some of these main areas of personal and social functioning and there is a broad consensus of opinion amongst experienced practitioners in the penal setting that early identification of the latent problem and intensive remedial programmes must be achieved if the numbers of grossly damaged men and women in our penal institutions are to be reduced. As long ago as 1952 Stott (1952) argued a convincing case for supported and intensive social work with multiple problem families as part of a strategy for the prevention of delinquency and the avoidance of inappropriate and costly institutional solutions. Fully evaluated and undiluted work of this kind is still awaited but it is work which could and should be undertaken by the personal social services as part of an imaginative programme of child and family care.

Any examination of the possibilities of prevention and early remedial intervention must consider the level of reliability so far reached in the systematic and objective identification of potentially persistent offenders. Rose's (1967) survey of a number of enquiries underlined the limitations of various devices used in attempts at early identification and the difficulty in applying any system on a scale which could be effective and which could improve on the subjective judgment of the skilled worker in contact with the child. Rose accepts, however, that general improvements in the social services may not necessarily reduce crime, 'but that they may well do so', and presses for the continuation of attempts at early identification of objective and subjective means. 'Whether or not delinquent behaviour is symptomatic of individual maladjustment, or an expression of anti-social sub-cultures, in practice it is no less and no more difficult to identify than other forms of maladapted behaviour, which are also necessarily described by their symptoms. The commission of an offence is no doubt a somewhat misleadingly positive event, but it is no more misleading than the numerous definitions of various other forms of maladapted behaviour, and persistent offending is, if symptomatic, undoubtedly behaviour injurious to the community and thus a symptom which we ought to identify, if only as a guide to the treatment of an underlying condition. To put it bluntly, there really is no reason why we should not try to identify any forms of behaviour, delinquency is no more difficult than others, and there are strong social reasons for trying.'

The now classical work of the Gluecks has led to their cautious claim that a method has been developed for identifying potential delinquent children and into the even more difficult area of remedial intervention. Sheldon Glueck (1964) suggests the development of a therapeutic project which would, amongst other things, seek to develop techniques for 'informing parents, tactfully and helpfully, of necessary modifications in their child-rearing practices' and which should include 'competent clinicians in a position to devote time and thought to furnish necessary prophylactic advice in the care of those children shown to be in substantial danger of developing into delinquents'. Those experienced in work with formally identified offenders and their families will apprehend the formidable difficulties which would be presented in such a project, but the current reorganisation of the health and social services and the implementation of the Children and Young Persons Acts of 1963 and 1969 should greatly diminish the major impediments to acceptable intervention.

Certain possibilities and indications may be quite simply outlined. Firstly, the movement towards a firm community base for generalised service activities must reduce stigmatisation arising from functional associations and increase the general acceptability and availability of service personnel. Secondly, the increasing provision of such amenities as day nurseries and the extended supervision of child-minding arrangements will bring into contact with caring staff a number of children already exposed to some degree of disadvantage and at risk of maladjustment and severe emotional disturbance. Thirdly, the consultations between the police and the local authority, established as part of the recent legislation affecting children, allow for a consensual approach to the problems of a child at risk, or the offending child, by parent, child, the police and the social services, and increased awareness of delinquent and anti-social behaviour in the earliest stages of development. Finally, a much closer working relationship between schools and field staff of the social services departments has been made possible. The generally existing arrangements for collaboration fall short of the service associations envisaged by the Seebohm Committee but increasingly teachers and social workers must recognise the inter-dependency of their services in work designed to reduce the levels of educational and social failure. With the obvious exception of the primary family situation, there is no factor more important in socialisation than school and no context which presents greater opportunity for the perception of maladaptation and emotional disturbance. An extension of formal attachment of social service department workers to schools, of the kind already established in some parts of the country, could without doubt further the growth of complementary programmes of objective and subjective prediction and inter-disciplinary care and treatment. Already, attention is focusing on the 'disruptive' child whose non-conforming or disturbed behaviour disrupts an educational pattern designed to meet the needs of positively motivated and emotionally balanced children. It would be massively regressive if policies of exclusion were adopted and equally disastrous if attention were not paid to views recently expressed by senior members of the teaching profession. The mover to a successful resolution of the National Association of Head Teachers (1972) asking for government enquiry into the numbers of disturbed and disruptive children in school described the difficulties in the following terms:

> These children are surely ill. They need help, but there is little to be had.
>
> Heads and senior staff become so involved they often cannot give their attention to the rest of the school for long periods; too frequently they become entangled in the web of disruptive or disturbed parents of disruptive and disturbed children in trying to resolve social problems which should have received the attention of the social agencies long before.
>
> If, as we think, there is a serious problem, the means must be found to assess it, the criteria to define it decided, and eventually action taken to find the solution.

The causal relationship between psychical and physical breakdown in the primary family situation and offending behaviour is irrefutably established and it is in the field of work directed at the preservation and enrichment of family life that the social services departments can most effectively contribute to the abatement of personally and socially damaging behaviour. The objectives, needs and benefits of such a strategy have nowhere been so succinctly stated than in the evidence of the National Association for Mental Health to the Royal Commission on Marriage and Divorce (1956):

> . . . childhood should be passed in an atmosphere of stability, consistent affection and security, where the extremes of neglect and indulgence are excluded. Emotional harmony, warmth and devotion in the home are the greatest factors contributing to good mental health in the adult. For any child to be deprived of such a background can often be shown to have serious effects on his subsequent personal development and mental health out of all proportion to the apparent disturbance.

In severe and persistent form delinquent and criminal behaviour must be subjected to effective constraint by the judicial and penal systems because 'the problem of crime, like the problem of disease, is not in any final sense soluble' (Morris & Hawkins 1970). But, as medical epidemiology has contributed to the reduction of a number of pathological conditions, so the maturing knowledge and skill of the social sciences and social work can reduce the incidence of gross character and behaviour disorder.

Clinical studies and operational research, typified in the work of Bowlby (1965) and Winnicott (1957) have contributed to a firm theoretical basis for the practice of family and child care and a general discussion of this area would be superfluous. Nevertheless, it is necessary to consider certain features of family dysfunction and defective nurture which may be seen as specific to the problems of offending behaviour and its treatment. Remedial, therapeutic and educational services have all been influenced by the relationship, now established, between defects in maternal care and a range of functional problems presented by the child and adult. In school, clinic and the home, contacts with mothers predominate and the lack of emphasis on defective paternal role functioning cannot lightly be explained by the distribution of service availability and the demands of male employment. Without fuller understanding of general changes in familial structures and greater recognition of the importance of nurturing behaviour in the male, effective strategies of treatment and prevention are unlikely to be achieved. For example, the rapid development of industrial technology and urbanisation in our society has impacted on the traditional roles of both mother and father and there is substantial reason to believe that the future impact will be increasingly significant in relation to the male's role within the family. The responsibility for economic support and protection which inheres in the male role has, in many important respects, been defined in terms of occupation. It is a man's work which tends to determine family status and to affirm his identity and authority within the family. It is also the perception of the man's capacity and ability to work his craft or skill which provides for the child positive educational learning paradigms. Residential or nursery care which ignores the importance of this dimension will almost certainly add to the difficulties of socialisation of children already deprived of the experience of a complete family. The author's own professional experience leaves no doubt that defective or colourless paternal models account for much non-aligned and disaffected behaviour amongst delinquents and that lack of colour and quality in paternal employment is an important contributive factor. Research undertaken in different social science disciplines adds substance to these personal impressions.

Bradley was amongst the first of the psychologists in this country to explore Margaret Mead's affirmation that the cohesion of society depends upon the learned nurturing behaviour of the male, and to seek a relationship between paternal defects and educational and social failure. A projective testing technique was used to provide evidence of a family dominance hierarchy and the results led to general conclusions about the relationship between paternal authority and nurture and the development of conforming, socially acceptable attitudes. Educationally well-achieved and non-deviant children of both sexes were clearly distinguishable from delinquent and deviant children in that, from seven years onwards, their fathers were increasingly identified as salient members in a family hierarchy. In contrast, breakdowns in the families of delinquents were impressively associated with defects in the role of the father. Disinterestedness or abdication of fundamental paternal responsibilities appeared to be far more frequently encountered in the families of delinquents and, while Bradley fully acknowledged the importance of both parents in the socialisation of the child, he argued that the role of the father was more vital than had hitherto been admitted:

> The father who chooses to abdicate or to dominate rather than to nurture or who, because of defects in his own rearing, is incapable of learning to nurture, adds to the difficulties of his children's socialisation and appears from the investigation so far carried out to be responsible in a large measure for his children's social deviation.

These views are in accord with those of Andry (1960) who describes researches in a similar field. Andry's conclusions were

> that delinquent boys (suffering neither mental defects nor diseases nor from broken homes) tend to perceive greater defects in their father's roles than in their mother's roles, whereas non-delinquents tend to perceive the roles of both parents as being adequate. Thus the prime differentiating feature between delinquent and non-delinquent, as far as parental role playing is concerned, is the delinquent's perception of the father's role as being negative.

More recently, a Home Office research unit study has underlined the significance of father/son relationships in the circumstances of 507 male probationers aged between 17 and 21 years. Parental over-indulgence was common and was linked with reconviction and almost all the fathers had the worst possible relationships with their sons. In general, it was noted that:

> mother–son relationships were rather more positive than those between father and son; but there was overwhelming evidence that it was the

> latter association which was the crucial one insofar as it was most closely linked with the lad's failure or success on probation. Easily the most important family factors in the successful avoidance of further trouble are that the father should be firm but kindly, and that there should be mutual warmth and affection between him and his son.

Defects in the nurturing behaviour of the father are also of significance in the creation of situations known to heighten the vulnerability of the child and in some circumstances actually to precipitate a delinquent reaction. Even short-term admissions to residential care tend predominantly to affect children already deprived of benign and helpful relationships within their homes and the Schaffers investigation of 100 families who made application to the local authority to have children taken into care during the mother's hospitalisation has demonstrated the extent to which one form of disadvantage can overlay another.

For each 'child care' case, a control case was chosen at random from the mothers present in the same maternity ward at that time. The criteria for selection provided for comparability of socio-economic background and for mothers in the control group to have older children who were being privately looked after. The extent to which the control group fathers took over the care of the children during the mother's absence in this exclusively working-class sample was 'surprising and unexpected' and indications suggested 'a basic difference between the two groups in the fathers' general participation in family life'. It was emphasised that most of the child care parents were not simply neglectful or rejecting in their attitude towards their children but were presenting one aspect of a general inadequacy or instability also shown 'in their geographical mobility, the father's work record and their lack of community integration'. The indications for social work focus of these and other studies are considerable. All too often the social work and health care contacts with the father are minimal and insufficient time is available for the solution of employment problems which, quite apart from the economic consideration, touch on the crucially important areas of self and family esteem. Societal expectations and psycho-biological factors combine to produce an overwhelming preponderance of males in the known population of offenders and it is this bias in the population which underlies a requisite treatment emphasis on subjective problems of employment and paternal role function.

It is evident that the established principles and method of social casework and residential care are generally applicable to the prevention and treatment of the offender. Nevertheless, the distribution of personality and social characteristics of identified offenders does represent an important determinant of treatment priorities and role relationships between workers and the client group. The social services departments are already assigned considerable responsibility for control, containment and treatment of younger offenders, many of whom will not present symptoms of serious psychological disturbance or, initially, wish to relinquish the satisfactions of established delinquency patterns. The differences which exist in role relationships have been suggested by Studt (1959) who expects in the social services 'a graded series of definitions of the client role which reflects the different abilities of individuals to take responsibility for themselves. At one end of the range the client position is designed to allow for self-determination in all areas of personal functioning. Such positions are usually found in private family agencies and in outpatient psychiatric clinics. There are intermediate positions in which the role definition of the client calls for submitting one or more aspect of personal functioning to shared decision-making with the worker, such as the economic area in public assistance, parent–child communication in foster home care, and the management of illness in the medical services. At the other end of the range would be positions for clients who enter the role involuntarily and are assigned to work with authority persons in relation to extended areas of personal functioning. Such positions are found in agencies dealing with parental neglect, in many institutions and in correctional services. All social agency caseloads fit within this continuum with variously designed positions for clients which reflect the nature of the need, the ability of the client to take responsibility for his own life and the potential danger to society in his behaviour.'

Even although Studt is here referring to the American organisational context, the described pattern of role relationships is clearly distinguishable within the caseload of the social services department and at the latter end of the continuum has specific application to the treatment of offenders. A mild but clearly discernible degree of authority and capacity to control is positively indicated in the treatment of many young delinquents and relationships, often involuntarily established in the first instance, can provide the base from which growth is possible and from which sensitive and effective casework can proceed. Much can be learned from well-established professional practice in the Probation and After-Care Service where enforced relationships are utilised (Hunt 1964) in treatment and in the stabilisation of those commonly encountered family situations where, because of difficulties in their own nurture, the authority of the parents is diminished, and their roles unhelpfully differentiated. Foren & Bailey's (1968) description of the shadings of authority necessarily present in diverse social work contexts, has contributed to a greater understanding of client perception and expectation of authority figures and agencies and acknowledges the therapeutic potential which exists in situations of control. Having reviewed ideas representative of the various theoretical standpoints adopted over many years, Foren and Bailey state a firm belief that 'there are good theoretical reasons for using assertive casework methods and setting limits in selected cases'.

At the moment, local authorities are primarily concerned with the structural design of the new social services departments and this process is taking place against a background of preparation for local government reform and health service reorganisation. In these circumstances, some loss of impetus in specific programme development is inevitable and it would be unrealistic to expect dramatic improvement on established provision and method within a period of some four or five years. Above all, the treatment of the offender requires a high level of practitioner aptitude, skill and understanding, and the dependency on national provision for professional education and training is such that the level of this provision will represent the major determinant of change. Given imaginatively trained staff in the requisite numbers, it will then be possible fully to utilise the resources of an integrated social service organisation and realise the full potential of the liberal and humane policies embodied in the Children and Young Persons Act, 1969.

It has already been suggested that the social services departments will make their major contribution to the treatment and prevention of offending behaviour in the field of care and support for families under internal and environmental stress. This service cannot be provided in isolation and must actively involve the law enforcement, education and health care organisations. In its social work with the adult offender in the community, the courts of civil and criminal jurisdiction and in penal establishments, the probation and after-care service enhances the possibility of family survival and endeavours to preserve a network of vital family relationships hazarded, for example, by marriage dissolution or parental imprisonment. Close collaboration between the probation officer and the members of the area social services teams will certainly extend the range and effectiveness of family casework conducted by both services and contribute to the necessary growth of non-institutional systems of treatment and disposal.

Studies of women shoplifters and of marital stress in the lives of sentenced prisoners have exemplified the extent to which health and social problems in combination can precipitate offending behaviour and Goldberg's (1968) study of social work in general medical practice, the extent to which these problems are referred to the general practitioner.

The increasing establishment of health centres and enlarged group practice is presenting unique opportunities for the effective meshing of services, particularly at local level and for expansion of social work help immediately available to the general practitioner. The absence of close collaboration in attempts to resolve the complex of health and social problems extensively presented to the general practitioner will certainly ensure that there is no reduction in the number of unwell and seriously troubled people who daily are to be seen in the magistrates' courts of this country. The response, even to short-term casework, of those who have committed offences where under acute stress suggests that many personal tragedies could have been avoided had the combined resources of medicine and social work been mobilised before the now classical 'cri de coeur'. The case for close professional association with the general practitioner may be applied with equal substance to the hospital and clinical situations but, at this point in time, no agreement has been reached on the ideal formal organisation of social work in hospitals and psychiatric units. In this sector, as in so many others, there is room for experiment and innovation but the small number of local authority and hospital administrations already establishing formal service arrangements are assembling substantial evidence of the benefits to the patients of coherent social work care and support offered as an institutionally based extension of the field service.

Reference has already been made to the relationship between the social service department and the school and the requisite interaction in the prevention of delinquency and its treatment. Now considered are those aspects of the problem in which the social services departments themselves become directly involved in diagnosis and remedial care in the residential or group setting. It is axiomatic that careful and perceptive evaluation of the child and young person's needs and potential must precede decisions concerned with specific care provision and treatment planning. Such evaluation must necessarily recognise the communication difficulties created by social and constitutional disadvantages of many kinds and limitations set by reliance on verbal contact; sensitive observation of spontaneous behaviour in inter-personal and group relationships forms an essential part of diagnosis. In spite of increases in the range of local authority observation and assessment centres there are still substantial deficiencies in this field of provision, and staffing establishments do not, in the main, acknowledge the importance of a multi-disciplinary team working as an integral part of the unit. Traditionally, staff of child guidance clinics have reinforced the diagnostic capability of assessment and reception centres, but the pursuit of greater effectiveness, continuity of perception and sophistication in evaluation points to the inclusion of certain skills, notably those of the clinical psychologist and remedial teacher, within the permanent membership of the assessment centre team.

Provisions of the Children and Young Persons Act, 1969 have been designed to diminish lack of flexibility in the use of residential care and the degree of geographic child/family separation compelled by the former organisation of the approved school system. The establishment of regional planning committees has given the necessary impetus to a form of strategic planning which not only can acknowledge regional variations in social structure and need, but also provide fluidity in the use of residential care and intermediate treatment. The static nature and restricted range of available placements has, for many years, impeded attempts to match specific treatment and social education to the individual maladapted and delinquent child. In numerous situations residential care has been unnecessarily protracted and the move to localise units will doubtless reduce problems of this kind. Even those community homes which provide education on the premises will be better able to draw on specialised educational services in the area and those planning programmes of intermediate treatment can already see very real opportunities for the joint involvement of education and social service personnel. The episodic nature of much delinquent behaviour calls for a capacity for short-term residential containment combined with a stabilising framework of intermediate treatment and developments in this field could well provide the most effective and relevant part of the programme of treatment, prevention and social education.

This discussion has attempted to illuminate some facets of a complex and acute social problem, and many aspects of challenge and opportunity have necessarily been omitted. It is, however, the recognition of complexity and the impossibility of finding single solutions which form the essential basis for planning and service development.

References

Ardenaes, J. (1968) 'Recidivism in Scandinavia', *Int. J. Offender Therapy* 12.

Andry, R. (1960) *Delinquency and Parental Pathology*. Methuen, London

Avison, N. H. (1966) 'New problems of Crime', *New Soc.*

Bowlby, J. (1965) *Child Care and the Growth of Love*, 2nd edn. Penguin Harmondsworth.

Bradley, J. (1963) 'Educational and social failure: an experimenta approach', *Nature*, 2 November.

Bradley, J. (1964) 'Educational and social failure: some further observa tions', *Nature*.

Children in Trouble (1968) Cmnd. 3601. HMSO, London.

Children and Young Persons Act (1963) HMSO, London.

Children and Young Persons Act (1969) HMSO, London.

Committee on Local Authority and Allied Personal Social Services (1968 *Report* (Chairman: F. Seebohm), Cmnd. 3703. HMSO, London.

Davies, M. (1969) 'Offence behaviour and the classification of offenders' *Brit. J. Criminol.*, 9, 39.

Foren, R. & Bailey, R. (1968) *Authority in Social Casework*. Pergamon Oxford.

Glueck, S. (1964) 'Potential delinquents can be identified. What next? *Brit. J. Criminol.*, 4, 215.

Goldberg, E. M. (1968) 'Social Work in General Practice', *The Lance* 552.

Hunt, A. W. (1964) 'Enforcement in probation casework', *Brit. J Criminol.*, 4, 239.

McDavid, J. & McCandless, B. (1962) 'Psychological theory, research an juvenile delinquency', *J. Crim. Law, Criminol. Police Sci.*

Morris, N. & Hawkins, G. (1970) *The Honest Politician's Guide to Crime Control.* University of Chicago Press, Chicago.
NAHT (1972) Conference report, *The Times*, 3 May.
Rose, G. (1967) 'Early identification of delinquents', *Brit. J. Criminol.*, 7, 6.
Royal Commission on Marriage and Divorce (1956) Cmnd. 9678. HMSO, London.
Schaffer, H. & Schaffer, B. (1969) 'Deprived children and their families', *Howard J.*, 12, 113.
Stott, D. (1952) *Saving Children from Delinquency.* University of London Press, London.
Studt, E. (1959) 'Worker-Client authority relationships in social work', *Soc. Wk.*, 4.
Trasler, G. (1962) *The Explanation of Criminality.* Routledge and Kegan Paul, London.
Walker, N. (1965) *Crime and Punishment in Britain.* Edinburgh University Press, Edinburgh.
Winnicott, D. (1957) *The Child and the Outside World: studies in developing relationships.* Tavistock, London.

6 *The aged and the social services department*

Maurice G. Speed

'When I grow old, I want to go back to the place where I was born and drink beer with the men who were boys when I was a boy.'
(Hilaire Belloc.)

In post-war years the elderly have been remarkable as the poorest members of our society, physically, economically and socially. The relief of old people from this unenviable situation has proved as difficult as the problem of reducing the chronic, mass unemployment of the thirties. The Seebohm Report (Committee on Local Authority and Allied Personal Social Services 1968, p. 11) identified 'very old people' as calling for special attention and the development of a comprehensive social service to meet their needs must be an important priority for the new social services departments.

The statistical pattern of an ageing population

The statistics of an ageing population are important but they can obscure the fact that the elderly have little in common except their age and relative poverty. With this reservation in mind, it is essential to identify the pertinent details and some of the social implications which emerge from the national census, as well as relevant research and surveys.

We have been aware during the last thirty years that the population over retirement age was increasing both absolutely and as a percentage of the total population. The number over 65 years of age will continue to increase until the end of the present decade, but the significant projection is for the very old (age 85 and over), which is not only rising faster, but will continue to rise until 2001 when it will be two-thirds as large as at present. The following table sets out projections drawn on the base of 1966 (Committee on Local Authority and Allied Personal Social Services 1968, p. 91):

TABLE 6.1

	1971		1981		1991	
Age range	*Number**	%	*Number**	%	*Number**	%
65–70	4,188	8.4	4,559	8.5	4,473	7.7
75 and over	2,268	4.6	2,725	5.1	3,062	5.2
	6,456	13.0	7,284	13.6	7,535	12.9

* in thousands

It is also significant that women out-live the men so that in 1971 while there were 79 men for every 100 women between the ages of 65 and 69, the proportion was 35 to 100 in the 85+ group.

Imbalance in the rates of increase for males and females reflects higher mortality of males than females at all ages and the loss of a million men in the First World War. However, the considerable improvement in male mortality at the younger ages is expected to affect the sex ratio over the next two decades, so that males will outnumber females up to 60 years. In addition, the movement through the age groups of the war-depleted male population is expected to produce a sharp increase in the next decade or so in the overall population of men of retirement age. However, the population of very old men, age 85 and over, will still be depleted in 1981 (Thompson 1970). Some conclusions can be drawn from the figures themselves which should influence both the size and the shape of the pattern of social services in the new departments. There will be a large number of women, single or widowed, living alone and highly vulnerable. Apart from the obvious risk of their frailty and isolation, they may be particularly susceptible to depression arising from loneliness, bereavement and the regular loss of old friends.

Many of our assumptions about family life reflect experience of the nineteenth and early twentieth century when the traditional pattern was of large families with very small numbers surviving into old age. The present situation is very different when the relatively small numbers born during the inter-war years are unable to support a very big increase in the number of their elderly relatives, of which a significant proportion are spinsters robbed of their marriage prospects by the First World War. For the very old, their own children will already be in late middle age, while the mobility of labour and the decreasing size of family accommodation place practical limitations on family support. It must also be recognised that to rely on relatives may seem to some older people a situation of dependence.

In 1970, Michael Meacher attempted to estimate the numbers of old people in high-risk groups, and although there may be considerable overlap between the different categories, the classification is valuable. The numbers are also based on 1964 estimates so that a 10% increase could be assumed for 1972. The original estimates are set out below.

TABLE 6.2

Estimated numbers of old people in high-risk groups (Meacher 1970)

Risk classification	*Number aged* 65 *and over*
Severe incapacity	350,000
Mental infirmity	277,000
Extreme social isolation	262,000
Age over 85	305,000

Meeting the needs of the elderly in the social services department

There are factual considerations affecting the elderly which make them different from the other groups who will be competing for the attention of the new social services departments. It is not only that the incidence of old age is different from, for example, mental illness or juvenile delinquency, but cultural attitudes and emotional reactions to old age are of a different quality and kind.

To grow old is a natural process and the infirmities of ageing fall like rain upon the unjust as upon the just. This is not to say that we welcome our inexorable fate in this respect, indeed, we deny or conceal the symptoms for as long as we can. At the same time our society lays little blame on being old even if it often fails to allow much opportunity for grace and dignity in retirement.

The sheer size of the retired population and the extent of their deprivation in terms of income, housing conditions and community role, call for a diversion of scarce resources to their relief well beyond the foreseeable means of the social serivces departments. Successive ministers with undoubted commitment and good intent have recognised the needs but have only been able to think politically in terms of percentage growth, when what was needed was a multiplication in the rate of expenditure.

The case for an exceptional expansion does not rest simply on the low level of present provision nor on the substantial growth of foreseeable need. A percentage growth of the order of perhaps 10% is most likely to encourage an assumption that the best policy is a steady uniform development. Better results might come from an imaginative exploration of the possibilities of a more radical approach. With the current decline in the likelihood of full employment, a doubling of the home help service would be practicable, particularly in development areas, and it is a policy which would be reversible and would not involve the delay inevitable in the erection of buildings or the training of professional staff.

Without such special consideration, many directors, particularly those with long experience of the unmet needs of other groups, see an imminent danger that even a minimum expansion of the services for the elderly will leave no additional resources available for the essential family service, let alone community development. There are no short cuts because all long-term support services are expensive, better domiciliary services will not avoid the need for many more residential homes, although they may abate the ultimate requirement.

The absence of a comprehensive approach to the problems of the new population structure which followed the spectacular increase in the normal life span, is underlined by the statutory framework itself. The way in which Parliament has provided for the elderly is curious if not devious. The National Assistance Act, 1948 imposed a duty to provide residential homes but apparently saw no need for the employment of social workers; sheltered housing is supported by contributions under the Local Government Acts, while the social needs of the elderly are covered by a section of the Public Health and Health Services Act, 1968—a section which only became operative in October 1971. Community nurses, health visitors and home helps who are now heavily engaged in supporting the elderly in their own homes were not mainly intended for this purpose. It is not surprising that there is no co-ordinated plan to meet the special needs of older people.

Local authorities generally show a surprising antipathy to any external measurement of their social services; the 'league tables' of performance are sternly rejected as being superficial and unrelated to local circumstances. Such an attitude could be justified if they were able to demonstrate sophistication and comprehensiveness in the assumptions on which they based their own planning; the fact of the matter is that the level of provision of old people's homes or sheltered housing is normally much more indicative of a commitment by the authority to a particular form of service rather than an analysis of local need. How else can one explain why, within a single county, the estimated need for sheltered housing by housing authorities may vary from as much as 250 dwellings per 1,000 persons over 65 years of age, to nothing at all?

What has not been fully explored is the effect on the demand for social services of the low level of the retirement pension and supplementary benefits. A subsistence income means inevitably the cheapest, which is often the poorest, housing accommodation and unsuitable diets; the rapid improvement in physical health which normally follows admission to a residential home demonstrates dramatically that apparent infirmities of old age may be symptoms of poverty.

The penury of retirement is a depressing prospect, but it is not the only reason why giving up work can fail to herald a different and satisfying part of the normal life cycle. At best, highly effective budgeting makes life possible, but it is a life in which monotony and drabness are constant factors. In a work-orientated society, there is an underlying assumption that economic activity is the main justification for existence. As a result, retirement can be a very painful and difficult process where men lack a sense of purpose at a time when there should be fruitful leisure.

In a period of high general unemployment, it may be easier to look realistically at the possibility of working after retirement age. During the immediate post-war period, the acute labour shortage suggested that the country could not afford to lose the economic contribution of those who wished to work after the age of 65 years even if this involved some retraining or working at a slower pace. When the economy cannot find jobs for men of working age, the argument loses its force and calls perhaps for a complete reappraisal.

In a farming community or amongst craftsmen, the old often have a natural status simply because they have so much accumulated knowledge and wisdom which is still relevant to everyday life and work. In modern industry, the situation is quite different and the rapidly changing technology makes much first-hand experience obsolete and irrelevant in a very short time. Although there is now some evidence that the greater diligence of older people may offset their natural difficulty in acquiring new knowledge, almost everything is in favour of the young worker in the present day.

For men engaged in heavy manual work such as dockers and coal miners, the inability to withstand the heavy physical strain is already a common cause of premature retirement. The shake-out of manpower by industry during recent years has made many professional and executive staff redundant and for these it has been increasingly difficult to find alternative employment.

The fact of the matter is, therefore, that retirement at 65 is more and more becoming inevitable and that it may be more realistic to talk of earlier rather than later retirement.

Although we are aware of the awkward adjustment which a breadwinner makes when he gives up this role and status, there is little knowledge about the number who retire easily and find enjoyment in their years of retirement. It could well be that one of the useful functions of an occupational health service would be to prepare workers for an easy and successful retirement.

During 1968, general practitioners with the help of the County Health Department established a number of retirement clinics in Devon and in his annual report, the County Medical Officer of Health estimated that at least 50% of the patients who attended would benefit to some extent. The striking comment in the report is, '*Depression* is a common finding and in widowed people it is the exception for it to be absent' (County Medical Officer of Health, Devon, 1971). The existence of such depression must be an additional handicap in facing the other difficulties of giving up work. Preparation for retirement is no new concept, but so often it has been pre-occupied with intellectual activities and middle class ideas. It is encouraging to recall that Mr. Vic Feather has now called for industrial workers to be given the opportunity in working time to prepare themselves for retirement.

The new social services departments face the classical dilemma of severely limited resources and unlimited demand; in particular, they cannot offer skilled social casework for all those with serious personal problems. One of the questions now being asked is whether the needs of the elderly justify a claim on the scarce time of qualified social workers.

Matilda Goldberg in *Helping the Aged* reports on a field experiment designed to test the value of social work training in meeting the needs of older people. The conclusions confirm in part the justification for using trained social workers in this way, but Professor Richard Titmuss in his preface says, 'One critical element justifying social work and justifying training is the listening role—an element often over-looked or misinterpreted by critics of the profession. . . . In other words, the trained workers functioned more selectively, they concentrated more practical aid and more psychological effort on those who appeared to need help most' (Goldberg, Mortimer & Williams 1971).

The view of a director of social services is necessarily different from that of Miss Goldberg and Professor Titmuss, and his expectations of the social worker will be crucial. It may be helpful to indicate the basis for the writer's own view that a comprehensive service for the elderly can only be used effectively if trained social workers are employed in this field.

While the elderly face many common difficulties, none of the personal circumstances will be identical and each person will rightly expect to be considered as a unique and special individual. The growing range of services may even increase the possibility that the best solution is not found. Variety has no value unless it increases the choice which is available and the older person requires skilled help if he is to make his own decision in moments of crisis and distress.

Too little has been said in the past about the value of casework or a casework approach with older people. They face many problems including the crises of retirement and bereavement, both associated with a great deal of pathological depression not always diagnosed or treated. They live in a rapidly changing world in which they are asked in addition to make drastic adjustments at a time of life when this is most difficult.

There may be no better example of the need for social work skill than the vulnerability of the older person forced by circumstances to consider accepting full residential care.

When old people apply for admission to a residential home, it is essential that the matter shall not be treated lightly or superficially. It will be necessary to ensure that the client knows what is involved in this step—the loss of independence, the reduction in personal identity, the limitation on privacy and the restriction of community life. Unsatisfactory living conditions are not a valid reason for admission to residential care, still less should an old person be over-persuaded by friends, relatives or even her doctor that 'you'll be far better off in a home'. Such an application may be a completely accurate statement of need, or it may be a cry for help because of other worries or needs; what is important is that the client is not encouraged to abandon her home too easily and that, first of all, every other possible solution is explored.

Although admission to hospital or a residential home will in itself indicate a high degree of physical or mental infirmity, this is seldom the immediate cause. The patient has not become suddenly very frail, more often there has been a breakdown in help given by family or neighbourhood which has left him unable to cope once the support is withdrawn. The sad fact is that few residents return home when the social situation has been restored. To neighbours and relatives who have been concerned with the safety of an old person, admission to hospital or residential home can appear to be a complete and final solution. It is important that the new departments develop effective ways of relieving the social situation before the crisis actually occurs or of encouraging the old person to return home when the difficulties have been overcome.

The experience of child care and some recognition of the limitations of full residential care in meeting emotional needs have, over the years, prompted the development of schemes for the 'boarding-out' of old people. The Hampshire County Council initiated a scheme in 1952 and there have been some half-a-dozen comparable developments in other areas since then; it is the failure to proliferate on a national scale that calls for comment, rather than the schemes themselves.

The choice of the name may in itself have been a mistake with the obvious assumption that the older person would be provided with something like a substitute family and also that his standing in the household would be that of a dependent child rather than an adult. The scale of the service may also have been disappointing for those who were seeking a radical reduction in the demand for residential care. Nevertheless the provision of suitable lodgings can be a valuable service in the individual case and justifies development as a particular way of helping those who cannot fit easily into either residential care or normal housing.

The family is the natural source of strength and support for old people. This is not to say, of course, that they will all be offered or will accept family or community support—those who have found it difficult to make satisfactory personal relationships in earlier life are likely to find it even harder in old age and will be specially vulnerable to isolation. But family rejection is not common.

The breakdowns of family support usually come when the family itself has been pressed to breaking point; help must be offered long before the burden has become too heavy to bear. Short-stay accommodation is probably the most effective way of doing this, but it is important that a wide range of services should be available, known to the family, and offered in an acceptable way.

The older person will usually prefer to remain in his own home or in the family home of a relative. Infirmity and shortage of money will inevitably mean that he cannot do everything for himself. He will need a home help for part of his domestic work, meals on wheels if he cannot cook regularly, but above all he will need suitable housing; any analysis of admissions to residential care will illustrate that bad living accommodation is a common and basic cause.

Sheltered housing—groups of dwellings with a warden service—has allowed many of those, who were too frail to live alone, to survive with independence and security when they would otherwise have been admitted to residential homes. The way is now open for bolder experiments by the statutory authorities in providing sheltered housing with a midday meal on the general lines of the Abbeyfield Society. The residential homes remain the most difficult service, mainly because they still fail to present an acceptable image. Within the community they are respected but a reservation remains—'I'm sure they are very good but I should not like it.' Our failure to define the role of the residential home has prevented a recognition of a professional element in the work of the staff.

To meet the needs for residential care and housing will involve a high investment of capital funds. If, however, these buildings are to improve the quality of life for the elderly, it is at least as important that they shall be managed properly and in the following pages an attempt has been made to indicate the ways in which the best use can be made of valuable resources.

Far better off in a home

The residential home today cannot escape from painful public memories of its direct antecedents in the workhouse, reformatories and bedlam. With this unhappy history, admission can still carry some vestige of shame for the old person and guilt for near relatives. Moreover, low standards of residential care can make it an unattractive last resort for those who cannot care adequately for themselves.

Little attempt is made architecturally to create a building reminiscent of ordinary domestic houses, too often the elevation and general design impress rather than please; method building and the authority's own architectural style combine to ensure that its public ownership is as unmistakable as that of the old workhouse. Many sites are unnecessarily large and laid out in the manner of a minor stately home; spacious grounds may gladden the heart of the authority and the staff but they meet no conscious wish of the residents and further highlight the separation of the home from its local community. The total effect is to emphasise that this is a public building and not an indigenous part of its residential setting.

Even given the ideal building, inappropriate practice and policy can make the care of residents irrelevant to their needs or even destructive of their well-being. The superficial assumption that ageing creates stereotyped needs can mean that the individuality of the residents is suppressed so that they fit the services provided by the home.

Any service which gives total care faces an ambivalence amongst the public which almost ensures that it cannot win. There is a general belief that the freedom and independence of the individual must be a prime concern, and yet the staff are expected to ensure that the same individual shall be protected from all foreseeable risks. To instance the dilemma for staff of an old persons' home; residents must be free to go out as and when they please, but staff must be accountable if the resident comes to any harm when exercising this right. In much the same way, there must be no risk to health or hygiene, which will encourage a clinical tidiness and a well-balanced non-fattening diet; most of us, however, associate the concept of a homely atmosphere with informal muddle and tasty, traditional food which for the elderly will be stodgy and fattening. Clearly, no compromise will satisfy such disparate views and it may be more helpful to clarify some of the more common needs of older people living a communal life.

Meeting personal needs in a residential home

There is a fundamental satisfaction in living in your own town with your family and friends around you; apart from the wealth of social contacts, a personal and community identity is established from a network of relationships, and a lifetime's contribution to the local community is well-known and remembered. In moving to a strange town all this is lost to the resident, for whom even the local newspaper has little meaning. It scarcely needs to be stated that these important needs can only be met if residents are as a matter of course admitted to their own local home. Some county authorities are still surprised to find that the opening of a new home produces substantial new demands for admission direct from old people; a simple enquiry of the old people themselves would have revealed a basic fact which has generally been overlooked for purely administrative reasons.

To move from the smallness and intimacy of a private house and to become irrevocably one of a group living together as a community is probably the greatest change of a lifetime for many older people; this will be particularly so for women, as men may have had a similar experience in the army, and women will be the great majority of residents in homes. The manifest loss of privacy can only be lessened by ensuring that each resident has somewhere they can go to be alone and to shut out the world. When applying for admission almost everyone asks for a single room; another simple statement of preference by those most concerned and yet often ignored in the planning of residential homes.

The common justification for including multiple bedrooms is a splendid example of crooked thinking and the bureaucratic need to have been absolutely right. The evidence is mainly based on the argument that residents do not really need single rooms because they often refuse a subsequent offer to move into a single room; such answers are more likely to demonstrate that change is uncomfortable and few will wish to reject a companion. If it were correct that a higher value is placed on company and security than on privacy, it might be expected that those in single rooms would ask to share—a request that is seldom made. Even authorities who accept the prime value of the single room may then fail to provide locks for the doors or if they do will shrink from giving residents the dignity of possessing the key; how can they imagine that the old lady who has meticulously locked her house against intruders for eighty years will not still wish to feel safe?

Personal possessions form part of personal identity and are often important links with landmarks of a long lifetime. In a bedroom which is necessarily of standard size and appearance, they can do more than anything else to avoid uniformity. It is often argued that it is administratively difficult to allow residents to bring their own furniture; an assumption normally made without consulting residential staff. There is also the bogey of woodworm, almost as if woodworm in furniture were a natural concomitant of old age. The abiding spectre of low institutional standards can sometimes result in a civic pride which is only satisfied by furnishing homes as though they were hotels and which would be shamed by the presence of a motley assortment of well-worn furniture. I am aware of no experience which does not support completely the great value of allowing residents to furnish their own rooms.

Most parents will be aware of the almost insoluble problem of allowing adolescents the right balance of security and independence. Within a residential home it is equally difficult to meet in full measure these same basic needs of the elderly in a way which will satisfy staff responsible for giving adequate care as well as residents trying to be themselves in a new and alien situation. There is a further complication in meeting the reasonable expectations of relatives and the authority itself.

Independence is vital for mental and emotional health and is quite distinct from liberty and freedom, although they cannot exist separately. Independence depends on the extent to which the individual can decide or influence significantly his own life. Within a community the scope for individual decisions is necessarily limited, but this makes personal choice and preference more and not less important. The answer lies firstly in ensuring that each resident is left with the maximum amount of discretion and that careful techniques are developed to allow the maximum participation of all residents in those matters which affect them. Residents' committees are not common and they certainly call for great understanding and no little skill from hard-pressed staff; there are obvious implications for future staff training.

Security is as important for some residents as independence. While ordinary family life provides the best chance for the individual to stand on his own feet and determine the course of his life, it can, for example, mean a marriage in which one partner dominates, making all the decisions, while the other is content to be managed and protected. Bereavement may leave a dependent woman who will be seeking the security of a new situation in which no demands will be made that she decides for herself. Apart from this special case, a proper sense of security will come from a clear and open definition of the place of the resident in the home, what he can and cannot do, what is expected of him, whether staff are expected to help him or manage him, in short, the answers to all the questions which will tell him where he stands. Primarily for the older person, security will be concerned with the permanence of his residence which means in terms of his reality whether he must always be prepared for a move to hospital.

It would be wrong to leave the question of independence and security without referring to the fact of great frailty, physical and mental, which may be the only common quality of residents. This makes it more difficult to ignore the possible consequences of their making bad decisions about themselves. The nursing aspects of care will be ever present so that the staff must have considerable nursing competence; this casts further doubt on the real value of transferring a resident to hospital because of temporary or terminal illness, particularly if the wishes of the resident are believed to be relevant.

It is impossible to over-estimate the need of the resident to remain in contact with his own family and yet so often the relatives create frustration for the caring staff. Few relatives can take an objective view of the care given. They will expect perfection to justify having allowed the admission to take place and yet will probably want to reassure themselves that it is not as good as they might have offered. Staff may find it hard to live with the resulting attitudes or to accept relatives who take advantage of the resident's need for their attention and company.

Housing—the critical issue

It is impossible not to be aware that the low standard of housing for the elderly is a major and continuing national scandal. The fact that slum clearance schemes could normally be directly related to the provision of small dwellings for the elderly speaks for itself—knock on any ten doors in a street of condemned housing and the chances are that nine will be opened by someone of retirement age. It is also necessary to look at some of the statistical evidence which is available to demonstrate the scale of the need.

The following evidence shows the poor housing conditions of the elderly and the relatively slow rate at which these are being improved:

(1) In England and Wales outside Greater London, the proportion of households without sole use of a hot water supply, and of a w.c. in or attached to the building was 36% for households with a head aged seventy or over, compared with 16% for households with a head aged 30–39 and 14% for those with a head aged 40–49 (Woolf 1967).

(2) A fifth of the residents in welfare homes need not have been there if adequate housing could have been made available (Harris & Clausen 1968).

(3) 27% of those over 65 in Britain did not have access to a bath and another 4% shared a bath with another household. 5% did not have a w.c. and another 34% only had access to a w.c. outside the house (Townsend & Wedderburn 1965).

(4) In a survey of the over-80s in Stockport, there was a high proportion of the houses lacking adequate facilities. Poor conditions increased down the social scale; nearly a third of the Social Class V respondents had no fixed bath, piped hot water, inside lavatory, coal store at living room level, or gas/electricity for cooking. Old people living together and those living alone, irrespective of social class, were gravely lacking in household amenities; of those living alone in Social Class V, 38% had no facilities at all (Brocking & Lempart 1966).

Towards a housing policy

Nothing is more destructive of independence than to give help in excess of need, and such extravagance cannot be explained except that civic pride is sometimes satisfied by offering an over-perfect service for a few and blaming shortage of money for failing to do anything for the rest. A good management precept is to deal with the smaller problems first, in social work terms to look primarily at the more simple and less expensive ways of overcoming the handicaps of old age. On this analysis, housing must be our starting point.

The need for adequate housing units for the elderly can be under-estimated by simply seeing them as constituting some 12% of the total population. In a West Country seaside town where there are some 25% of the population above 65 years of age, the census shows that half the households are headed by someone of that age, merely confirming that older people live alone or as couples whereas younger people live in much larger groups. In spite of the fact that the elderly must necessarily need proportionally more houses or flats, few housing authorities have grasped the implication of this and are then surprised to find that they have many three-bedroomed houses occupied by elderly couples at considerable cost and inconvenience to themselves.

Too much is often made of the reluctance of older people to move into smaller accommodation. There is all the difference in the world between making a decision and making a decision hurriedly. The housing authority which allows tenants ample time to reflect on the advantages of a more convenient and less expensive dwelling, is seldom disappointed. When planning special housing for the elderly, one rural district council invited older tenants in family housing to consider applying for tenancies when the site was being purchased. Over the succeeding months as the building progressed, the applications flowed in. The elderly are on the whole practical and sensible, which means that they make very good use of any time they may be allowed to think about their problems.

There are excellent examples from both voluntary organisations and local authorities of attractive housing developments which meet the special difficulties of older people. It is not uncommon to see small groups of flats and bungalows, well designed and well sited, and above all, built by housing authorities with manifest and unusual pride. There are many examples of sheltered housing which combine, with a nice sensitivity, independence, privacy, security and opportunity for social activities. Unfortunately, it is comparatively rare to find an adequate range of houses on council estates so that a couple may move into a smaller house without leaving their friends and familiar places.

The challenge to housing authorities is to identify the best of present practice and then to ensure that future housing programmes produce an adequate supply and variety. It is an insult to offer the warden's service of sheltered housing to married couples who are quite competent to support each other and it is wasteful to compel those who are frail to accept full residential care when sheltered housing would have been quite enough to cover the risk involved. Much more is needed, but with the emphasis shifting rather more to independent dwellings in counties and to sheltered housing in the cities.

Sheltered housing

In the early 1950s, Dorset County Council, in association with several housing authorities, pioneered sheltered housing for the elderly mainly as a way of avoiding the unnecessary admission of older people who were at some risk into residential homes. A simple pattern had been developed which involved 20–30 small bungalows designed to meet the needs of the elderly, for whom a resident warden would be available through a call-bell system.

Such housing schemes developed quickly in county areas, but are very seldom found in the large towns. Part of the explanation may lie in the way in which they are financed; the county council make a grant to housing authorities for this purpose and grants are peculiarly effective in stimulating all local authorities. It could also be that with all the stresses of urban and industrial life, the security of the fully residential home seems more important than the relative independence of sheltered housing. This could explain the relative failure of such housing schemes to develop in Scotland.

Local government is always vulnerable to accepting a good idea as a panacea and there is a danger of this happening with sheltered housing. There has been a tremendous proliferation of this service, but comparatively little attention has been paid to the way in which it could or should work. Even after nearly 20 years, there is still no agreed salary scale for the wardens, no recognised form of training and very little has been written about the right way of handling the relationships between the housing authority, the warden and the tenants.

At best the warden will be clearly seen by the tenants as someone on whose help they can call, but who will not otherwise intrude into the privacy of their home nor attempt to manage their lives. At worst, the warden is established as a supervisor who will visit each house every day whether the tenant wants this or not and who will be vested with an authority to inspect the bungalow and to take decisions about the tenants' private affairs.

The role of the warden does not arise solely or mainly from the interaction between the warden and the tenants. Much more important will be the views of the housing committee and the involvement of the local community. If, for example, the housing committee are reluctant to accept the possibility that one of their tenants may suffer an unfortunate accident for which they might be blamed, then they are likely to insist on the tenant's independence being restricted to the point where accidents are unlikely to happen, or if they do, that they will be discovered almost immediately. The warden may equally be pushed into an authoritarian role simply because neighbours and relatives hold her accountable for the constant supervision and safety of every tenant.

Ideally, each tenant should feel confident that the warden will wish to respond immediately to any call for help, but that it is entirely a matter for the tenant to decide when this is necessary. There will be occasions when health risks will make a tenant so vulnerable that a daily visit by the warden will be essential, but this is a precaution which should be dictated by medical considerations and the general practitioner should convince his patient that the alternative to such an arrangement would be an admission to residential care or even hospital.

There is a similar danger that the warden will be expected to provide personally a home help and nursing service for tenants. Apart from imposing an intolerable burden on the warden, this would deprive the tenants of the normal service of a community nurse and a home help and is undesirable for that reason also.

There can be little doubt that sheltered housing has been a successful way of meeting the needs of elderly people who would be at significant risk living completely alone. There has, however, been little attempt to assess the scale on which this should be provided, although there is an unacknowledged yardstick of 50 units of housing per thousand people over 65 years of age. Even more disappointing is the way in which such housing is often used by the housing authorities, when tenants may well be above retirement age, but their need is for a small dwelling rather than a warden service. In other words, it is quite common for the service to be denied to many old people genuinely at risk, simply because allocation must follow a formula and practice which was developed in relation to general housing needs.

Many former welfare authorities confidently believed that the provision of sheltered housing would avoid the need for residential homes, and Peter Townsend in *The Last Refuge* added substantial authority to this view. Curiously enough, there has been little attempt to justify this assumption, and there is even a contradictory minority view that one of the advantages of sheltered housing is that it makes it more easy for the old person to accept communal living, particularly if the sheltered housing was linked to a residential home. Sheltered housing is a valuable service in its own right and may become more effective if it is not regarded as a direct substitute for residential care.

Because it is probably true that most older people would prefer to remain in an independent housing situation, this should be the first objective unless it is too dangerous or impracticable. Undue emphasis on this assumption can be an unspoken censure on those who are seeking shelter and support from all the demands of independence. A proper social policy requires an open-minded approach in which the wishes of the individual are accepted as important and relevant even if they do not conform to the department's general beliefs about security and independence.

In the long run it will be essential to strike the right balance between residential care and the facilities for older people to live more independently in small dwellings; it is easy to evade this difficult and complicated decision when all services are demonstrably inadequate. Planning of this sort must look initially at the needs and wishes of the elderly themselves but cannot ignore the costs. Much of the development of sheltered housing has followed an assumption that it was very much less expensive in terms of public expenditure than full residential care, although the only evidence normally adduced in support of this view was that it called for a lower contribution from rate funds.

The recent publication of a cost-benefit analysis commissioned by the Essex County Council has suggested that domiciliary care can be a feasible alternative to residential care, particularly where admission to such care arises from social breakdown rather than permanent infirmity. In attempting to estimate the relative costs of maintaining the person in the community or in a home the report concludes:

> Although the benefits of maintaining the elderly independent in the community were not valued, the rather marginal difference overall between the cost of residential care and the likely resource cost of intensive domiciliary care suggests that a greater 'return' would be obtained by the relative diversion of resources in the future away from the expansion of residential facilities into a selective domiciliary care programme for those in substantial need of support (Essex County Council 1972).

The voluntary contribution

Visitors from developing countries are often confused to find that families in Britain do not provide complete care for aged relatives. In the long run, they too may find that a substantial increase in the expectation of life and the mobility of labour demanded by an industrialised society make it impossible for families to sustain themselves. By contrast, the same overseas visitors are often incredulous of a purely voluntary contribution to social need and the contribution to the welfare of the aged from voluntary effor has fulfilled all the best traditions. Certainly the needs of the elderly are ever present and in such variety that every volunteer has something useful and valued to give.

The flexibility and adaptability of the voluntary organisation is well demonstrated by the WRVS who switched easily from war to peace and adapted an emergency feeding of the victims of bombing during the last war into the meals on wheels service. The meals service is also important because in addition to the nutritional value of the meal itself there is no doubt that the regular visit is also valued, and the preparation of house and person for the visit create a sense of purpose.

In the immediate post-war years many of the first small homes were provided by housing associations on a voluntary basis and the local authorities encouraged to make similar provision themselves. With an emphasis on maintaining the dignity and individuality of their residents the voluntary homes established valid principles which were sometimes ignored in local authority homes. Against these advantages it must be said that voluntary homes were often too reluctant to admit the non-conforming resident and they were seldom distinguished by offering good staff accommodation or an adequate status to their matrons.

The Abbeyfield Societies introduced a new concept by converting small houses to provide bed-sitting rooms for four or five tenants, with a resident housekeeper providing a midday meal. Inflation of house prices and the low remuneration paid for the very demanding job of housekeeper, have limited the development of the Abbeyfield movement, and local authorities in general have shown scant interest. The Abbeyfield Society was established in 1955 by Major Richard Carr-Gomm and a number of local societies have been formed in subsequent years. Abbeyfield Houses normally provide a small number of bed-sitting rooms where tenants live independently but can rely upon a resident housekeeper for midday meals and general support.

At national level, we are fortunate in having two highly effective voluntary bodies, Age Concern and the National Corporation for the Care of Old People which in their very different ways are making important additions to our understanding of old age. Age Concern with its trendy new name and enthusiastic executive is clearly determined to throw off the avuncular role associated with its older title of the National Old People's Welfare Council; the current militancy in favour of higher pensions is a recognition, long overdue, that a little more money in the pocket may be more welcome than advice on running a club.

The National Corporation has followed its thoughtful secretary along a very different road. Over the years they have sponsored a number of direct projects including special housing and a home-finding service. This is a valuable organisation which clearly sees its role in research and the exploration of new ideas.

At the grass roots level, old people's welfare committees have done much to encourage recreational activities, especially with clubs and holidays. It is perhaps unfortunate that they have too often remained unnecessarily separate from the Old Age Pensioners Associations, almost as though they were too genteel to become involved in the politics of protesting about poverty.

What then does the director of social services expect of voluntary organisations and volunteers in the altered situation following the reorganisation of the social services?

In brief he needs more and not fewer organisations and very many more volunteers.

The enlarged departments will, like all other large concerns, be especially vulnerable to those changes which alter the basic factors on which they formed their own assumptions about need in old age. There must be independent and well-informed groups who can act as pressure groups when official policies become inappropriate or irrelevant; such groups will lack credibility unless they draw heavily and manifestly upon the elderly themselves. Local old people's welfare committees need a wider cross-section of the population and in this context the most encouraging news of recent years is that Jack Dash has retired from the London docks and is now active in this field, which is surely a natural occupation for the retired trade union leader?

Conclusions

More resources are clearly required for substantial expansion over the full range of services for the elderly, but this must not prevent a new emphasis on quality. High standards have been achieved but they are by no means universal and perhaps more guidance is necessary to raise poor standards—effective evaluation is needed—and the results must become available nationally. There must be variety and flexibility and this necessarily means opportunities for voluntary organisations and volunteers to play a full part. The greatest contribution will come from less patronising attitudes which will allow the elderly themselves a greater measure of real choice and full involvement in deciding their own futures; above all, a sensibility in the providers of service which will not undermine confidence nor injure a tender pride.

References

Brocking, C. F. & Lempert, S. M. (1966) *The Social Needs of the Over-Eighties*. Manchester University Press, Manchester.

Committee on Local Authority and Allied Personal Social Services (1968) *Report* (Chairman: F. Seebohm), Cmnd. 3703. HMSO, London.

County Medical Officer of Health for Devon (1971) *Report*. DCC.

Essex County Council (1972) *Care of the Elderly*. IMTA, London.

Social issues and the social services

Goldberg, E. M., Mortimer, A. & Williams, B. (1971) *Helping the Aged.* Allen and Unwin, London.

Harris, A. I. & Clausen, R. (1968) *Social Welfare of the Elderly,* Vol. 2. HMSO, London.

Meacher, M. (1970) 'The old; the future of community care', *in The Fifth Social Service,* ed. P. Townsend. Fabian Society, London.

Thompson, J. (1970) 'The growth of population to the end of the century', *Soc. Trends,* 1, 21.

Townsend, P. & Wedderburn, D. (1965) *The Aged in the Welfare State.* Bell, London.

Woolf, M. (1967) *The Housing Survey in England and Wales,* 1964. HMSO, London.

7 *Black people and the social services departments: problems and perspectives*

J. Wallace McCulloch and Robert Kornreich

There is a need to identify scientifically a social problem, and distinguish symptoms from causes, for otherwise one may not merely obscure the real problem, but even amplify it. This is particularly relevant with regard to what has come to be known as the immigration problem. We shall discuss black people, partly because there is scarcely any comparable research on the large number of white immigrants in Britain, and partly because black people's problems tend to arise from racial rather than ethnic differences, but largely because the term immigrant has come to include black natives as well as those born outside the United Kingdom.[1] In order to emphasise the relevance of correctly identifying the problem, we would point to the 1971 Immigration Act. This Act, to which we shall later return, incorrectly identifies social problems in Britain, and will have a direct bearing on the practice of many social workers (British Association of Social Workers 1971a, Hewitt 1971b). The issue under discussion here is how to identify the problems of black people, how they attempt to resolve them themselves, and whether, if their problems are taken to social workers, they are solved. Does social work, as presently constituted, deal with the problems of all citizens? One of the difficulties here is that the information on this issue is inadequate.

Scientific research and research pitfalls

In order to focus on the relevance of research on this issue it is first necessary to discuss the general relevance of scientific research in social work. Many social workers aspire to professional status. A generally accepted requirement for this is a scientifically-derived specific body of knowledge about practice. This is why the recent reorganisation of social work has implemented the Seebohm Committee's (Committee on Local Authority and Allied Personal Social Services 1968) recommendation that research should become an integral part of social work. One aspect of this would be research upon social workers themselves. Another generally accepted requirement of a professional is that he, unlike a trader, deals with clients as distinct from customers or consumers: the client is a sovereign as well as a voluntary consumer. This conception of the social-work client, with particular regard to self-determination, is an integral part of social casework theory. Whether this conception of the professional task in social (casework) practice is desirable, or even valid (Leonard 1965), is not here at issue, but it is an important aspect of social workers' occupational ideology. Thus, if only for this reason, another fundamental of professional social work is 'consumer research'. The Seebohm Committee's conception of the professional social worker was such that their enquiry into changes in organisation was undertaken without any consumer research.

A problem here is the type of consumer research to be carried out. Most research concerning the social welfare services and race relations simply concerns the issues of national aggregate use, expenditure on and contribution by black people. Such research is relatively irrelevant to the operation of social service departments. It is also inadequate for the social welfare services in general. This is not simply because it does not separately analyse high-density immigrant localities, but because such research ignores the social relationships and ideas making up such transactions. Because people act partly in terms of their 'definition of the situation', as well as the material situation, in order to explain the demand, supply and use of the social welfare services, we need to understand what the potential recipients think of them as well as the views of their potential suppliers.* This, as Pinker (1971) points out, is an essential aspect of social work research.

However, the crucial problem is the necessity for scientific research: the issue of objectivity, the relationship of knowledge and interest. Many factors influence the choice of a research problem: the values and interests of sponsor and researcher, the pressures and interests of government, practitioners and academics. These factors vary in different subjects. Practitioners in the area of social problems, compared with medicine, often note that knowledge is so inadequate that little professional guidance occurs. Consequently more knowledge is a necessary, although not sufficient, means for policy change and problem resolution. The need is for scientific, critical research, for there is the possibility that the identification of a research problem itself, and the use made of the findings, can become part of the scapegoating process whereby the phenomenon being researched becomes spuriously defined as *the* social problem. This is not a question of the researcher's values intruding, and his 'cooking' the facts, for the facts are always socially constructed. It is, as Horton (1966), Allen (1969) and Moore (1971) point out, more a case of research methods being at fault, with an uncritical formulation of research problems and research method.

Possibly the greatest source of this problem is a type of applied or policy-oriented research. This involves a piecemeal social engineering outlook, a non-historical concern with immediate 'practical' application, and hence ad hoc research. The underlying assumptions of such research are that deviants, in this case black immigrants, can be incorporated into British society without radical change to the consensual status quo, and that agencies of the state are not only willing but able to take the necessary action to do this. Such research is usually carried out in non-scientific ways with, for example, uncritical research into officially defined problems, little concern with theory, and reliance upon conventional wisdom. This results in a low concern for the relationship of race to other social issues and the non-critical use of concepts, which often leads to racism being condoned. It also results in

* *Editor's note:* The authors of this chapter are themselves engaged in a substantial study of the utilisation of the personal social services by immigrant groups and their perception of them. The study, sponsored by the Home Office, is likely to be published during 1974.

inadequate research designs. In order to discover whether black immigrants have specific characteristics, one must compare them with white immigrants, and black and white natives.

One must not reduce the research to that of consumers, to merely allowing the client to speak, for this omits not only those who are in need but do not use social services, but also those people who are applicants but do not become clients. Another inadequacy of such research concerns data-gathering techniques: the uncritical use of official records or the sole use of attitude surveys, when it is known that, because there is often a discrepancy between words and deeds, the extent of prejudice tells us little about discrimination. This applied perspective tends to dominate Rose's study (Rose, Deakin, Abrams, Jackson, Peston, Vanags, Cohen, Gaitskell & Ward 1969) which, though not sponsored or published by a government agency, starts by contrasting black immigrants with a supposedly culturally homogenous and equal native citizenry or community. The study does conclude by correctly locating the black population in a Britain of great class and regional inequalities (Westergaard 1972). However, the authors remain uncritical of the basic role of policy-makers and ignore the history of British imperialism which Cheetham (1972) regards as highly relevant in explaining current race relations.

We would not wish professional social work research on this issue to pursue the inadequacies which many race-researchers have noted about their own work (Oretton 1971). This concerns not only the uncritical location of the research problem, but also the assumption of a rationalistic and consensual model of policy-construction: the belief that conflict is solely due to lack of knowledge about consumer demand and that better communication will necessarily lead to policy change and problem resolution. As all social workers know, it is the use made of insight that matters.

Figures and trends

Leaving aside the issue of research, it is important to know how many people may be involved in the issue under discussion in order to be aware of maximum eligibility and any changing trends in that population. This population includes native-born black people as well as immigrants, because, as we shall show, the real issue for social services departments is not one of geography but one of culture, colour and class. Problems may arise from ethnic differences, even in native-born blacks, or from the factor of colour, even when black people are ethnically British. Some black people who are immigrants will not be alien to British culture, but problems may arise for them also because of their colour. As a result of these considerations, and because not all the black population are potential users of the social service departments, the figures we are presenting are an overestimation.

International migration is not a new phenomenon to the British. Since the middle of the nineteenth century, there has been more emigration from than immigration to Britain. Rose *et al.* (1969) show that the majority of black immigrants came between 1956 and 1966, there being different patterns of entry for different ethnic groups. This immigration tended to follow the level of labour demand until 1961 when the fear of immigration restriction led to a 'beat-the-ban' rush and a 'bulge'. The 1962 Commonwealth Immigrants Act restricted the number of black people entering and by means of a work-voucher system, restricted the number of semi-skilled and unskilled immigrants, the issue of unskilled vouchers ending in 1964. The majority of black immigrants now entering are the wives and children of husbands already present and the re-uniting of families has become more difficult with each Act, the 1971 Immigration Act giving black Commonwealth citizens, like aliens, no right of entry.

The number of black people in Britain is difficult to discover, for the Census does not identify black people directly, but rather does this by inference from birthplace, making it difficult to estimate the number of black natives in England and white immigrants born in Asia. According to Rose *et al.* (1969), the number of black immigrants in England and Wales in 1966 was 710,900. In addition to this figure there were approximately 213,300 native-born black people, making a total black population in England and Wales in 1966 of 924,200. Rose estimates that this was 1,113,000 in 1968, will be 1,522,000 in 1976 and about 2,000,000 in 1986, some 4% of the population of England and Wales. However, more important than this national aggregate is the distribution of the black population, for some departments will have to care for many more black people than others. These variations cannot be accurately presented in terms of the total black population, but in 1966 for black immigrants alone the proportions range from 0.4% in Liverpool to 7.4% in Brent (Institute of Race Relations 1970), and Rose *et al.* (1969) estimate that there were only about 13 local authorities with a proportion of black immigrants greater than 5%.

Not all of these black people are potential social services department users, either because they have no need, or because they have need but seek aid from other sources. It is not the role of a social service department to force help on people who feel that they have no need of it, but it is well within their remit to ensure that people who seemingly don't want help (because they don't ask for it) do know what help is available should they, at some stage, decide that they require it.

The Seebohm report stated that part of the role of the social services departments is to support other appropriate and satisfactory sources of aid. This is particularly relevant to the issue under discussion because of the cultural factors involved or to combat real or perceived racial discrimination.

Black people's problems

Although we are specifically concerned with the black clients of the social services department, we must see the issue in a wider context, which would at best be that of the history of imperialism. This is partly because the social welfare services are an integral part of British society. A better reason is that this is the only really practical way to judge the causes of the problem, the desirability, type, degree and source of change required and the resources available. One could deal with those things about which something could easily and immediately be done, but this would not be scientific or efficient in the long run. We shall not deal with the wider context of general problems of British society in detail, but compare and contrast black people with whites in order to ascertain the extent to which they have specific problems.

While the research we present refutes racist arguments about the effects of black immigration, it should not be thought that even if we found these arguments factually correct we would accept immigration control, ghettoes and repatriation.

Leaving aside the issue of whether records should be kept on black people's application for and use of services, it is the case that many central and local government departments do so. However, these official records are often invalid and unreliable for research purposes (Butterworth 1969) and most of the adequate research is specific research projects. Daniels (1968) and Rose *et al.* (1969) reveal discrimination as well as prejudice which is both deep-rooted and widespread. Rose *et al.* (1969) show that there are important differences in culture, ability and knowledge between Indians, Pakistanis (including those who are now Bangladeshis) and West Indians, and between localities and local authorities, but these studies show a general discrimination against black people in the crucial areas of employment, housing and education. They show that this is usually racial discrimination as it occurs even to black natives who have the same culture, abilities and knowledge as white natives. Furthermore, Daniels (1968) shows that black people did not exaggerate this discrimination, on the contrary, they underestimated it, for they tended to avoid discriminatory situations.[2]

It is necessary to locate the present position of black people in Britain—or at least the position in 1969—and see what changes have occurred since the middle 1950s. Following Butterworth's discussion (1969) of the three stages of Asian settlement in Bradford, we should examine the labour demand and changing aspects of culture and power. The first stage is the settlement of largely unattached men. Problems here concern the type and conditions of employment, housing (with large numbers in multi-occupation) and physical health. The second stage is the entry of dependants. The previous problems remain, although they change in form, and education and welfare are added. The issue now is one of mutual cultural penetration and problems of adjustment. To a large extent these are now dealt with by the extended family. The third, and present, stage concerns the emergence of large numbers of adolescent black natives (second generation immigrants), who have had all their formal education in Britain. The problems now tend to be those of a minority-group status, of lack of power, of race and class rather than cultural differences. Butterworth (1969) believes that it is at this stage that contacts with social work agencies are more likely to occur.

With regard to employment, Rose *et al.* (1969) show that there is no evidence that black immigrants cause unemployment: areas of high unemployment tend to be areas with small black immigrant populations and vice versa. A higher proportion of black immigrants than the native population is employed, because of their ages but in a recession they are among the first and the longest unemployed. Because the majority of unemployed black immigrants do not register at unemployment exchanges, they are not eligible for benefit. Thus black immigrants contribute more to national insurance than they benefit from it (Jones & Smith 1970).

Black Commonwealth immigrants were actively recruited in the 1950s as a source of semi- and unskilled labour in a period of labour shortage in Britain and Europe. Rose *et al.* (1969) show that black people still tend to constitute a sub-proletariat in industries which white natives are leaving and we would agree with Allen (1970) that their problems can best, although not solely, be explained as deriving from this role. They tend to be in unskilled and semi-skilled jobs even when they have the qualifications for other positions. Several researchers have maintained that racial discrimination is practised by the Youth Employment Service as well as by employers. Officers often regard black 'second generation' immigrants as having 'unreliable aspirations' although they have comparable ability with white native youth (Deakin *et al.* 1970; Allen 1969). One writer (Special Correspondent 1972a, 1972b) has argued that racial discrimination is also practised by the Department of Employment, as a principle, rather than by individuals, as it operates a 'green wafer' system to identify unemployed black but not white immigrant workers.

Further problems in this area will arise for black immigrants from the Immigration Act, 1971. Like previous Immigration Acts, this one is more concerned with regulating labour skill rather than numbers. However, the disciplinary legislation of the present Act is an innovation for Commonwealth citizens (*Race Today* 1971; Hewitt 1971). The Act extends the labour conditions of the Aliens Act, 1919, to black British citizens ('non-patrials'), for such workers can only come for specific jobs for specific employers and have to have their work-permits renewed yearly by the Department of Employment on their employers' notification of 'good conduct'. Termination of the permit results in deportation of the worker, and the whole family. This clearly reduces the black workers' power to fight for better pay and conditions and brings the status of such Commonwealth citizens to that of Continental contract labour. Furthermore, the Immigration Act complements the Industrial Relations Act, 1971. The Industrial Relations Act is designed to curb rank-and-file union militancy and unofficial industrial action (Simpson 1971). The two Acts complement one another in that they can create, however unintentionally, a body of indentured, docile, dispensable and geographically mobile black 'scab' labour.

One writer (Special Correspondent 1972a) has suggested that the 'green wafer' system would be part of this operation and Macdonald (*Race Today* 1971) maintains that the Department of Health and Social Security can also play an important role here due to the power of Supplementary Benefits Commission to pay the fare home of families who have become a burden on the state. That is, officials can persuade black immigrants to take low paid employment or scab labour by threatening either the withholding of social security payment or repatriation. The Immigration Act therefore raises great problems for both white and black workers as it divides them by fostering racism.

In the area of housing, government reports and other research as well as that of Rose *et al.* (1969) show that black immigrants have not caused shortages and decay; that they are not to blame for the lack of homes suffered by both black and white workers. In fact, much of the housing problem, as well as the pattern of black immigrant settlement, can be explained in terms of the changing native class structure of housing; as the rich move away from the decaying city centres to the outskirts, the poor move into the centres, black people suffering in particular. This is an area of subtle as well as blatant discrimination, by central and local government as well as by private landlords.

It should not be thought that the relatively good housing conditions for black immigrants and race relations in some areas are simply due to the efforts of the local authorities. Rather, they may be due, as in Bradford, to the relatively adequate supply of housing (Rose *et al.* 1969). The 1971 Immigration Act will worsen the situation, for since black immigrants will have to renew work permits every twelve months, it will make it even more difficult to get facilities for credit and comprehensive insurance, and mortgages.

In education, as in other fields, Rose *et al.* (1969) show that black immigrants have not caused educational deficiencies. The problems are due to inequalities already existing in the society and the changing structure of cities. These problems exist for all working-class children, but are particularly severe for black children. This is not simply because of immigrants' cultural and language differences. It is because in addition to the problems of the white native working-class child resulting from the parents' employment and housing situation there is often racial discrimination, expressed in both official policy, for example, in the collection and presentation of statistics (Bentley 1972), and teachers' discretion. False stereotypes are established and, through prejudice and discrimination, become a self-fulfilling prophecy. This is not due to a conspiracy on the part of teachers, but rather to middle-class white people's common-sense ethnocentric evaluation of black people or another culture as inferior (Hill 1971). The lack of 'culture-fair' tests and racialism may explain the reason for the disproportionate number of West Indian children in schools for the educationally subnormal (Deakin 1970).

The forced dispersal policy, often involving bussing, was officially established in 1965 to prevent any school having more than one-third of 'children of Commonwealth immigrant parents' and many reasons were given for its introduction. In fact, black children tend to be dispersed on the basis of race and not language ability; low ability seems to be viewed as necessarily associated with being an immigrant child. The reason given for the policy of separate language centres is that they can give more attention to children with special needs, following a policy of 'separate but equal' aid, but there is evidence that both teachers and pupils often have inadequate resources in the immigrant reception centres, educational centres and remedial classes.

In the area of crime, Rose *et al.* (1969) show that with the exception of illegal drug trafficking, the black population has a lower crime rate than the white, even though black people tend to live in the areas of high crime rates. While this may show a lack of racial discrimination among the judiciary, it does not show this for the police, for the evidence concerns prosecutions and not apprehensions or arrests. Research on the police shows not only the existence of racial stereotypes and prejudice, but also discrimination largely due to police discretion (Lambert 1970). It may also be a normal reaction of those enforcing law and order against those who merely rebel in an unjust society (Davis 1971).

The chairman of the Police Federation has said (*Race Today* 1971) that the 1971 Immigration Act is likely to increase tensions between the police and black people. Although registration of 'non-patrials' is now being carried out by employment exchanges rather than the police, the latter have to enforce the law and the impossibility of immediately telling a non-patrial black from a patrial one is likely to lead to harassment by the police. The Police Federation was not initially consulted about the Act. Another problem arising from the Act is that it provides for a recently arrived black immigrant offender of seventeen to be deported, cancelling the intentions of the 1969 Children and Young Persons Act.

There is a widespread belief that black immigrants introduce epidemics and are a burden on the medical and social welfare services. This is false, as they are concentrated in areas where such services were already not up to strength. For example, Butterworth (1967) maintains that in the Bradford area West Indians make use of the social services in much the same way as native whites, while Asians use them less. On balance their contribution is higher than their cost due to their ages and the high proportion employed, especially in such services (Jones & Smith 1970). Most writers (Rose *et al.* 1969; Dodge 1971) distinguish between imported diseases peculiar to the immigrants' part of the world and diseases acquired from area of settlement. The former diseases are screened at entry and in 1968 only 0.11% of black immigrants were refused entry, this proportion being lower than that for aliens. Furthermore, these diseases present little problem and are only temporary. However, Hood, Oppe, Pless & Apté (1970) show that West Indian infants are significantly at risk with regard to physical health due not only to their parents' adverse environmental conditions but also due to cultural differences regarding health practices. There was little evidence of physical neglect and a higher proportion of such mothers regularly attended the infant welfare services than did the comparison group. However, some research by Butterworth in Bradford shows that the pattern of health is assuming social class rather than ethnic characteristics (in Rose *et al.* 1969). Dodge (1971) suggests that more important than either of these two types of health problem is mental illness, and suggests that this is due less to the stress of migration and adaptation than to racial prejudice and discrimination. However, research does not really enable one to come to any general conclusion here, largely because of the unreliability of diagnosis and the lack of 'culture-fair' criteria (Bloom 1969). The Immigration Act, 1971, will create problems in this area for black immigrants and social workers, as it provides for the 'removal' from the United Kingdom of non-patrials receiving in-patient treatment for mental illness (BASW 1971a).

With regard to the hospital services, Rose *et al.* (1969) shows that in general black immigrants make less use of them than natives do. The exception to this is the greater use of maternity beds, particularly in certain areas. This is due to a number of factors: the concentration of black immigrants in certain areas, the temporary high birth rate due to the wives' ages, the 'bulge' as wives join their husbands, and the poor amenities making home confinements unsuitable. There are problems, as Cheetham (1972) shows, of unattached men, all-male households, the difficulties of the entry of fiancées, illegitimacy, spouse conflict, deserted children and parent/child conflict. This last may be due to the child's separation from the parents by migration or by conflicting cultural demands, which is felt particularly by native-born adolescents (Rose *et al.* 1969). Actually there is little research on the type of problems of black people in social work, particularly in casework, and whether the problems are specific to them. However, discussion with colleagues and some published work indicate two prominent problems which concern children of mixed race and the position of women, in particular Asians. There is even less research on the conflicts the social worker may face if contrasting solutions to these problems are suggested by client, family and native culture (Hutchinson 1969).

The causes of black people's problems are often difficult to unravel. It is not clear why there is such a large number of 'non-white' children in local authority care (Rose *et al.* 1969). Studies show that a very large proportion of children in care are of mixed race, generally black fathers and white mothers, and are significantly different from both wholly white and black children in that they are younger, stay longer and are referred for illegitimacy (Antrobus 1964; Davies 1969; Foren & Batta 1970). The reason may be white racism on the part of the grandparents. Some Children's Committees, showing concern about the apparent difficulty of finding good foster homes and adoptive parents and what they regard as a burden on the tax-payer, are operating repatriation schemes. Child Care Officers are told that facilities exist to send non-white children 'home', if this is in their best interest, to be cared for by relatives or foster parents under the Children and Young Persons Act, 1963, with investigation by the British branch of the International Social Service. While Holman (1968) and Raynor (1970) deny that there is great difficulty in fostering and adopting such children, and Antrobus (1970) and Jay & Halpin (1970) differ over whether for many of these children staying in Britain is in their best interests, all agree with the Director of the British Section of the International Social Service (Rowse 1970) that careful investigation needs to be made into the provision of care for such children in the other country. It is also unclear whether the large number of West Indian children in care is due to cultural preference or material deprivation on the part of the parents (Rose *et al.* 1969). The disproportionately large number of West Indian children in the charge of child-minders who give an inadequate environment seems to be due to the large number of West Indian mothers working rather than preference (Jackson 1971).

There is a danger that social workers will view black people's problems in the same way as many diagnose poverty, as due to personal inadequacy, and blame the victim rather than seeing the problems as features of social inequality and oppression. There is also a danger, as Cheetham (1972) points out, that social workers will see the problems they deal with as the fundamental problems and social work as the fundamental solution. Most research shows the black population caught in a vicious circle of badly paid jobs, bad housing and poor education, although there are different views over the primary cause and solution here. Their problems derive not only from cultural differences but from a British ethnocentrism which diagnoses cultural differences as inferiority ('cultural deprivation'), and racialism.[3] The heading of this section is deliberate: the immigration problem or race problem is the problem of white racism (Rose *et al.* 1969).

We have noted that black people's problems may arise from common-sense racial discrimination by individuals or as a principle, as institutionalised racism, in the social welfare services. This may arise for social service departments from the 1971 Immigration Act, for if State hostels are established for black immigrant workers, as on the Continent, the social services department, may have to operate them. It is therefore clear that there is cause for concern by social workers, for they may find themselves in day-to-day practice acting as social control agents for white racism as expressed through the State (Hewitt 1971b).

We conclude this section by examining some of the specific government provisions with regard to this issue. These are contradictory. For example, while most educationists note the ill-effects of streaming, the similar procedure of language centres is operated for black children; while most official spokesmen speak against the separate provision of welfare (Rose *et al.* 1969) this is being established under the 1971 Immigration Act. The situation at the moment is that the Home Office is responsible for both immigration and race relations, for the co-ordination of government grants under the Local Government Act, 1966 and the Urban Programme, and for the activities of the statutory Race Relations Board and Community Relations Commission. The United Kingdom Immigrants Advisory Service, a voluntary body with members of the CRC on its executive, is totally grant-aided by the Home Office. A Commons Select Committee on Race Relations and Immigration was appointed in 1968 to review government policy, the Race Relations Act and the work of the Race Relations Board and CRC, and has investigated the problems of black school-leavers and housing. But what is government social welfare policy on this issue?

As Rose *et al.* (1969) show, before 1966 a policy could not be said to exist and local authorities were not given specific government guidance and funds. The 1965 White paper terminated this stage as it was the first systematic government recognition of the situation. However, it saw black people's problems as simply different in degree, not also in kind, to the white native population and therefore capable of being remedied in the same way, for example, by building more houses and by the same type of welfare services. Furthermore, while it refuted the claim that black immigrants had caused problems, by other statements, immigration control and the lack of funds to local authorities, it pandered to the belief that they amplified them. While under Section 11 of the 1966 Local Government Act there was a 50% government rate support for local authorities where special provision was made for immigrants, application was left to the authorities' initiative and there was still no overall guidance or overall policy. However, in 1968, there was a clear change in this situation, related to changes in general social welfare policy (such as the Plowden policy of compensation (Central Advisory Council for Education 1967) or 'positive discrimination' in educational priority areas and the housing priority areas) which culminated in the Urban Programme. Also the Community Relations Commission was established under the 1968 Race Relations Act and its role, through local Community Relations Councils, partly financed by local authorities, was to be the focal point for the encouragement and aid of harmonious community relations. This largely concerns liaison with the town hall and the provision of training courses and conferences rather than social work, or casework (Hill & Issacharoff 1971). Some of these conferences on social work and cultural differences also compound many of the errors noted earlier regarding the immigrant problem. In 1971 the Commission's role was extended to cover immigration and race relations policy (although it was not consulted over the 1971 Immigration Act which it opposes) and a greater administration of the Urban Programme. This phased programme, established in 1968 to last at least six years, was created through the 1969 Local Government Grant (Social Need) Act and it involves the Home Office, DES and DHSS. It is concerned with urban renewal (Holman 1971). Similar to the 1966 Local Government Act, the government gives a 75% grant to applicant local authorities in areas of concentrated social deprivation, one of the criteria of need being the mere existence of large numbers of immigrants. The Programme's provisions include nursery education, children's homes, playgroups and community development projects as well as language courses for black immigrants and multi-racial playgroups.

It is clear that government policy is to view black people as a problem, and social welfare policy regarding black people is constructed in terms of general policy. Similarly we must view citizenship in the general context of changing British society. There is now a situation of high unemployment with taxes and rising prices outstripping pay rises, and of underdevelopment of certain regions, rising rents, little educational reform and the disintegration of the welfare state; a situation caused by the Industrial Relations Act and the Immigration Act, and the increasing demand from some quarters for law and order rather than civil rights (Hewitt 1971). This may lead to a situation where white aliens from the Continent have freer access to Britain than black Commonwealth citizens now that Britain is in the E.E.C., where there is conflict between Government and independent researchers on race relations policy, and more Government-sponsored research. It is in this context that we must try to understand black people's problems and the organised development of racism. It is difficult to diagnose as irrational, as do Rose *et al.* (1969), the misplaced white native working-class racial prejudice and discrimination.

Social work with black people

We are not suggesting that the problems which black clients—immigrant or native, voluntary or non-voluntary—bring to social workers are, objectively or subjectively, their most pressing problems. Nor is it to be inferred from this discussion that social work, by any method—or, indeed, social welfare in general—offers the most effective solution for the black population, client or otherwise. Such a position would be strange given the great concern regarding the effectiveness of the psycho-therapeutic orientation of social casework with white native clients.

It would be appropriate to discuss the British research on this issue, but there is scarcely any. The research on the extent of West Indian families' use of the health services (Hood *et al.* 1970) and that on the Community Relations Councils is relatively inappropriate. The research on inter-racial adoption (Raynor 1970) is also largely on the availability and characteristics of adoptive parents. There is nothing for the social worker in Britain like Miller (1969) or Turner (1968). It is only if we include the police as a welfare or service organisation that we can say that any sophisticated British research exists (Lambert 1970).

However, Kent, a caseworker, has established a framework from the sparse, conceptually confused and largely clinical literature on social casework with black people in Britain which, although not definitive, is of great aid (Kent 1965; 1968a; 1968b; 1969). The following discussion draws heavily, although not uncritically, on her work. Kent, as do the present authors, sees the problem in the context of British society and general issues within casework. She starts by emphasising the importance of culture in human conduct; human characteristics are not inborn but largely acquired. The materialist concept of instinct, or, in its genetic version, race, cannot adequately explain human conduct (Jehu 1968; Rose *et al.*

1969). Culture, consisting of a structure of rules, not only concerns what one should do but also what one should not do, that is, culture is social control. The process of learning cultural roles, about one's relation to others, is socialisation. Social control does not consist solely of surface culture or external controls, which are possibly coercive, but also of inner controls or rules which the person has internalised. This aspect of culture is part of one's basic personality, deriving primarily from parental influences in childhood. The common-sense ways of life of a group become part of a person's ego-identity/super-ego and social reality. While intercultural tension and clash is common, and while some people are more cosmopolitan than others and less prone to stereotyping, if the internalised culture is radically challenged by other cultures, then threats to personal identity occur.

No society is culturally homogeneous. Every nation and state contains diverse patterns of socialisation, social control, and hence sub-cultures—even counter-cultures. In fact, urban industrial societies are more diverse than rural pre-industrial societies. But not only are societies culturally heterogeneous, they are also unequal. They are stratified, and one sub-culture will be hegemonous and pervade the mental and material life of the whole society so as to be the primary reference group. Hence one form of social control will tend to dominate the whole society (Miliband 1969).

Human deviance or social problems is not a disease inherent in individuals, but may be culturally specific or relative and a manifestation of culture clash. Indeed, the stigmatising reaction may result from a non-existent or spurious clash of cultures and social control. It may amplify or even create the deviance or social problem by translating such a spuriously labelled culture clash into reality by means of a self-fulfilling prophecy. This is Young's explanation (1971) for the development of the drug problem, and Butcher (1970) suggests that a similar process sometimes occurs in the transactions between social workers and their clients. Since deviance may be due to conflicting cultures as well as to inadequate common socialisation, it cannot simply be cured or solved by informing the deviant of the moral code and commonly-held rational conduct, for there is disagreement over what this is. Social education may further be inadequate in that deviance or culture clash may be so fundamental as to involve internalised social control and hence personal identity. It is within this context that

Kent locates the issue of British social casework with the black population, implicitly utilising aspects of the stranger/ethnic, colour/race and class perspectives in race relations theory.[4]

Kent maintains that in contemporary Britain, the dominant sub-culture is that of the English upper-middle class. The normality, the thought and conduct that permeate British society are primarily those of individualism: independence and achievement through geographical and/or social mobility are admired. There is also emotional reserve.

Social control, as an aspect of culture, is a natural aspect of human conduct; all roles and organisations have a social control aspect dealing with deviance. However, in urban industrial societies, there have developed specialised social control organisations and agents, often employed by the state. These range from those primarily involving coercive repression, like the military, through the penal system and police to those primarily using manipulative persuasion like education and social work (Miliband 1969; Leonard 1965). While the official theory and formal organisation of social work employs non-directive or enabling methods, expressive rather than instrumental techniques, and cosmopolitan concepts of ethical neutrality, social work is none the less concerned with social control. The issue is social control and legitimation, and Kent maintains that the more professional the social worker the more he is acting as a social control agent, not simply for British culture but for the middle class. In this sense social work may be viewed as a functional alternative to coercive forms of control, casework with its psychological approach flourishing in a period of economic boom. Kent maintains that this form of social control occurs, whatever the workers' intentions, for two basic reasons. First, social casework was established as a specialised legitimation agency. If the occupational culture clashed to an important degree with the dominant sub-culture, social workers would be unable to obtain the moral and physical resources which would enable them to work. Secondly, because social workers are either recruited from the British middle class or socialised into it before and during occupational training, they will identify with its interests. Hence, Kent maintains, caring for failures or solving deviance is an attempted restoration of clients to a state of at least minimal disapproval of dominant values and hence a re-inforcement of them. Social workers are thus seen as concerned with assimilation or possibly integration but not with pluralism, which would maintain deviant identities. It follows that there will be tensions or even contradictions of interest, perhaps overt conflict, between social workers and many of their clients.[5]

British culture is not universally applicable to other societies nor an integral aspect of it; but it has created Anglo-American social casework. Kent makes this clearer by giving a detailed analysis of casework principles. Anglo-American casework is primarily based on a liberal-democratic, abstract humanistic philosophy. This emphasises individualism in aiding clients to recognise every person's intrinsic worth and non-fatalism in helping them make and implement their own choices. Kent maintains that the correct application of these basic concepts are distasteful to some immigrants because of their contrasting culture, and illustrates this by showing the seven needs that a basic casework text, Biestek's *The Casework Relationship* (1961), says all clients bring to the casework situation. These would be inappropriate in kin-centred societies in which the individual is subordinated to the group or where fulfilment is in terms of the group where decision-making is in terms of age; where great emotion is normal or where emotion is not normally shown. Many of these examples are actually characteristic of Mediterranean and Asian cultures.

For Anglo-American educated social workers, then, there are several problems of diagnosis. For example, some conduct may be an effect of immigration as such: the trauma of disorientation. However, the diagnostic problems which Kent discusses are those due to cultural differences regarding normality and, therefore, deviance. For example, the social worker may diagnose as a problem conduct which the immigrant regards as normal, while the immigrant may regard British culture, and social work, as the problem. The social worker may interpret some immigrants' different conception of immorality or a normal cultural prohibition of emotion, particularly aggression, as a resistance and a manifestation of extreme personal guilt. Alternatively, the normal volatility of some immigrants, by anger or sorrow, may be diagnosed as an acute personality disorder. In such cases, treatment will create tensions and not meet the needs of the client. Furthermore, the black client may expect racial prejudice and discrimination and this would lead to treatment problems. The racist element in British culture may result in the caseworker having a culturally imposed low estimate of a black person's ability to overcome his problems. Since success is partly a self-fulfilling prophecy, such a poor prognosis, such 'prior culpability' (Davis 1967), is likely to become accurate due to the lower expected standards of achievement and ability.

As a result, social work with black people, natives and immigrants, is faced with a dilemma for both parties. This is not primarily the dilemma for workers which Hutchinson (1969) maintains often occurs with native-born adolescent girls of Asian families, whereby a culture clash between the client and her family may leave her isolated from them as well as the white native British. Rather, it concerns the social worker's role of control for British culture, an issue seemingly ignored by Cheetham (1972). Even if an individual caseworker, or the profession as a whole, knew of the background of culturally alien black immigrants, the problem would arise as to how far social workers can themselves tolerate their clients' different expectations and conduct in practice, since these may negate the workers' personal internalised values. There is also the possibility of racial prejudice and discrimination regarding black natives. Furthermore, even if workers knew about and wanted to maintain black client's identity and were not racists, and managed to establish a rapport, empathy, transference and counter-transference, this would be difficult to sustain due to the influence of the wider society—not the least of these difficulties being the employer. Kent therefore regards pluralism as impossible, integration as improbable and recommends a policy of minimal assimilation or acculturation as a solution for social workers to these problems: the social worker's role is to contain 'deviance' within tolerable limits by enabling his clients to meet minimal British middle-class prescriptions. She maintains that this policy, in itself, implies a dilution, if not negation, of basic casework values since, in this respect, the social worker is giving priority to British middle-class needs. Consequently, it would appear that ethnocentricity and a strategy of assimilation, racism at worst and integration at best, but not a pluralist policy of client autonomy, is institutionalised in social casework with black people, immigrants and natives, and their needs cannot be met and they cannot be treated as citizens.

Kent's analysis is useful because it is not bogged down by unnecessary detail, treats general issues in social casework, and locates casework historically in Britain. The earliest paper is in an issue of a journal on general problems in social work (*Social Work*, London 1965) and asks who social work really serves. This as Baski (1971) notes, is very relevant in the current reorganisation of the personal social services and their integration into the state. Kent does not view the social work as a closed and stable system of practitioner and client, and hence she adequately identifies the problem and the solution and does not reduce the issue of power to one of administration.

What is the answer?

Most studies on social work with black people show that this issue is closely related, but not in any simple manner, to the problems and solutions for social work clients in general. For example, Hutchinson (1969) starts his discussion of this issue by noting the relevance of client power and the political role of the social worker.

An answer can best be considered by discussing Kent's (1965; 1969) suggested solution in greater depth. She argues that there is conflict, or at least tension, between black immigrants and white social caseworkers and suggests reducing this by an admix of cultures in favour of white, upper-middle-class British culture. However, we shall argue that she does not pinpoint the exact nature of the dilemma of self-determination and that her suggestion for overcoming it is impractical for some types of client.

In contrast to Kent, few social casework writers view client self-determination as an absolute principle. In fact the work of Mayer & Timms (1970) and Whittington (1971) suggests that the dilemma and process which Kent sees as occurring with black immigrant clients occurs with clients in general, though in particular with the white native working-class client (*Social Work* 1965). This is a process whereby the social worker distinguishes between the client's wants and needs and tends to pursue client self-determination in terms of his own conceptions. Hence the dilemma is unlikely to arise very often.

Where it does occur, Kent's solution for overcoming the dilemma is equally simplistic. For example, if a voluntary client and a social worker were faced with such a dilemma, a control process would occur similar to that which Kent argues occurs with regard to social workers themselves. Either the applicant would not become a client, or else the social-work relationship would end prematurely (Mayer & Rosenblatt 1964). Such a process, of course, need not be carried out by the applicant or client. Compliance, and the avoidance of the dilemma, can be achieved by the screening of applicants by social work gatekeepers (in which case a high success rate will be achieved) or by the social worker referring the client elsewhere at the intake interview or during treatment. The dilemma is also avoided with an involuntary culturally alien client for the person is rarely referred as a casework client but rather treated by means of relatively coercive measures where self-determination is not attempted. As Kent almost explicitly argues, the only type of client with whom an effective therapeutic alliance can be forged is one who is already highly integrated into British, white middle-class culture. In this situation either the conflict does not occur because the black immigrant wants to learn the worker's culture, or if it does, it is not at the level of internalised values. Here Kent points out that the worker plays an informational role, only needing to be aware of cultural differences and, knowing where the client is, of the variations of the role to which the client aspires in order to vary treatment goals: the worker merely has to educate such black clients about the minimal tolerable standards of role performance. However, this could only be a small number of black people, for such people are not only less likely to become clients but even if they do they will not have culturally specific problems.

It would therefore appear that the effective area of principled social casework with culturally alien black people—or indeed with any deviant—is necessarily a restricted one. Most of the writers on this issue, particularly Kent, are concerned with non-material differences, rather than material inequalities. However, research shows that prejudice exists against black people who are culturally British. Black people are treated as scapegoats for inequalities within the native white society, though there is not in reality much hostility to cultural differences (Baski 1971). A social work solution, therefore, which does not involve changing the society that fosters racism and is intolerant of cultural differences can be of little help to black people and social workers. Baski (1971) argues that there is a role for effective and efficient social work with black people, but that this can only be in terms of general social policy, not simply casework. The question is often asked whether one should instruct black people to use the existing white native welfare services or whether they should be provided with separate ones (Rose *et al.* 1969). These are inadequate alternatives. We suggest that there is a case for discrimination regarding black people, but that this should be of a compensatory nature, not exclusively oriented towards black people and part of a general social welfare policy. This type of social policy is in line with the earlier ideas of social work (Lees 1971).

This type of policy which Cheetham (1972) seems to advocate, can be made clearer by analysing some policy recommendations regarding social work with black people in terms of the two-part question posed by Gilbert (1972): who gets what in social policy? The *who* aspect concerns eligibility in a more complex manner than the orthodox universality–selectivity dichotomy. Gilbert points out that selectivity is not necessarily means-tested, but that it can be pursued by attributed need or by technically assessed diagnosis. The *what* aspect concerns the source of aid and whether it is material or non-material. From 1968, with the Urban Programme, there was some attempt to increase certain types of aid as part of national general social policy. The recommendations of Rose *et al.* (1969) for the development of the programme include compensation and specific provision for black people in order to create equality as part of general compensation for all people living in areas of social deprivation, the establishment of a local authority advisory service as well as continuing support to the Citizens' Advice Bureau, and special in-service training for social workers in contact with black people.

Kent omits from her analysis radical changes in the society of which social work is a part, and that this was a reason for her pessimistic conclusion. An important social work writer who does not do this is Davies (1967; 1969). Although his recommendations specifically concern child care, we shall consider them together with those of Rose *et al.* (1969). Davies asserts that we must first recognise the problem. His final recommendations concern the need for us all to involve ourselves in the building of a new, genuine, multi-racial society in Britain. His view of the problem and the solution is different not only from that of Kent but also from that of Rose. Although Kent and Rose differ over the likelihood of a solution, they both explicitly locate the specific issue of the black population and social welfare services in the context of the general cultural and power differences in Britain rather than in terms of immigration or race. It is for this reason that Rose *et al.* (1969) reject a policy aimed solely at black people.

Rose *et al.* and Davies's further recommendations, unlike Kent's, are based on the idea of integration, desire for co-operation by black and white people, brought about by an increased knowledge of one another's cultures. Due to the present existence of racism and culture conflict, Rose's recommendation regarding an information service, also made by the Seebohm Committee (Committee on Local Authority and Allied Personal Social Services 1968), would be ineffective without an accompanying policy to reduce racism and cultural hostility. As Gilbert (1972) notes, one should not assume that the eligible would want to become recipients even if they had knowledge of the sources of official aid. Following Kent, one could more validly infer that there would be less voluntary use of the social welfare services by the black population if there was greater knowledge of them. Davies's recommendation that social workers learn more about the black immigrants' culture again either misses the point or merely leads to a subtle assimilation policy. Similarly the mere dialogues between white and black social workers in the U.S.A. (Lide 1971; Beasley 1972) are inadequate. It might appear that Davies's recommendation that more black immigrant social workers should be employed would overcome many of the difficulties. A community Relations Officer (*Telegraph and Argus* 1971; Mujahid 1971) has argued that it is impossible to train a native British white social worker to deal with Asian culture. However, there is no necessary relationship between country of birth, race and culture and it is likely that because of class position and occupational socialisation, black immigrant social workers would be almost as alien to their compatriots as white, native ones. A similar point can be made about Davies's recommendation that black immigrant representatives should be co-opted on to relevant local authority committees where there are no black immigrant councillors. Such a criticism is implied in Hutchinson's (1969) comment that black immigrant middle-class people and officials are westernised and hostile to their working-class compatriots. It can, therefore, be seen that without the concomitant implementation of a general social policy programme the implementation of the other recommendations would have only trivial effects.

We can now discuss Rose's first recommendation in detail: a positive discrimination programme for working-class people with separate but equal facilities for black and white people. This can be done by following Pinker's (1971) proposals for social policy. Pinker, like the Seebohm Committee, argues that if the under-privileged poor are to be effectively aided, they must be distinguished and society must discriminate in their favour. Overt discrimination policies already exist in terms of negative discrimination against the poor or positive discrimination in favour of the rich, e.g. tax relief on mortgage interest payments.

But who is to be the unit of positive discrimination: individuals or categories of people? Both these approaches are likely to arouse humiliation amongst potential recipients and, legitimately, arouse hostility from other deprived categories of people. Pinker, like the Seebohm Committee, suggests as the unit a social priority area in terms of a community setting. A development of this type of priority area would be separate but equal services within a selective, positive discrimination programme. This would require research into the needs of the population and the location of social service departments similar to that carried out by Deacon and Cannan (1970). But what is the aid? The Plowden Report (Central Advisory Council for Education 1967) a model for such policy, saw the educational priority area as involving housing and social welfare as well as education. Pinker (1971) argues that such a programme should concern public utilities (for example parks, transport and public health amenities) as well as the social (environmental) services and personal social services. This concerns the relationship between central government and the local authority, between social services departments and other sources of aid.

Pinker then turns to the management of innovation. What are the agencies for such a change? Throughout the book, he rejects the Marxist concept of welfare as a capitalist device to 'cool out' revolution. However, Pinker, unlike Rose *et al.* (1969), does not rely on the state for the implementation of social policy. He argues for pressure group activity on the government. These groups, as Lees (1971a) points out, can be interest groups of either clients (Claimants Unions) or social workers (BASW) or attitude groups of non-participants (Child Poverty Action Group). Pinker's (1971) conceptions of the role of citizen participation in social policy is similar to that of the Seebohm Committee that we must reduce stigma by reducing the rigid distinction between givers and receivers. He suggests that social workers should have the most important role, and it would not seem to include working with black power groups as Naik (1972) recommends. Pinker's elitist strategy fails to recognise what Lees (1971a) points out: social workers as social control agents for the state are not the best people to defend their clients' interests. The weakness in Pinker's (1971) analysis, although it is a sophisticated plan, is that he primarily advocates pressure group politics to aid the disadvantaged. Such a strategy is based on an incorrect pluralistic model of society with the state as a neutral arbiter between equally powerful and competing pressure groups. His own evidence indicates the presence of vested local and national interests hostile to the redistribution of resources to the poor. A similarly Fabian manner of reducing politics to administration is found in his argument that social policy research will become increasingly used due to the (assumed) increased use of positive discrimination policies which require technically assessed diagnoses and selection. Here Pinker operates within the consensual model of policy-oriented research which we earlier highlighted as a possible pitfall.

We regard as necessary for adequate social work with black people a general positive discrimination programme within priority areas, combined with separate but equal provisions for different groups according to specific categories of need. The policy would involve many local authority departments (housing, education, transport and, of course the social services department and the Council of Social Service (Baski 1971). It is important that the local authority should not be over-burdened by costs and central government has to play an integral role in this policy for the underprivileged. Within the general plan, the social service department would advise on all aspects of the wants and needs of the people involved, as against the more concrete aspects of such a political administrative and physical venture.

Carrying out a plan of this nature would require more resources for the Community Relations Commission, Urban Programme and the social services departments, redevelopment of the inner cities with real citizen-participation and the repeal of the 1971 Immigration Act. We are not particularly optimistic that this policy will be implemented. Baski's (1971) challenge remains for all social workers: 'A force for conformity to hierarchical society or a force for non-conformity in an equal one?'

Notes

[1] Terms or words are not mere labels but part of the way in which a person's identity and conduct can be constructed and controlled. Euphemisms abound in the field of race relations and the term black is used here to include all non-whites, Asians as well as Africans and West Indians. It is used in preference to the equally imprecise term coloured in order to confront explicitly race labelling. Bentley (1972) discusses conceptual collusion with racism in greater detail, arguing that the collection and presentation of the Bradford Education Authority's official statistics are one such example. By immigrant, we mean a person resident in the United Kingdom but born outside it. A citizen of Eire resident in England is an immigrant. This legalistic definition does not imply that such a person is culturally or ethnically alien. By ethnicity, we refer to national culture but there is no simple relationship between country of birth and ethnicity. By race, we refer primarily to colour (black or white), not the concept of genetic inheritance. The terms assimilation, integration and pluralism are often used interchangeably, but there are important differences between them (Horton 1966; Rose *et al.* 1969). By assimilation we mean a unilateral uniformity to one culture or ethnic group; by integration we mean a bilateral amalgamation or synthesis to form a new, emergent culture, and by pluralism we mean a situation of diverse ethnic groups in an egalitarian situation: separate and equal. By racism (or racialism) we mean adverse verbal prejudice or physical discrimination against people solely on the grounds of race. This can be either by individuals or expressed in organisational terms, when it is institutionalised racism.

[2] Daniels (1968) is an abridgement of the 1967 PEP Report and Deakin (1970) is an updated abridgement of Rose *et al.* (1969). The Facts Paper (IRR 1970) is the most concise and comprehensive source. Cheetham (1972) includes much of the above data with particular reference to social work.

[3] It is relevant that in a period of increasing international migration and the development of multi-national businesses, white immigrants on the Continent are becoming a sub-proletariat (Special Correspondent 1972a). This suggests even more strongly that the position of black people in Britain should be viewed primarily in terms of an international class analysis.

[4] Cheetham (1972) deals with these different frameworks at length. Kent's articles are highly eclectic. Her work may be located within the ego-psychological theory of the culture-personality school (Lindesmith & Strauss 1950) or weak structural-functionalism (Coulson & Riddell, 1970). Her work should not be confused with the

transactionalist approach to deviance which would reject her concentration on the super-ego and on an oversocialised (deterministic and consensual) concept of man and society (Butcher 1970; Cohen, ed. 1971). However, she avoids a criticism of this approach for she does locate deviance and the specialised social control agencies in the wider society (Cannan 1970).

[5] For a more detailed analysis of such conflicts manifested *within* a welfare organisation, see Allen (1967).

References

Allen, S. (1967) 'Structural Aspects of Medical Social Work', *Med. Soc. Wk.*, 20, 67.

Allen, S. (1969) 'School leavers: problems of method and explanation', *Race Today*, 1, 235.

Allen, S. (1970) 'Immigrants or workers', *in Race and Racialism*, ed. S. Zubaida. Tavistock, London.

Antrobus, P. (1964) 'Coloured children in care: a special problem group?' *Case Conf.*, 11, 39.

Antrobus, P. (1970) 'Policy of sending children away', letter in *Guardian*, 5 November.

Baski, J. (1971) 'The Seebohm proposals and community relations', *Race Today*, 3, 223.

Beasley, L. M. (1972) 'A beginning attempt to eradicate racist attitudes', *Soc. Casewk.*, 53, 9.

Bentley, S. (1972) 'Identity and community co-operation: a note on terminology', *in Race*, 14, 69.

Biestek, F. J. (1961) *The Casework Relationship*. Allen and Unwin, London.

Bloom, L. (1969) 'The social aetiology of schizophrenia in immigrant groups: a notice of caution', letter in *Race Today*, 1, 255.

British Association of Social Workers (1971a) 'Immigration Bill', *Soc. Wk. Today*, 2, 16.

British Association of Social Workers (1971b) 'Immigration Bill', *Soc. Wk. Today*, 21 October, 17.

Butcher, H. (1970) 'Deviant labelling and the social worker', *Soc. Wk. Today*, 1, 16.

Butterworth, E. (ed.) (1967) *Immigrants in West Yorkshire: social conditions and the lives of Pakistanis, Indians and West Indians*. O.U.P., London.

Butterworth, E. (1969) 'Local Government and the presence of minority groups', *Race Today*, 1, 206.

Cannan, C. (1970) 'Deviants: victims or rebels?' *Case-Con.*, 1.

Central Advisory Council for Education (1967) 'Children and their primary schools' (Plowden report). HMSO, London.

Cheetham, J. (1972) *Social Work with Immigrants*. Routledge and Kegan Paul, London.

Cohen, S. (ed.) (1971) *Images of Deviance*. Penguin, Harmondsworth.

Committee on Local Authority and Allied Personal Social Services (1968) *Report* (Chairman: F. Seebohm), Cmnd. 3703. HMSO, London.

Coulson, M. A. & Riddell, D. (1970) *Approaching Sociology: a critical introduction.* Routledge and Kegan Paul, London.

Daniels, W. W. (1968) *Racial Discrimination in England.* Penguin, Harmondsworth.

Davies, J. W. D. (1967) 'Thursday's Child Has Far to Go', *Case-Conf.*, 14, 8.

Davies, J. W. D. (1969) 'Immigrants—part two—in Britain', *Child Care*, 23, 55.

Davis, A. Y. (1971) *If They Come in the Morning: voices of resistance.* Orbach and Chambers, London.

Deacon, B. & Cannan, C. (1970) 'Social Priority Areas and Seebohm', *Soc. Wk. Today*, 1, 94.

Deakin, N. (1970) *Colour, Citizenship and British Society.* Panther, London.

Dodge, J. S. (1971) 'The impact of immigration on medicine in Britain', *Brit. J. Hosp. Med.*, 5, 47.

Foren, R. & Batta, I. D. (1970) ' "Colour" as a variable in the use made of a local authority child care department', *Soc. Wk.* [London], 27, 10.

Gilbert, N. (1972) 'Who gets what: perspectives on choice and social policy', *Appl. Soc. Stud.*, 4, 2.

Gretton, J. (1971) 'The race industry', *New Soc.*, 11 March, 385.

Hewitt, M. (1971a) 'Immigration Bill', *Case-Conf.*, 4, 3.

Hewitt, M. (1971b) 'Effects of Immigration Bill', letter in *Soc. Wk. Today*, 2, 31.

Hill, B. (1971) 'Who are the E.S.N.?' *Times Ed. Supp.*, 9 April, 12.

Hill, M. J. & Issacharoff, R. M. (1971) *Community Action and Race Relations: a study of community relations committees in Britain.* O.U.P., London.

Holman, R. (1968) 'Immigrants and Child Care Policy', *Case-Conf.*, 15, 255.

Holman, R. (1971) 'The urban programme appraised', *Race Today*, 3, 227.

Hood, C., Oppe, T. E., Pless, I. B. & Apté, E. (1970) *Children of West Indian Immigrants: a study of one-year olds in Paddington.* Institute of Race Relations, London.

Norton, J. (1966) 'Conflict and order theories as competing ideologies of social problems', *Amer. J. Sociol.*, 71, 701.

Hutchinson, P. (1969) 'The social worker and culture conflict', *Case-Conf.*, 15, 467.

Institute of Race Relations, (1970) *Fact Paper on the United Kingdom*, 1970–71, 3rd edn. IRR, London.

Jackson, S. (1971) *The Illegal Child-Minders: a report on the growth of unregistered child-minding and the West Indian community.* Priority Area Children, Cambridge.

Jay, P. & Halpin, H. (1970) 'The overseas child in public care', letter in *The Times*, 17 November.

Jehu, D. (1968) 'Developmental issues in inter-racial adoption', *Case-Conf.*, 14, 345.

Jones, K. & Smith, A. D. (1970) *The Economic Impact of Commonwealth Immigration.* Cambridge University Press, Cambridge.

Kent, B. (1965) 'The social worker's cultural pattern as it affects casework with immigrants', *Soc. Wk.* [London], 22, 14.

Kent, B. (1968a) 'Casework with Immigrants (1)', *Inst. Race Relations Newsl.*, 14.

Kent, B. (1968b) 'Casework with Immigrants (2)', *Inst. Race Relations Newsl.*, 286.

Kent, B. (1969) 'Casework with Immigrants (3): some tensions', *Inst. Race Relations Newsl.*, 130.

Lambert, J. R. (1970) *Crime, Police and Race Relations.* Oxford University Press, London.

Lees, R. (1971) 'Social work, 1925–50: the case for a reappraisal', *Brit. J. Soc. Wk.*, 1, 371.

Lees, R. (1971a) 'Professions, the underprivileged and the political process', *Appl. Soc. Stud.*, 3, 155.

Leonard, P. (1965) 'Social control and class values in social work practice', *Soc. Wk.* [London], 22, 9.

Lide, R. (1971) 'Dialogue on racism: a prologue to action?' *Soc. Casewk.*, 52, 432.

Lindesmith, A. K. & Strauss, A. L. (1950) 'A critique of culture-personality writings', *Amer. Sociol. R.*, 15, 587.

Mayer, J. E. & Rosenblatt, A. (1964) 'The client's social context: its effect on continuance in treatment', *Soc. Casewk.*, 45, 511.

Mayer, J. E. & Timms, N. (1970) *The Client Speaks: working class impressions of casework.* Routledge and Kegan Paul, London.

Miliband, R. (1969) *The State in Capitalist Society.* Weidenfeld and Nicholson, London.

Miller, R. R. (ed.) (1969) *Race, Research and Reason: social work perspectives.* National Association of Social Workers, New York.

Moore, R. (1971) 'Race relations and the rediscovery of sociology', *Brit. J. Sociol.*, 22, 97.

Mujahid, S. (1971) Personal Communication.

Naik, D. (1972) 'Social work in a multi-racial society', *Brit. Hosp. J.*, 82, 513.

Pinker, R. (1971) *Social Theory and Social Policy.* Heinemann, London.

Race Today (1971) 'The 1971 Immigration Bill: a special report', *Race Today*, 3, 3.

Raynor, L. (1970) *Adoption of Non-White Children: the experience of a British adoption project.* Allen and Unwin, London.

Rose, E. J. B., Deakin, N., Abrams, M., Jackson, V., Peston, M., Vanags, A. H., Cohen, B., Gaitskell, J. & Ward, P. (1969) *Colour and Citizenship.* Oxford University Press, London.

Rowse, W. I. (1970) 'Children in Transit', letter in *The Guardian*, 7 November.

Simpson, T. (1971) 'BASW and the Industrial Relations Bill', *Soc. Wk. Today*, 2, 3, p 31.

Social Work (1965) 'Culture and communication', *Soc. Wk.* [London], 22, 4.

Special Correspondent (1972a) 'Green wafers, white racism', *Race Today*, 4, 61.

Special Correspondent (1972b) 'Black unemployment', *Race Today*, 4, 174.

Telegraph and Argus (1971) 'Migrants "Not in Welfare Force",' *Telegraph and Argus*, 8 October.

Turner, F. J. (ed.) (1968) *Differential Diagnosis and Treatment in Social Work.* Free Press, New York.

Westergaard, J. H. (1972) 'Sociology: the myth of classlessness', *in Ideology in Social Science*, ed. R. Blackburn. Fontana, London.

Whittington, C. (1971) 'Self-determination re-examined', *Brit. J. Soc. Wk.*, 1, 293.

Young, J. (1971) 'The role of the police as amplifiers of deviancy, negotiators of reality and translators of fantasy: some consequences of our present system of drug control as seen in Notting Hill', *in Images of Deviance*, ed. S. Cohen. Penguin, Harmondsworth.

8 *Voluntary enterprise and social services departments*

W. B. Harbert

The extension of statutory social services in recent years has forced voluntary organisations to change rapidly. At a time when social needs are changing, and when statutory services are developing rapidly, it is necessary for them to reconsider their role and redefine their objectives. The process of self-examination can be painful and there are reports of internal strife and dissension, as many of the old established voluntary bodies struggle to find a new sense of purpose.

The major responsibility for the provision of services must rest with statutory bodies. Organisations which were once the pacesetters have had to accept a lesser role as work which they have pioneered for decades is taken up by statutory services. There has always been a high mortality rate amongst voluntary organisations and those that cannot or will not adapt to new conditions die whilst others take their place.

It is against this background of change and uncertainty that the new social services departments have been established and directors of social services are keenly aware that their efforts to create a new and improved pattern of local authority services are being studied with great interest by the voluntary movement.

Since Henry VIII dissolved the monasteries people have been talking gloomily about the declining role of voluntary organisations in the provision of social welfare services. After every government report or Act of Parliament on social welfare, the rumour is heard that improved statutory services will obviate the need for charitable effort. Yet voluntary organisations obstinately continue to thrive despite the pessimism all around them. In a democratic society, in which people are free to express their views and develop interests, men and women will always want to right wrongs, to press for social and political change and to help the oppressed, the deprived and the underdog. The quality and quantity of statutory services for the under-privileged have no correlation with the desire of men and women in the general community to effect social change by their own personal efforts. The more affluent a nation becomes, the more are its members freed from the drudgery of ensuring economic survival and the more they turn their minds and resources to improving their own, and other people's, social conditions.

But the growth of voluntary services at the present time is more than a product of greater leisure. It is a reflection of the changing public attitude towards authority, towards the 'they' who shape our lives; it is a reaction to the growing impersonalisation of life, to large-scale industry, large-scale housing and large-scale government; it is a way in which ordinary members of society can assert their individuality in an age of mass production and mass living. Unlike nineteenth-century philanthropy, the current upsurge of voluntary enterprise is a mass movement stemming, not just from the comfortably-off middle classes, but from a broad cross-section of the population. We have in fact come to recognise the vigour and abundance of voluntary enterprise as the distinguishing marks, not only of a free society, but also of a healthy community.

It is significant that at a time when travel and communications are becoming easier and when so much of human existence is dominated by large and impersonal social institutions, we are rediscovering the social value of the small community and local neighbourhood. Many of the recently formed voluntary bodies are tenants' organisations, community associations and other groups of people who come together in a particular geographical area to bring about some desirable social change. Their frame of reference is the local community. Although most of their members would deny that they were operating in the social welfare field, many of these bodies make a sizeable contribution to social welfare by encouraging good neighbourliness, by organising activities for the lonely and isolated and by the personal fulfilment which the organisations bring to their participating members.

The development of area-based social work teams by social services departments must inevitably encourage social workers to examine the relevance of community groups as a means of achieving their objectives. Many social problems have a community pathology and must be treated on a neighbourhood, rather than a family or individual, basis. The concepts of working with communities as described by Younghusband (1968) and Leaper (1971) have been accepted by present-day social workers at least as eagerly as their predecessors accepted the philosophies of Freud and Jung. The extent to which community work can be an effective tool of social services departments remains to be seen; meanwhile, it is clear that it adds a new dimension to the provision of social welfare services.

Some departments are extending their work with communities into what the Seebohm Committee described as community development. That is to say, they are moving beyond the use of community groups as resources for social welfare activities and are assisting neighbourhood organisations to express the needs of the community and to take collective action to meet them. It is debatable whether social services departments are the most appropriate agency for carrying out this function as community needs extend across the full range of central and local government services but staff in social services departments see very clearly the potential value of this work and now have the command of resources to implement plans.

Community work and community action are increasingly seen as instruments for social betterment by social workers and others but there is a marked lack of enthusiasm for existing social institutions through which the community's needs are expressed and met—the local authority and the elected member. Watts (1972) says 'the rapid growth of community action—of self-help—groups over the last few years carries a serious warning for local government. It suggests that the established democratic processes are failing to involve large sections of the urban community which are nevertheless becoming increasingly politically conscious'. If the local government machine is too large and too remote to reflect the will of the people, small neighbourhood groups are too fragmented to command the power and resources necessary to provide services and amenities of a satisfactory quality. The next decade is likely to see massive confrontations between community groups and local government—confrontations like those recently seen in London about squatting.

It is traditional in this country to praise voluntary effort and even to be patronising and condescending about it. Robin Huws Jones (1967) has said that there is more sentimental humbug talked about the topic of the volunteer than any other in the social welfare field. An assumption is often made that voluntary service of any kind must be valuable simply because it is voluntary. However, Broady (1972) told a conference of representatives from voluntary organisations that perhaps 75% of voluntary organisations were doing work of such poor quality that they were not worth supporting; such a statement shatters cherished dreams but is probably realistic. Where voluntary organisations exist to provide for the social or intellectual needs of members from their own resources, there is no need for the rest of us to assess their value, but when they undertake to meet the social welfare needs of others and ask for financial assistance from the public purse it is right that they should be subject to close scrutiny. Services to the public should not be third rate because they are being provided by voluntary effort.

There are many gaps in the social services that can only be filled by voluntary effort. For example, the domiciliary care of the elderly and handicapped and the provision of advice and friendship to unsupported mothers and others are mammoth tasks which can only be tackled by mobilising all the community strengths and resources that are available. In earlier generations the family and the immediate neighbourhood offered spontaneous support to people in distress, but changes in technology, in women's employment, in housing and in social attitudes, make it necessary now to provide support by organisational means. Professional social workers, unaided by the general community, can make little or no impact on such problems. There are opportunities here for close collaboration between social services departments and groups of volunteers in the community, with the local authority, perhaps in co-operation with training bodies, providing short training courses and offering consultation.

Social workers are becoming increasingly aware of the fund of good will in the community which is ready to be tapped. At Christmas some organisations are swamped with offers of toys, food parcels and even cash for distribution to the needy. Many of these offers are quite unsolicited. The new departments must find ways of harnessing this good will, of putting it to greater use, of strengthening it, of spreading it throughout the year and applying it to the needs which are not at present apparent to the donors.

People respond to urgent and obvious social needs. A baby is found abandoned on a doorstep and ten people clamour to adopt it. A pensioner loses her possessions in a fire and from nowhere come donations of money and furniture. Unorganised voluntary effort can easily become frustrated unless it is given encouragement and potential givers are discouraged by seeming indifference on the part of professional staff. As social services departments begin to operate at neighbourhood level they will be able to exploit these human and material resources more fully.

If the social services are to welcome a greater involvement from individuals and from voluntary organisations in the provision of services, it will be necessary for local authority staff to become much more involved in the life of the communities they serve. Community-based social work is not an extension of paternalism by authority to the underprivileged with consultation added to make it more acceptable. It implies a new relationship between public services and the public—a relationship in which no one part has a monopoly of resources, power, initiative or ideas. Social workers will be required to adopt the role of adviser and consultant, helping neighbours, voluntary visitors and club leaders. As David Jones (1969) has said, they may also be expected to seek out those persons in the community to whom people in distress naturally turn for help, and support them in their helping role without trying to convert them into self-conscious volunteers. In some areas social work staff employed in the public service now play an enormous part in stimulating voluntary enterprise in their private capacities and in their spare time. Some voluntary bodies have been created out of the concern of social workers to see improvements in certain fields of work and are almost entirely managed by them.

Professional social workers have mixed feelings about volunteers and have been slow to recognise their value. Voluntary organisations have pioneered the use of volunteers and they have done so largely without the help of professional social workers. Social work training courses now equip students to embrace the philosophy of community based social work but have generally failed to prepare them for work with volunteers.

If voluntary workers are to be deployed in a systematic way by social services departments they must be given adequate training and supervision. As the Aves Report (1969) suggested, in some instances it may be better to avoid using the word 'training' and adopt the word 'preparation'. There is no need to be afraid of insisting that volunteers undertake some kind of preparation; experience suggests that good volunteers demand it.

Formal training is sometimes difficult to arrange because volunteers offer themselves at different times and there are practical problems involved in training people in small numbers. Sometimes a university, an extra-mural department, a council of social service, a college of further education, or the WEA may be persuaded to provide courses for volunteers covering several agencies including voluntary and statutory bodies. A method adopted by the National Citizens Advice Bureaux Council and described by Pridham (1969) is to advertise widely for volunteers, provide a training course and make a selection from those candidates who complete the course.

Staff require assistance to understand the needs of volunteers and in busy departments where there is understaffing, there is a danger that staff may see themselves as competing with voluntary workers for the attention of seniors and there may be friction if junior staff find themselves continually carrying extra burdens because volunteers are inadequately supervised or unreliable. Nevertheless, where volunteers are deployed in social services departments, there are advantages in them working alongside area teams and being responsible to area social workers rather than being segregated, as this provides a good learning experience for both staff and volunteers.

The volunteer, eager to assist his fellow man, poses management problems for social services departments. His is a spontaneous expression of concern, springing from a genuine and powerful desire to be of service to the community and those in need. He has a built-in suspicion of bureaucracy and wishes to retain complete freedom of action in his relationships with his clients. He is usually not so concerned about overall policy, accountability and record keeping as with meeting the personal and day-to-day needs of people in distress. He wants to feel that his efforts achieve success and he responds to need in a positive and direct way. These facets of voluntary service are a strength and a weakness: a strength because the volunteer can show real care and kindness and offer spontaneous friendship to people who might otherwise receive no help, and a weakness because it is difficult to regulate and to measure what is done since the volunteer wants to help the client—not the social services.

There have been a number of successful examples of volunteers undertaking domiciliary social welfare work directly for statutory services. This trend will no doubt be accelerated in coming years although experience suggests that volunteers identify more readily with a voluntary organisation than with a statutory body. It may therefore prove easier to involve volunteers in the work of social services departments by working with and through existing voluntary organisations. There is scope, too, for volunteers of all kinds to offer services in residential day care establishments.

The value of community activity as a means of promoting individual maturity and a sense of responsibility is being increasingly exploited by government agencies. The Schools Council (1968) has underlined the character-building aspects of community service and urged that it should have a positive connection with the school curriculum. The Wootton Committee (1970) proposed that certain offenders should be required to perform a specified number of hours of service to the community in their spare time; it recommended that reliance should be placed primarily on voluntary agencies for the supply of tasks. Provision for community service orders is contained in the Criminal Justice Act, 1972.

The Department of Health and Social Security (1972) has published a guide called *Intermediate Treatment under the Children & Young Persons Act, 1969*. Forms of treatment are available to the juvenile court which allow a child to remain in his own home while at the same time bringing him into contact with a different environment and new experiences. The report says, 'a great deal of the most suitable provision will lie outside the public sector and many of the facilities included in schemes will be provided by voluntary bodies and individuals.'

This kind of official patronage will increase the scope of voluntary enterprise. It will also provide greater opportunities for social services departments to work with volunteers. Nevertheless, there will be problems of deployment and supervision to be overcome if both statutory and voluntary bodies are to make full use of these captive volunteers. The increased financial support from government agencies to voluntary organisations which is inevitable if such schemes are to be effective, and the relationships which must be developed between the statutory and voluntary agencies concerned, will still further blur the edges between voluntary and statutory organisations.

It is in the field of experimentation and pioneer activity that voluntary organisations have made a major contribution in the past. They have been quick to take up new ideas, to test out theories and to take risks. They have been willing to develop services which are unpopular and to provide help for people whose problems have not been fully understood by the public at large. There is always a danger that local authorities, responsible for providing wide ranging and comprehensive services within defined geographical boundaries, will be unable to devote adequate time and skill to deal effectively with particular problems.

The freedom of action of voluntary organisations to start new services and to experiment is in sharp contrast to the constraints imposed on statutory services. The latter cannot pick and choose their clients and they cannot select the kind of problems they will handle. Often the exercise of statutory duties leaves no staff-time or resources for more imaginative work. Some local authorities could deploy all their social work resources on the prevention of family break-up and on providing for children under their care. These are tasks which a local authority must carry out before it can attempt to meet other pressing needs. It is therefore clear that the kind of service undertaken by the voluntary sector is likely to vary in different parts of the country as social needs and local authority provision varies.

Good organisations, both statutory and voluntary, continually experiment with their structure and their way of presenting services to the public; the role of pioneer and innovator is not confined to voluntary organisations. There is room for many small-scale experiments on ways of publicising services and of encouraging people in need to use them. A good example of this activity is the publication by the Liverpool Personal Service Society (1969) of a guide to welfare benefits for use by local social workers. The booklet gave details, in a readable form, of sixteen benefits provided by central and local government in Liverpool. For the first time details of benefits made available by nine different authorities and departments were brought together in one publication.

The booklet was prepared because the Society was concerned that many people failed to obtain benefits to which they were entitled. It was an immediate success. Although it referred to benefits available in Liverpool, copies were ordered by local authorities, voluntary organisations, libraries, universities, industrial welfare organisations and social workers from all over the country. Within six months ten organisations had sought to copy the format of the booklet for use in their own areas and similar booklets began to appear, published not only by other voluntary organisations but by local authorities too. The central office of one of the major political parties requested permission to distribute the material to all its parliamentary candidates. Central government departments showed considerable interest as did a number of members of Parliament.

Here is a good example of a provincial voluntary organisation recognising a problem, attempting to meet it and arousing public interest and concern. As a result, authorities providing benefits were made aware of the need to review their publicity and it is known that the rules pertaining to one benefit were changed following adverse publicity caused by the booklet. It may be that the evidence the booklet provided of the need for more and better information about services and public discussion on this issue which was thereby generated, were two of the factors which influenced the Supplementary Benefits Commission to produce the Supplementary Benefits Handbook in the Spring of 1970.

Much more experimentation is required to find effective ways of presenting services to the public. Statutory services have in the past been crisis-orientated; they have come forward when the family cannot cope. Voluntary organisations have provided a more preventive service, assisting people with their problems and referring clients for specialist help when necessary. Voluntary bodies have made a significant contribution in the area of legal advice. It is known that people in need of legal advice frequently do not come forward for help and experimental advice centres are beginning to fill this need. In some areas the services provided by the rent officer are not used fully. Tales of old people and unsupported mothers failing to claim supplementary benefit, rate rebates and other benefits are legion. These are all areas of need in which opportunities exist for voluntary organisations to experiment in making services more accessible.

Local authority social services have, up to now, largely assisted the under-privileged, the poor and the socially disadvantaged. The Seebohm Committee went so far as to suggest that there has, in the past, been a stigma about being a client of the social services. Unfortunately, a social services district office, even if it succeeds in being physically near the population it serves, may not be accessible in every meaning of that word if a significant proportion of the population in need feels a certain stigma about asking for help. A district office can easily become regarded locally as the place where delinquents are looked after or where the mentally disturbed, problem families, the poor or neglectful mothers are interviewed. Serious thought must be given to how this obstacle to the effective provision of services can be overcome.

The Seebohm Committee said that experiments should take place associating a social services district office with other locally based services such as health centres, schools, libraries and day nurseries. There may also be advantages in providing services in association with voluntary groups. Community associations, tenants' groups and other neighbourhood groups are showing a keen interest in neighbourhood advice centres which can, with expert help, provide a wide range of information and advice and carry out advocacy work for the local population. Such centres can be focal points from which community work is fostered. Local authority services can, with advantage, work alongside such organisations, sharing premises and common services. The next decade is unlikely to see a major breakthrough in our knowledge about social problems or the development of new techniques in the provision of social care. Improved services will come from a reshaping of the structure of services and by using our present knowledge to greater advantage. The voluntary movement has a major part to play in this process of change.

Unlike other areas of human knowledge, the social services have no laboratory in which experiments can be made in clinical isolation, in which ideas can be formulated and tested and in which new techniques can be perfected. Experimentation must take place in the open and must be carried out on living people with acute and often distressing problems. Furthermore, it must take place in full view of the public and endure the glare of publicity that is likely to follow mistakes. Any worthwhile experiment must have an element of risk, a risk that the results will prove disappointing, that money will be misspent, that people will not be helped, and experiment is open to the criticism that the money could have been better spent in providing services which are badly needed. For these reasons, and others, there will always be scope for voluntary organisations to test out new ideas.

With health services reorganisation in 1974, the pattern is set for six largely self-contained administrative units for meeting social needs. These are social welfare, education and housing through local authorities, health, through area health boards, and income maintenance and employment services administered by central government. However well these pieces of machinery dovetail with one another there will be gaps between them and grey areas in which services are not fully developed. There will be opportunities here for voluntary bodies to experiment with new services and to press for the needs of particular groups of clients to be met more adequately. Already, for example, some voluntary organisations are showing interest in the needs of the under-fives. For this age group responsibility is divided between the health service, which provides medical and health visiting services, social services departments, which have responsibility for residential and day-care services including playgroups and day nurseries, and education authorities which provide nursery schools. Without continual vigilance services for the under-fives may not be fully developed and some children may receive inappropriate care.

Other areas of social need which may not be fully explored by local authorities in the immediate future are those for special school leavers, discharged hospital patients, the unemployed, the so-called work shy, unmarried mothers and adults and children suffering from psychosomatic disorders. All these potential clients are on the margin of two or more administrative empires and risk being overlooked or neglected while so many new developments are taking place. At the same time, the clients concerned do not push themselves forward for attention. In a sense they require a pressure group to speak up for them and demonstrate their needs. The social services still tend to operate on the principle that people with problems will draw attention to themselves or that needs will be recognised by other agencies and the client referred for help. This has resulted in services being provided for the articulate, for those with acute and obvious problems and those who present problems to other public agencies. Voluntary organisations can show the extent to which the silent majority have problems which require attention.

Another area requiring exploration and study by voluntary organisations lies on the boundary between social welfare, youth work and community development. We need to know more about how the social needs of young people can be met, the ways in which they can best serve the community, what kind of personal service they can provide, what supervision is appropriate and what administrative framework is most likely to encourage this activity and meet their own needs.

At a time when local authority social work is developing a generic approach, the value of voluntary organisations which provide a service to specific categories of people or which speak on behalf of them must be kept under review. It remains to be seen how far social services departments carry the generic principle, but some specialisms will certainly remain. A rationalisation in social work training should produce social workers with a knowledge of a wide range of social situations but it may also whet the appetite of the student for studying certain problems in depth. Thus it should be possible for social workers to carry largely generic caseloads whilst specialising for part of their time in an area of work of their own choice. New specialisations may emerge and they may well be narrower than in the past. For example, some social workers may wish to specialise in work with the under-fives, in psychiatric patients with organic diseases, in psychopathic husbands, neglectful mothers, battered babies or the employment problems of the physically handicapped.

As knowledge about social need is extended, so opportunities arise to develop new skills and specialisms. A glance at industrial technology shows that only by the division of labour and by freeing people to specialise are the boundaries of knowledge extended. It is to be hoped that voluntary bodies do not too readily abandon specialisms at this time. They have built up a considerable expertise and an understanding of problems which are a vital springboard for innovation and experiment.

Voluntary organisations are not immune from the problems that affect other social institutions. They are sometimes turned inwards on themselves and they act like any bureaucracy to preserve their interests; as Schorr (1969) has said, 'they answer first to the needs of their own survival and security'. It sometimes happens that they hang on too long to activities which should be passed to statutory bodies. New legislation, even new government regulations, can suddenly transform statutory services; and tasks which have been the responsibility of voluntary initiative since the dawn of civilisation, become part of the accepted pattern of state services. The leadership of voluntary organisations must therefore be in the hands of people who are not dismayed when statutory services lunge forward to accept responsibility for work traditionally undertaken by voluntary bodies. Their allegiance must be to those in need and not to any particular organisational structure. Annual reports produced by some voluntary bodies frequently display a defensiveness and even hostility towards statutory services which reveals their latent fears about their own future.

In the world of commerce and industry the consumer of a service relates his satisfaction to the cost involved to decide whether or not he has made a good buy. His future pattern of consumption will depend upon this which will, in turn, determine the quality, type and extent of services offered to the public. Where services are paid for through rates and taxes, however, these decisions are not left to market forces but rest on political judgments. This makes it difficult for the consumer to have a direct influence on the level and quality of services provided and almost completely rules out choice. It confines the social services to a level determined by government or local government instead of by the collective action of consumers. This is particularly so in the social services where consumers are generally not well organised to make their demands known.

The growth of the movement towards greater consumer participation, which is discussed in Chapter 10, is clearly making its mark but the consumer of social services is usually placed in the position of having to accept what is offered. Our society, which provides a wide choice of refrigerators, washing machines, clothes, shoes and motor cars and which considers it important to ensure alternative newspapers and television programmes, frequently denies the users of the social services an element of choice. In a free society only the convicted criminal should be made to feel that he has forfeited the right to exercise choice in the goods and services he consumes.

A strong argument can be advanced for voluntary organisations being encouraged to offer services alternative to and alongside statutory provision. This is particularly necessary in the field of residential care for the elderly and handicapped. Voluntary services help to mop up demand not being met by statutory services, point to those areas of need which, for various reasons are not adequately covered, give an opportunity for consumer demand to express itself, and offer some degree of choice to the public.

For a proportion of people it will always be vital that local services contain an alternative door on which to knock. The man who is by nature against authority will never be satisfied with statutory services. For some, the local authority social worker will appear to be a very powerful figure indeed. Get on well with her and she will make sure you get your welfare rights; she will speak to the Department of Health and Social Security about your supplementary allowance, she may even settle some of your bills; she may chase up your landlord about repairs, speak up for you with the Housing Department for a new house and generally look after you. But, disagree with her and you may be marked down as a trouble-maker or, worse still, as a scrounger, and all these benefits may be denied. Some countervailing force is surely needed; a force which will speak for disgruntled clients. Information and advocacy services provided by voluntary organisations can help to fill this role.

As social work training follows a national pattern geared to meet the requirements of social services departments, there will be an even greater need for men and women with independent views who can formulate their ideas from a close knowledge of the service but without the blinkers which almost inevitably affect the judgment of people trying to be objective about their own service. There are advantages too for students in training to have practical placements in voluntary organisations. In this way they learn to appreciate the importance of agency function in moulding professional thinking and action.

A pioneer of voluntary social action said, sixty years ago, 'to labour casework which does not affect policy is to plough the sands while to shape policy except in the light of casework is to build on them'. It must be the function of every social work agency to look beyond its day-by-day work and consider the implications of what it is doing for public policy. It has a duty to use its knowledge about social problems to advance understanding of social issues and to stimulate new thinking. Statutory services find no shortage of people willing to give advice about the provision of services and the level of spending. They are more likely, however, to listen with a keen ear when the organisation proffering views is one which itself is deeply involved in providing services and which therefore speaks from considerable knowledge. This was clearly implied by Sir Keith Joseph at the Annual Conference of the National Association for Mental Health in February 1972 when he said that he respected the Association as 'a stimulus, a critic and a participator'. He congratulated the Association for being both 'a lobby and a service'.

Expenditure in the social services, particularly new expenditure, is not decided in isolation but is considered against the needs of other public services. Good schemes do not therefore automatically receive financial support. Social services departments are competing for funds with housing, health, highways, libraries, baths and other local services. Voluntary organisations serve an invaluable role in assisting public discussion about priorities for spending. However, they must work within certain constraints.

The Charity Commissioners do not permit charitable status to be bestowed on voluntary bodies that include among their purposes the object of bringing influence to bear directly or indirectly on parliament to change the law. This ruling has been widely criticised in recent years, but it presents little difficulty to the locally-based charity that wishes to draw attention to social evils. It is surprising what can be said in an annual report, in carefully phrased press releases and in occasional letters to the local member of parliament, town clerk or council leader. Many charities are empowered to carry out research studies; a research report can carry concluding recommendations suggesting how public authorities should remedy situations described in the report. By ensuring that politicians serve on the executive committee of a charity it is possible for the organisation to have direct access to the seat of power.

A variety of economic, technological and social factors are leading to larger units of organisation in industry, commerce and local government. The same factors must influence the future development and viability of locally based voluntary organisations.

Social work, like other occupations, has been increasingly professionalised in recent years; standards have risen enormously and so have salaries. Many small voluntary bodies have been unable to offer the kind of salaries needed to attract qualified staff; they survive with dedicated, often inspired staff who, nevertheless, often work inefficiently. Too often, the poorly paid secretary of a local organisation deals with the accounts, appeals for funds, writes committee minutes, makes the tea and does many other things that in larger organisations are shared between a number of specialists. Organisations run on this basis often do good work but there is little doubt they are inefficient and that they will find it increasingly difficult to attract staff of the right calibre.

Closer collaboration between voluntary bodies could bring enormous benefits both to the voluntary movement and to the public they serve. In most of the large conurbations there are overlapping casework services provided by two religious denominations as well as secular bodies, for poor families and unmarried mothers. Such a fragmentation of effort is wasteful of resources and leads to misunderstandings on the part of the consumer. It is wasteful in terms of office accommodation, publicity, fund raising and administrative support; it leads to difficulties in attracting social work staff in that it offers a poor career structure and reduces opportunities for high quality supervision and consultation. The co-ordination of voluntary effort is not the responsibility of local authorities. It is an important function that must be undertaken by the voluntary movement itself, albeit with advice and support from the local authority. Nevertheless, grant aid provides local authorities which a powerful instrument which, if used with skill and understanding, can reshape the pattern of social welfare services, stimulate voluntary initiative and provide opportunities for community services on an unparalleled scale.

If voluntary organisations are to remain an influential force at local level and are to prove themselves worthy to receive larger and larger sums of public money by way of tax relief and grant aid they must make sure that they are efficient and also broadly based. Murray (1969), who studied voluntary organisations in Scotland, urged that voluntary bodies should undertake continual reviews of their structures and financial arrangements. In their survey of voluntary visiting for the elderly in twenty-three areas, Shenfield & Allen (1972), found that the organisational structure of the voluntary bodies was 'the least satisfactory part of the voluntary efforts studied in this enquiry'. Voluntary bodies must also be firmly rooted in the communities they serve. Too often, organisations which accuse local government of being unresponsive and undemocratic are themselves controlled by self-perpetuated cliques responsible to no one. Such organisations seeking greater public involvement in the social services could well start by examining their own constitutions.

The creation of social services departments has led to much speculation and anxiety among locally based voluntary organisations. They have been eager to ascertain how the new director of social services views their activities and to discover what his policies might be with regard to grant aid. Unfortunately, during this period, social services departments have been fully engaged in their internal problems. Combining three separate services into a unified whole, creating an organisational structure, making provision for new services laid down by Act of Parliament and at the same time maintaining services to the public, has taxed the energies of senior staff to the full.

The Seebohm Committee suggested that mutual criticism between local authorities and voluntary organisations is inevitable and even desirable. Certainly, informed discussion between voluntary and statutory bodies providing services is valuable but, too often, criticism on both sides is based on ignorance and shrouded in misplaced anxieties. There is a tendency for protagonists to assume that 'their' service has a monopoly of genuine concern, care and understanding for clients in distress. Many attempts at communication have floundered because one or both parties have adopted a 'holier than thou' attitude. Some directors have followed the suggestion of Foren & Brown (1971) and appointed an assistant director with special responsibility for co-operation with voluntary bodies but a tremendous responsibility rests in the person of the director of social services to ease communication and placate groundless fears and anxieties. He must come to be seen not only as head of the local authority social services but also as a professional adviser to voluntary bodies in the locality. As such he will have a divided loyalty and may sometimes be tempted to influence voluntary organisations away from independent and vigorous policies to a subservient role under the local authority.

The statutory social services that we know today evolved from voluntary initiatives of the past. Great reformers and innovators have, through voluntary enterprise, demonstrated the value of new methods of helping those in need or, more commonly, shown that current practices are out of keeping with changing social values. In turn, the reformers have helped to mould public opinion and hastened the time when their views of what is just and what is desirable are accepted generally.

Social policies result from a continuing dialogue between public services and a host of voluntary organisations. Thus, ideas which are 'radical', 'advanced', or 'progressive' are incorporated into public policy and in their turn become old hat, to be scorned by succeeding generations of bright new reformers. Such is the history of the development of the social services in this country. We must continually examine the processes by which individual and corporate initiatives are formulated and make their impact if we are to anticipate some of the friction points in the new departments and understand how changes will be brought about in social policy.

References

Aves, G. (1969) *The Voluntary Worker in the Social Services.* Bedford Square Press, London.

Broady, M. (1972) *The Future of Voluntary Organisations.* Liverpool Personal Service Society, Liverpool.

Department of Health and Social Security (1972) *Intermediate Treatment.* HMSO, London.

Foren, R. & Brown, M. J. (1971) *Planning for Service.* Charles Knight, London.

Huws Jones, R. (1967) *The Functions and Preparation of Voluntary Workers in the Social Services.* (Conference Report.) National Council of Social Service, London.

Jones, D. (1969) *Community Involvement.* (Report of Centenary Conference.) Family Welfare Association, London.

Leaper, R. A. B. (1971) *Community Work.* National Council of Social Service, London.

Liverpool Personal Service Society (1969) *Welfare Benefits.* Liverpool Personal Service Society, Liverpool.

Murray, G. J. (1969) *Voluntary Organisations and Social Welfare.* Oliver & Boyd, Edinburgh.

Pridham, J. (1969) *The Volunteer in C.A.B.* National Council of Social Service, London.

Schools Council (1968) *Community Service and the Curriculum.* (Working Paper No. 17). HMSO, London.
Schorr, A. C. (1969) *Independence as a Function of the Agency.* (Report of Centenary Conference.) Family Welfare Association, London.
Shenfield, B. & Allen, I. (1972) 'The Organisation of Voluntary Service', *Polit. Econ. Planning*, 533.
Watts, N. (1972) 'Community in Action', *Munic. Publ. Services J.*, 80, 433.
Wootton, Baroness (1970) *Non-Custodial and Semi-Custodial Penalties* (Report of the Advisory Council on the Penal System). HMSO, London.
Younghusband, E. (1968) *Community Work and Social Change* (Report of Gulbenkian Study Group). Longman, Harlow, Essex.

9 *Health and the social services*

Robin Huws Jones

In the history of the social services there are periods of ferment in ideas and swift changes in administration. They may be splendid to look back upon ('bliss was it in those days to be alive') but they are often uncomfortable and perhaps painful to live through. Examples include the period round the Franco-Prussian war; the first decade of this century when the Webbs and their colleagues were producing plans for the break-up of the Poor Law and the mid-1940s when ideas (some of which had been gestating for decades) were suddenly recognised, welcomed, and passed into legislation.

We appear to be passing through a ferment, though a mild one, in the early years of this decade. The Local Authority Social Services Act became operative in 1971; local government (outside London) is to be radically recast and, also in 1974, the nation's health services are, after a quarter of a century, to be reorganised in the hope that this will produce one unified National Health Service. Although it will be entirely outside local government, the official claim is that this new health service will be better adapted to recognise and respond to the particular needs of the local population and that it will work closely with the local authority education, social services and housing departments. These important legislative changes do not stand alone. Since the Local Authority Social Services Act came into operation and before the new departments could get their machinery in running order, they have been called upon to meet fresh demands probably unparalleled in peacetime: the white paper on Better Services for the Mentally Handicapped, the 1969 Children and Young Persons Act, the Morris Act on chronically disabled people, and wider powers (and thus higher expectations) for helping the elderly. These are major operations, especially for a patient still convalescent after massive organ transplantation and still manifesting some rejection symptoms. R. A. Butler once described the Education Act of 1944 as 'a programme for a generation'. The Local Authority Social Services Act will, I hope, not take the whole of a generation, but no one could reasonably expect it to take much less than a quinquennium.

For many workers in these services one of the most painful changes is what they describe as the separation of the Health and Social Services. The Local Authority Social Services Act removed those personal social services which until 1971 were within the public health department, to the social services department. After 1974 the work of the medical officer of health will be transferred to the new National Health Service and it seems certain that, subject to a variety of 'safeguards', responsibility for social work in hospital will pass from the health authority to the local social services departments.

These changes have led to serious opposition and sometimes violent criticism from some members of the medical and nursing professions, from local authority members and also from some groups of social workers, especially those who work in hospitals. Of course there *are* grounds for complaint and it is right also to bring into the open anxiety about services to patients and their families during a transition period, though it is easy to overlook the patients who needed social work and other social services under the old regime and who failed to get them. There has also been a display of resentment in some quarters, for 'human nature is very prevalent'. There is, in particular, a tendency to attribute all the difficulties in collaboration between health and social services to 'Seebohm' and to the threat in the further separation that will follow local government reform, and to argue that these difficulties are new, or at least vastly worse than they were before the changes.

But—and this cannot be said too clearly—overall and with splendid exceptions, the record of collaboration between these services has not been distinguished by its closeness. Some even seem to query whether this collaboration is basically a good thing. A writer in *Nature* (McMichael 1971) challenged the recommendation in the Todd Report about the early teaching of behavioural and social sciences because it might dilute the doctor's competence in physical and functional illnesses. 'A sick society', says this writer, 'needs sociologists, but the individuals need doctors.' Let me confess my prejudice and say I believe that both may need both.

There is a weight of evidence that doctors fail to use the social services that their patients need and that are available for them. In the opinion of physicians who carried out one important study, many doctors were positively reluctant to suggest appropriate social services, thus indicating that they were not oriented towards them.

A recent and still unpublished study (Revans & Bacquer 1972) of co-ordination of services for the mentally handicapped, supported by the Hospital Centre, found small evidence of contacts between the various services, and the writers add—with how much irony I cannot say—that one possible explanation is that professionals do not see co-ordination as one of their important functions. The studies by the Queen's Institute of District Nursing (1966 & 1969) on collaboration between hospital, general practice and community services found little evidence of rational distribution of care between hospital and community services; communication between district nursing and general practice was, in one Queen's Institute report, described as minimal. A report by the National Institute for Social Work (Goldberg, Mortimer & Williams 1971) showed that old people in Southwark needed services many of which were actually available in the borough but the doctors failed to refer them to these services. Furthermore, the social workers in the borough often did not appreciate the simple medical needs of these old people and did not help them go for examination and treatment.

The need for collaboration is acute and growing. Almost every family doctor you talk to tells you that his regular and common jobs today and for the foreseeable future lie not so much in coping with dramatic episodes and people who are acutely ill but with long-term patients, people handicapped in mind or body, the aged infirm who will live on for a decade or more. It is helping people to live with situations—not just diseases—which will continue as part of their lives and this task calls for a team that includes a variety of fellow workers.

Sir George Godber is quoted as estimating that one-third of all patients in acute wards could be dealt with on an out-patient or day basis. In hospitals for the chronically ill or handicapped, the proportion who need not and should not be there is far higher. Nevertheless, the number of old people in hospitals for the mentally ill and handicapped has risen sharply over the last five years and is still rising. They are there because of our failure to match our policies to our aspiration; we have kept people alive without thinking enough about the sort of lives they are living. We have willed the end without providing the means; our investment is totally inadequate in home helps, sheltered housing, day care, hostels, residential homes, home nursing, in voluntary effort and in the positive encouragement of good neighbourliness.

This failure to establish a regular pattern of working together should not be attributed simply to the perversity of social workers or doctors, though doubtless both have their share of that characteristic. Collaboration is not—as we have misleadingly assumed—the easy, the natural, the obvious thing to happen. Co-operation doesn't just happen even within the branches of one profession, and problems of collaboration are not confined to health and social services. Basically the problem is one of departmentalism within ourselves and within our social institutions; it is a problem of loyalty which is raised to the point where virtue may become a vice. Some have raised the question of whether sharply separated professions are appropriate to contemporary society and whether perhaps families of professions are indicated instead.

Difficulties of collaboration may unintentionally be created by the ideals we uphold, the organisations we build, the styles of government we establish, and by the way we educate for the professions. We should therefore all welcome warmly the working party set up in the Department of Health and Social Security on collaboration between the new local authorities and the new health authorities. Its terms of reference are: to consider the need and scope for collaboration and co-ordination—including any factors likely to impede or prevent them—between the local authorities and the health authorities, both from the point of view of those receiving services and the public generally and in order to ensure the most effective and efficient use of staff, building, and other resources; and to make recommendations to the Government on these matters.

The setting up of this working party was in itself a momentous step; it meant that co-operation, in planning, in day-to-day work and in evaluation, was recognised as a problem to be understood and solved, not something to be achieved simply by exhortation, good intentions or assuming that 'everything will come all right in the long run'.

In this working party a group of experienced practitioners from all the services concerned (doctors, social workers and administrators) have met with representatives of central government to examine the difficulties in collaboration between the new regional and area health authorities on the one hand and the local authority social services departments on the other; especially the administrative machinery, the sharing of professional skills, and relations with the voluntary sector.

The recommendations coming from this working party are likely to be much more significant than their diplomatic and somewhat bland phrasing may suggest. They develop the theme, set out in the White Paper, that the health and social services should each rely on the other for the skills which each can best provide, social work skills being based in the local authorities and medical and nursing skills in the health authorities, each service having a statutory duty to support the other. There is even a hint that if either service finds that the support provided locally by the other is inadequate for it to fulfil its statutory duties, then it should exceptionally be able to recruit its own staff, the health service appointing social workers and the local authority employing doctors or nurses. In this way the projected joint consultative machinery would in the last resort have teeth as well as a bark.

The proposals urge that, to facilitate collaboration in day-to-day working and in planning, the operational boundaries should coincide as far as possible, National Health Services district boundaries following local government districts and local authority social service 'areas', so organised that an area team or a district group of area teams, matches each National Health Service district. Co-terminous boundaries (where they can be applied without violence to the convenience of people on the borders) should help a lot in simplifying contacts. I once asked the chairman of a medical group in a large hospital if he saw much of the director of the social services department. 'Which one?' he replied, 'we have twelve to work with.'

The proposed joint consultative committee will, it seems likely, be encouraged to ensure that the community resources of voluntary organisations and voluntary workers are mobilised to make their maximum contribution to health and the personal social services.

One cannot have co-operation without agreement on common objectives, or at least without clarity about where objectives differ. But these objectives are not always simple to state, partly because they are not confined to patients or clients. A survey published in *Community Medicine* confirmed that the major burden of caring for highly dependent people falls on the family, and that service for the family *as a unit* may be as important as services for the dependent patients themselves.

The terms of reference of the Department of Health and Social Security Working Party did not—could not—cover everything that is involved in removing obstacles and setting the scene for positive and creative collaboration. After 1974, what might be called 'the styles of government' of local authorities and health boards will be radically different. The health boards will consist of appointed members with no direct local accountability and with inevitable ambiguity about their responsibilities and powers. The elected member is above all locally responsible. The appointed body spends money which it does not have to raise, and cannot raise; the elected body can determine its own budget but it has to defend the rates it levies. These styles of government may not be irreconcilable, but their mutual impact has not been sufficiently explored. Interlocking membership is valuable, but we know the limits to this when it comes to the crunch of a conflict of interests, when for instance a hospital restricts the admission of severely handicapped patients because it is grossly overcrowded, and the local authority members know directly from their constituents of the agonising strain this may put on, for example, elderly parents of difficult mentally handicapped patients or on other children in a family.

Sir Keith Joseph, speaking as Secretary of State for Health and Social Services, has pointed out that though there have recently been substantial increases in expenditure in the health services, there is never enough money—and never likely to be—for everything that ideally requires to be done. Nor he adds, are there ever enough skilled men and women, despite considerable increases in recent years. This familiar comment applies with equal force to the present social services; almost by definition, there never can be enough resources, especially as better services create more demand.

Resources, of course, influence collaboration because they affect the adequacy and the dependability of the services that can be offered. Dr. Henry Miller in the Marsden Lecture for 1971 complained that nearly a quarter of our county boroughs still have made no special provision for housing the elderly and that nearly half our county councils provide less than fifty home helps per 100,000 of the population; he complains of a Treasury which, in his phrase, turns a wilfully blind eye to steeply rising social needs authenticated by incontestable demographic data.

In the city of Leicester, a report in 1972 published on the social services by a firm of management consultants (their words strangely carry more authority than the words of others, even though they say the same thing!) indicates that by 1976 Leicester should be spending more than four times as much on community mental health services as it spent in 1970. When it is impossible to meet needs, doctors—and the direct consumer—should be told why. Rationing is unavoidable; but if the rationale of rationing is not planned and explained it is much more likely to seem arbitrary and unfair.

The Department of Health and Social Security Working Party did not, as far as the writer knows, consider how financial structures can act as impediments or spurs to collaboration. It is not too much to say that the present pattern of finance acts as a powerful deterrent to co-operation. It makes it beneficial in the short run for one service to pass the buck and for others to resist it. This has arisen lately in connection with official proposals for better services for the mentally handicapped; a number of local authority members and officers saw these proposals as a way of passing to their care—without equivalent financial support—those who would otherwise be the responsibility of the centrally funded hospital services.

The same forces are at work, equally powerful and affecting even more people, in provision for old men and women who can no longer look after themselves. The readiness of local authorities to receive from hospital and into their care frail old people who need a high degree of social support must be affected by the fact that this not only adds greatly to the authority's capital and current expenditure, but relieves central government funds probably by an even greater amount, as hospital care is more costly. Yet tens of thousands of these old people, who do not require (or get) intensive medical or nursing care, should be living in appropriate housing in the community because this can ensure a livelier life for them and an economy of scarce resources for the nation as a whole. I was told not long ago of a local authority that was asked to adapt a patient's house so as to enable him to go home to die, and this was what he wanted. The work would have cost about £60 and the local authority decided against it as the man was likely to live only a few months. So he stayed in hospital where the gross cost at a moderate estimate exceeded £40 a week, and of course hospital treatment was denied to some other patient.

Moreover, the present financial system does not—at least so I gather—make easy the experiments in joint provision that might in fact benefit health authorities, the local authorities, the public and the patient or client. These joint experiments in running hostels, in day provision and joint appointments, are none the less taking place and growing; they are among the hopeful signs. They are still far too few and, in my experience, proposals for joint work of this kind are often greeted with icy politeness—one of the most impenetrable of barriers.

Even if it means we have fewer new co-operative ventures, however, I suggest that we should monitor and advertise those that are taking place including their weaknesses and failures so that we and others can learn from our experience—for example from health centres that are also centres for other social services, from the various ways of linking social services for hospitals in order to ensure continuity for patients as well as for hospitals, and this does not generally happen at present. A project that does involve monitoring is taking place, to choose one example, in the public health and social services departments of the Borough of Camden where a social worker is currently working with *two* large general practices, to learn how social work services can be provided economically in general practice. Other encouraging signs include the appointment by the London Hospital of a community services officer whose job, as I understand it, is to develop co-operation with general practice, local authority departments and voluntary organisations in the area served by the hospital.

The King Edward VII Fund's Hospital Centre has provided resources for a co-operative enterprise involving the Society of Medical Officers of Health, the Association of Directors of Social Services Departments and the National Institute for Social Work Training. These bodies decided to look for examples of effective collaboration between public health and social services departments, the growing points where new ways of meeting the needs of the public are being developed. When this material is analysed, it will form the basis of useful seminars, such as those already held between the Royal College of General Practice, public health nurses and workers in social services departments.

Given space it would be possible to reel off a sizeable shopping list of jobs that ought to be done together by the health and social services, not only because doing these jobs together would be an economy, but because this could yield the most complete and the most fertile results.

The difficulty of co-operation between the health and social services is only an illustration of the problem of co-operation between professions and even within professions. All professions (including social work) involve some conspiracy against the laity and all tend to become associations for spreading the doctrine of self-importance. Professions, especially the older ones, often assume they have quite special codes of ethics and this assumption may be used to justify a refusal to co-operate with others. Yet, as I see it, the ethical basis of all professions must be essentially the same; it is always a choice between alternatives, as illustrated by a medical friend who said that for him the touchstone was, are you only for the patient? 'If I'm satisfied you are', he said, 'then I'm likely to share confidential information; if not I won't share it, even if you are a doctor.' This is part of the dilemma: are we likely to help the patient best if we look at the problem only from his point of view, ignoring his family, his school or work-place and his neighbourhood, when the trouble is for example mental ill health or venereal disease? The answer cannot be easy.

The Seebohm Report (Committee on Local Authority and Allied Personal Social Services 1968) recognises the traditions which lead to present difficulties on confidentiality but argues that today serious problems are rarely dealt with by the individuals but by *teams*, and the work assumes that confidential information will be exchanged. 'A new code of practice is essential', says the Report, 'to meet the changing situation and we think the professions concerned should initiate discussions among themselves, and with members of the public, through which such a code could be formulated'. Discussions of this sort could well prove more influential than the formulation which emerges from them and they should therefore take place locally as well as between national bodies.

It has been said that responsibility for achieving the closest co-ordination among the clinical and social services will be the first task of the community physician of tomorrow; let me add that it should also be among the first responsibilities of the director of social services. Not only should these responsibilities be admitted and faced; the social services departments should leave colleagues in the health services no doubt of their concern, their interest in contributing and their anxiety to understand how the transitional period is creating difficulties, as it is said to be doing particularly in the field of mental disorders, including mental handicap.

I have said elsewhere that as a shoemaker I must affirm there is nothing like leather. We shall know each other's services better and use them more effectively when learning about other services is recognised as indispensable in professional education. This may, as the Todd Report of Medical Education (Royal Commission on Medical Education 1968) suggests, sometimes be achieved by classroom teaching provided in common with people training for other professions. But practice is learnt through practice; students (and even experienced practitioners) in all the helping professions have to acquire the habit of *using* the knowledge they gain about what other professions can contribute. This presumes an inbuilt inter-professional training which, so far as I am aware, no one has yet worked out, and it will not be easy to achieve this with the necessary economy of time and effort, with professional curricula bursting at the seams. We must also consider how the *continuing practice* of team work can be taught, not only in education that leads to professional qualifications but in the successive retooling operations now seen to be necessary in all professions. In other words, inter-professional practice must be rooted in a measure of inter-professional education and this calls for fresh work by appropriate teaching institutions in the health and social services.

Finally, collaboration is needed—as those in the social services departments know well—with other professions in addition to medicine and nursing. Education, housing, probation and the police all relate or should relate closely to the personal social services and a strategy of continuing co-operation is essential with these services also.

References

City of Leicester (1972) *Management Survey*. Leicester CC, Leicester.

Committee on Local Authority and Allied Personal Social Services (1968) *Report* (Chairman: F. Seebohm), Cmnd. 3703. HMSO, London.

Goldberg, E. M., Mortimer, A. & Williams, B. (1971) *Helping the Aged*. Allen and Unwin, London.

Jones, R. Huws, (1971) *The Doctor and the Social Services*. Athlone Press, London.

McMichael, J. (1971) 'Medicine in society', *Nature*, 9 July.

Miller, H. (1971) Marsden lecture delivered at Royal Free Hospital (unpublished).

Queen's Institute of District Nursing (1976) *Feeling the Pulse*. Queen's Institute of District Nursing, London.

Queen's Institute of District Nursing (1968) *Care in the Balance*. Queen's Institute of District Nursing, London.

Revans, R. & Baquer, A. (1972) *Coordination of Services for the Mentally Handicapped* (unpublished). Hospital Centre, 24 Nutford Place, London W1.

Royal Commission on Medical Education (1968) *Report* (Chairman: Lord Todd), Cmnd. 3569. HMSO, London.

10 *Community participation and the social services department*

Ken McDermott

If you cannot belong to someone, then to belong somewhere is the next best or the only thing left. 'To be?' is both the question and the problem. The basic issue confronting mankind today is the pace and complexity of growth and change. The development of technology is outpacing man's capacity to systematise a 'feedback' which can be swiftly quantified and put through educational processes whereby the vast mass of the people can be aware, informed and therefore capable of participating and sharing effectively in the direction of as well as in planning the forms and shapes of services required to produce congeniality of living, if not outright survival.

The enormous growth in the fields of discovery and invention, together with their by-products, has produced rapid and dramatic changes in life styles and expectations so that only those with the equipment can adapt, manage and manoeuvre in order to maintain or improve their situations. People who are ambitious and able are stretching out ahead of the vast mass of the people and, in the gap between the two groups, distrust and dissatisfaction are breeding. The results are isolation and alienation on personal and collective bases with the concomitants of powerlessness, deprivation and conflict.

This state of affairs, while present everywhere, is more serious in towns and cities, especially in the U.S.A., but latterly in Great

Britain. Until the time of the Industrial Revolution and indeed for some generations later, people still depended on local needs and cultures, and the process of evolution was slow. Experience, methods and means gradually accreted to meet dawning demands.

Kinship and township networks evolved accordingly in relatively easily assimilated fashions and some semblance of security in time and place prevailed. Change was imperceptible and not altogether comprehensible, and as a consequence, in this orderly scheme of things, the organs and servicing systems of Church and State had their positions and their relationships fixed in terms of appropriateness, authority and power.

However, industrialisation created urbanisation by which man's original place in this scheme became disturbed, and this disturbance has increased as needs and demands have increased both in number and sophistication.

The original role of the village as a self-sustaining community had been incorporated into the township concept as a means of communication, marketing and protection. Indigenous communities and cultures survived or gradually intermarried and a common community identity developed where slow, settled, barely shifting norms and controls produced socially acceptable standards of propriety and performance.

This base was steadily eroded throughout the nineteenth century when the teeming townships were swollen to bursting point. Speedy adaptation at a personal and physical level became necessary. Dickens and Hogarth clearly and painfully portrayed the price of personal frailty, professional folly and political indifference.

Despite, or perhaps because of, the adverse circumstances, kinship and community networks grew and sustained the individual, without which survival would have been well nigh impossible. Opportunity for mobility, upward and outward, was severely restricted and so, tight and often taut, family fabric unfolded. Its spread was across a small geographical area encompassing and overlapping, promoting resourcefulness and filling gaps in meeting or modifying the effects of want.

The family, as an institution, grew in size and capacity, to meet the basic needs of its members, as it has done so often in the evolutionary process; but the conditions conducive to such development have as their corollary the need for change in proportion to the pressure of such circumstances. These circumstances were, as they invariably are, of a totally adverse if not alien nature.

These circumstances, these pressures, in the forms of poverty, disease, overcrowding and community strife, required political solutions which were only slowly and partially achieved. In large measure this was due to those holding the power to affect change being so insulated against the pain of the immediate problems that their reaction was often belated, and often inappropriate. The problem had moved ahead of the solution. The institutions responsible for service changed, and became remote from the society they were there to serve. They were out of step; in fact, as time went on their ability to grasp the real problems diminished. Since the last war particularly, they are regarded by the citizens as being unhelpful or irrelevant to their needs and aspirations.

Throughout this time, quite naturally, other significant changes were taking place, the implications and impact of which are being felt acutely by the present generation. Two changing attitudes that have affected the roles, communication and the performance of all institutions, from the family to Church and State, are attitudes towards authority and leadership and towards female emancipation.

Many, if not all, the organs of state derive their authority from the function enacted by the early Church of Christendom. The influence of the Church in respect of who plays what role with what duties and power vested in that role, especially within the family structure, is still discernible in communities within and without the British Isles.

The claims and teachings of Darwin, Freud, and the Abbi Mendel dealt body blows from which all institutions are still suffering today. The origins of man, his motivation and behaviour, together with his genetic make-up, were vital areas which hitherto had been regarded with a simplicity which made for comparatively clear-cut decisions and responses. The questions, uncertainties and disaffections which have ensued have made decision-making, the capacity to command, the ability to lead and indeed to follow the more difficult and hazardous on the one hand, but, possibly, the more just and satisfying on the other.

They are slowly emancipating man from the bondage of the rigid and the ritualistic exercises where ceremonial trappings consume the interest and resources which nowadays are being gradually transformed into more practical and demonstrable expressions of concern.

Nevertheless the effect upon all institutions, and these include settlements as small as a tenement block to groups as small as a street-corner gang, is only gradually being appreciated and understood as part of evolutionary development. Those who interpret and enact authority as well as those who react or respond to it no longer share the same basic belief or motivation. The days of delineated roles springing from a well-defined place in an ordered scheme of things no longer prevail, and in the absence of role-definition, communication breaks down and confusion follows.

As this state of affairs was emerging another fundamental crack appeared in society's primary structure, the family, which was to spread widely; the emancipation of woman. Her change of role has meant readjustments at all levels of society where meeting her needs and aspirations has affected still further the shape of authority in what was originally a man's world. The roles of both sexes, inside and outside the home, have undergone quite dramatic change. The behaviour of spouses and children towards each other and towards those with whom they relate has meant shifts of emphasis and often complete changes of role, which institutions of all kinds have been ill-equipped or unprepared to meet and match.

The need for change in the presence of change is not always consciously considered and, even if it is, the difficulty of the prospect is often a limiting factor. The natural conflict inherent in change is played down or avoided and the general aim of a painless stability with its built-in obsolescence is pursued. One of the basic sources of trouble and causes for alarm is the unwillingness or inability of existing social institutions to adjust to present realities. 'The art of progress is to preserve order amid change and to preserve change amid order.'

In this process we should seek to conserve what is good and change what is not, and recognise that harmony consists of opposing tensions. 'Inter-action between opposites is essential to the evolutionary process which, if understood, many contradictions will be transformed into complementaries and humanity will accelerate human evolution.'

Taking risks and making mistakes must become more acceptable otherwise information, and lessons from which valuable conclusions could be drawn, will be lost. Strategies should seek to avoid the pitfalls of Utopia and consensus.

But how to recognise and adapt to changing realities is the issue confronting all types of social institutions. The peddling of panaceas, political and otherwise, has made deception a way of life. It is an illusion that technical and professional expertise is matched by political and economic capacity to take curative and preventive action. Much of what is done or attempted is based on short-sighted attitudes which produce 'structured poverty and not cultural richness'.

Despite the ignorance and apathy within the social institutions, there was the occasional insight. For example, a far-sighted civil servant, Derek Morrell, was the inspiration behind the Government's Community Development Project. He recognised in the 'race from the cities' which had been taking place for a generation the breakdown of community, the loss of responsibility that one human being should have for another and the failure of institutional policies to come to terms with fundamental changes in society's structure. He persuaded his Government colleagues that by sinking 'probes' into a variety of community settings, an intelligence service could be established whereby feelings (which are as important as facts) might be sounded out, and an appreciation gleaned of the reality of life. He contended that to give 'relief' by producing 'more of the same' was the policy of the bankrupt and that only by a conscious and careful discrimination in favour of the deprived would equilibrium, trust, and confidence be restored to the lost and the alienated. His sudden death late in 1969 robbed the Project of its spearhead and advocate.

None the less, his commitment and compassion had converted many to his sensitive and far-sighted policies. His intention had been to instigate an experiment with national coverage where the laboratories would be twelve geographically different but socially similar environmental areas. The chemical agent would be an action team working within the community and involving itself at the same time with all institutions, statutory and voluntary, clerical and lay. The entire Project was supposed to have been underpinned by research from its inception. It would have been helpful to have had research from the beginning but, as it turned out, the acquisition and harnessing of research teams to the action teams proved much more difficult than could reasonably have been anticipated.

There was a surprising dearth of suitable research talent, at least within the price range laid down. This, together with the novelty of the proposed action, the researchers' unwillingness to become closely involved, and university commitments, contributed to delays which meant that by the time research was 'on the scene' the action teams on the first projects at Liverpool and Coventry had already embarked upon their role of change-agent.

Overall research plans centred upon Southampton University under the direction of Professor John Greve. His was, and is, the unenviable task of trying to muster scarce resources and relate them effectively to an ever-changing and not infrequently discordant set of widely differing social, political and professional circumstances. To provide succour, security, intelligence and direction to his teams and at the same time to interpret and to inform those to whom he was accountable, as well as the much larger 'public interest' group, is a burden few of us would wish to shoulder.

The stated objectives of the Community Development Project are:

1. *Needs and aspirations*
   To study the needs and aspirations of people suffering social deprivation; to help them to find ways of meeting their needs and aspirations.
2. *Community development*
   To help people exercise increased control over their lives, including enlarging their opportunities in directions which they themselves see as desirable, to reduce their dependence on the various social services, while also enabling them to use them more effectively.
3. *Services response*
   To increase the capacity of the relevant services to respond to both needs and aspirations more effectively, by a better understanding of the causes of need and by providing help which is more acceptable, intelligible and lasting in its effect.
4. *Social planning*
   To develop hypotheses about the causes of, and solutions to, social deprivation and through further testing of these hypotheses to develop criteria for allocating resources to meet such needs.

As already intimated, undertaking these objectives required research and analysis if a planned action based on realistic indices was to be measured as to its effectiveness and be repeated elsewhere.

It is the fundamental aim of the operation to illuminate the locale, test out the action, feed back the consequences, and thus influence social policy at national and local levels. The difference and distances between theory and practice became, quickly and painfully, apparent.

Over the past twenty years, it has become evident to workers of all disciplines, who are familiar with conditions of the under-privileged in our towns and cities, that failure to take account of surrounding circumstances produces a scandalous waste of precious resources. To concentrate solely on individual treatment or personal attention without reference to the adverse environmental forces amounts to professional myopia at best, or at worst fraud and injustice.

It is the responsibility of all those professionally concerned with people suffering from the effects of social malaise to employ the knowledge which they have acquired to alleviate the conditions which contribute to social breakdown.

Those engaged in professional social service of one kind or another, whether policemen or priests, teachers or social workers, have discovered that the process of isolating individuals from their social context for specific treatment is often futile and frustrating on both sides.

It is not suggested that there is no place for the one-to-one therapeutic encounter, but it must be employed on a far more selective basis. The resources so released would permit a specific part of the workload to be devoted to ameliorating those social circumstances, the inimical impact of which offsets whatever benefits are sought by this form of treatment.

Whether the worker should formally structure his strategy in the fashion, or whether his agency should permit or advocate such an approach, raises questions which have been mulled over these past few years, though as yet there has been little evidence of any serious answers. There is ample evidence, however, of the conflict that such considerations promote.

In the early sixties in Liverpool a groundswell of community interest slowly developed, which eased its way across the city and subsided, towards the end of the sixties, leaving behind a loosely co-ordinated system of community enterprises centred upon the Liverpool Council of Social Service. A lattice-work of community groups stretched across the face of the city, whose original spontaneity had taken on a semblance of organisation, the potential of which has yet to be fully recognised and explored.

This movement was started by a few professional groups who felt that their professional service was too limited, and wanted to share ideas and information with city members, in districts in which they worked, where, out of mutual concern, some means could be devised upon which trust, co-operation and change might ensue.

None initially was aware of the concept of community development, nor did any have knowledge of what had been attempted elsewhere. They wanted to start a movement which would gain its legitimacy from the sincerity and fidelity with which views were projected that sprang from the people who were the recipients, the consumers, of their varied professional services.

It was against this background that the Community Development Project was launched late in 1969. The area selected by the City Council bore all the signs of acute deprivation.

Their decision was, in great measure, influenced by a recent report by the City Planning Officer, Francis J. C. Amos (1970). This was a study in social malaise, where, with the co-operation of other Chief Officers and interested agencies, a list of statistical indices was compiled which reflected many aspects of the social problems of the city. It was hoped that the study would help to guide the allocation of social service resources and the establishment of community development programmes. Its aims were stated thus in the introduction:

> In order to achieve the basic objective the study can be conveniently divided into two major elements. First by noting areas where there is a high incidence of social malaise statistics, it is possible to select areas of special social need, that is, areas where the present deficiencies might be remedied by an influx of extra physical and social resources along the lines suggested in the 'Seebohm' Report.
>
> Second, the Study explores the interaction between the social malaise indices themselves, and the census indices, on a city-wide basis. This enables certain key factors (e.g. possession orders) to be isolated, which can be used to predict the occurrence of other forms of social malaise; it demonstrates the close relationships that exist between different social problems, assisting in the co-ordination of social service agencies and providing background material for caseworkers; and, finally, it traces the influence of housing and economic factors on the distribution of problem areas, pointing to forms of aid not usually within the sphere of social service agencies.

The publicity given to the launching of the Community Development Project engendered expectations and suspicions to an alarming degree inside and outside the projected area. A rumour had been spread that as this was an attempt to discriminate in favour of the deprived, a vast amount of cash was lying somewhere waiting to be tapped. Quite understandably, there were other similar areas and many smaller pockets of poverty who were pained at being denied access to this resource. However, the worst of these could not muster the required amount or stability of population while the presence of the E.P.A. and S.N.A.P. (Shelter) Projects elsewhere in the City were held to be complicating elements in an enterprise which was supposed to 'start from cold' and be 'researched' all the way.

The Project's offices were located in the Liverpool Corporation's Town Clerk's Department and despite the uncertainty of what C.D.P. might really be about, it would be petty indeed to be critical of the co-operation received, while the sympathy extended at both personal and professional level was a continual source of strength and encouragement.

Funding was on a shared basis between the Local Authority and the Home Office under the auspices of the Urban Aid Programme, while professional accountability was directly and immediately to the Deputy Town Clerk, Mr. Alfred Stocks. His ability and reputation is such that his 'presence' was a key factor in the new project, while his supporting staff's knowledge of the ways of bureaucratic men and their procedures prevented many pitfalls and provided access points to aid and information.

Mr. John Banks, Principal, Home Office, was in overall charge of the national programme. His wide experience and ability to get on with people made his leadership heartening during the crucial early days when expertise was at a premium and natural conflicts at their height. An advisory group was set up at the Home Office to consider day-to-day possibilities and practice. Expert and keen to assist though its members were, the primary social problems, their recognition and the form of response, could only be gauged by perambulating the streets day and night and meeting the residents singly or in groups. Consequently the first months were spent in trying to establish, with some precision, those issues upon which to build some action programmes and upon which, therefore, an overall strategy could be devised at local and national level.

The original aim to describe and then assess the selected area proved difficult and time-consuming. The need to establish and maintain mutual trust was felt, but the Project Team was greatly assisted by Planning Department whose officials produced substantial data.

Although the residents were deprived of services and adequate social conditions which many of their neighbours took for granted, they were none the less blessed with indigenous intelligence and leadership which quickly sought to evaluate this Project, a word which in itself meant nothing, but quite probably stood for some kind of well-meant imposition in which they would, as usual, have little influence and less understanding, and from which 'somebody would get a thesis'.

Just prior to my appointment in November 1969 as Project Director, I attended a public meeting held within the Project area, at which reference to the new Project was being made by the only community association, the Scotland Road Residents' Association. The basic purpose of the meeting was to provide an opportunity for the local people to express themselves to the local politicians. and professionals about recent violence and vandalism. More than five hundred people assembled in a well-appointed school hall—over one-third of the audience were men—and for over two hours there were many heartfelt exchanges between 'them' and 'us'. It was a graphic demonstration of both problem clusters and growth potential, where helplessness in the face of institutional irrelevance was underlying much of the sentiment expressed.

The schools were blamed for contributing to the permissive society, in that they were not strict enough; the police criticised for 'pandering' about in cars instead of on foot; the priest criticised himself for organising bingo which attracted the parents whom he, in turn, criticised for not ensuring oversight for their children; the politicians were castigated for their inability to provide protection against the vandals, deteriorating physical conditions, traffic problems etc.; while the politicians railed against the systems, of which they were part, for their insensitivity and lack of response to their attempts to reflect local pressures.

Every institution and agency was mentioned in one way or another, but interestingly there was no comment at all about the personal social services. They did not appear to figure at all in the residents' way of life. The police were blamed less, as one of the three officers representing the Force was required to render resuscitation to some of those present, while one of the absentee members of the local patrol was at that time on the danger list in a nearby hospital having been savagely beaten the night before outside the hall in which this meeting was taking place.

The local superintendent had already addressed the meeting on local police policy and, with seeming justification, asserted that there were people present who had witnessed the episode. However, the fact that he took the opportunity to ask for witnesses to come forward, while understandable and appropriate enough in one social context, only served to demonstrate the failure to understand the implications of such a request in that milieu.

The failure to respond to this request from the police was condemned as apathy and indifference. This is a label often affixed to such communities when the truth is that persistent disillusionment, repeated and futile attempts to affect change, have bred the feeling of helplessness in the face of all-knowing and all powerful 'them'. People were resigned, and muttered, with arms outstretched, 'what's the use?' and 'we're cannon fodder in war and factory fodder in peace'. Shafts of humour, however, relieved the scene and eased the tensions. Wisdom born of brutal experience was discernible, a sense of belonging and the remnants of kinship networks were evident, and a genuine sense of concern was shared by all. But, as with many big meetings, something practical was missing. Prominent speakers, obvious spokesmen for special interest groups, ideas and complaints went unrecorded. Opportunities for future action organisation poured out through the doors at the end. This was no fault of the local organisers, only a handful, whose resourcefulness was not matched with the necessary resources. It was a lesson, and a lesson needing a deal of repetition before it was hammered home, that preparation, commitment and 'after-care' were required if the people were to acquire confidence in their capacity to exercise influence over local circumstances.

The list of issues and complaints was painfully similar to that which could be drawn up in any so-called deprived community which is part of any substantial conurbation in the greater part of the western hemisphere.

The difference here is that there may yet be time upon which to build some constructive compensatory models which are rooted in the reality of the community, whose needs they are there to meet. This, of course, is conditional upon the community's fundamental qualities being recognised and organised, most importantly of all, by the community itself. Enabling the community to do this was the Project's raison d'être.

As the strategic aim was a renewal of relationships between institutions and the needs of those they were to serve, it meant a change in the established order of relationships between the people, the 'professionals' who provide the services and the politicians whose function it is to provide the policies and the resources. To simplify a little, this requires approaches along the three levels of people, professionals and politicians as well as the vertical considerations of policy and its implementation through the management and allocation of resources.

An obvious problem in casework is to avoid initial entanglements in family circumstances with those who might inhibit future developments. Dealing with the self-appointed 'saviours' in the early stages of involvement with the community demands insight and skill while concerning oneself with the sensitivities and legitimacy of any organisations already operating within the area delineated.

An assessment as to how the patient (community) came to be in the condition that he is in, is a prerequisite which also entails collating social and demographic data, highlighted by 'pictures' drawn from life by the residents upon how they see and feel about their personal and physical circumstances. Through a process of street-by-street and block-by-block involvement, concentrating on issues raised by the residents themselves, the framework of district organisation evolves, from which are drawn representatives to form an area council, upon which sit the professionals and politicians who serve the area. Here the implications, political, managerial and otherwise, of the more localised casework is taken up from which the conclusion might be drawn that a mini-Whitehall/Town Hall establishment is required to respond with alacrity, appropriateness and comprehensiveness to the multi-problem nature of many of the issues.

Whether seeking to achieve this aim at the localised level of immediacy will ever bear fruit is a moot point; it is possible that if communications between the people and the services become more open, the objective will be modified in the light of changing demands and could therefore ultimately be very different from the one which was originally devised.

Putting this kind of plan into practice makes an 'informing' or educational input necessary, so that those involved can appreciate that the process rather than the product is the vital element. It is just as vital, perhaps even more vital at first to establish confidence in the team. This comes about through their responses to the obvious difficulties of the residents in their day-to-day life. Part of the team's workload has to be set aside to resolving the difficult problems of planning, housing, house repair, pollution, protection etc., which in themselves provide information and experience upon which to build relationships, special interest groups and links between professional agencies.

As well as activating group interest at street and then district levels, this development helps to channel expression in a variety of forms. Among those employed have been producing a community newspaper as professionally as possible; promoting individual and group connections with servicing agents both voluntary and statutory; establishing an information centre; creating an accessible, comprehensive servicing centre at local level with the management shared between political, professional and community representatives; suggesting the idea of a Community school by demonstrating in the area the results and kits produced by the nearby E.P.A. project; harnessing local industrial and commercial interests; and involving the local university and W.E.A.

At the same time, but ideally beforehand, the professional and political levels would have been at least informed, if not sensitised, agencies, and especially local and central government departments, to these community developments. The political implications of local managerial models of community-rooted multi-departmental servicing have yet to be seriously considered, while the problems that such an enterprise poses for decision-making will be the subject of research as, of course, is all else attempted within the Project.

Preparing local authority administration for the upward thrust of an informed community demands some re-education. Pressure means politics and to employees of statutory agencies, whether directly or indirectly concerned, this unavoidably produces changes in attitude and roles and disruption in communication.

When a community group asks the professional responsible for implementing policy to join them in discussion at street level about the problems involved, how is the professional prepared for the encounter? Where is the data bank upon which he draws his information? To whom does he return to advise of the results and feelings expressed in the discussion? How is the experience regarded, employed and fed-about the bureaucratic system so that the next or other encounters proceed along a graph of increasing skill, success or satisfaction? Problem areas lie in personal differences in perception, because of origins, experience and function; in distances, geographical and otherwise, between bureaucratic departments; between different departmental philosophies, objectives, time-scales and priorities; and in administrative boundaries and party political influences.

It is nevertheless slowly becoming apparent that information and knowledge, broken down into readily assimilated and employable forms, produce a power shift from the centre to the periphery. The recognition by all is that, because of this, disequilibrium is the norm rather than the fashion and that the inevitable dynamic prohibits the settled and static shape of institutional response. This should mean that change, conservation and innovation are accepted as the process through which participation, relevance and usefulness take the place of alienation, irrelevance and decay.

Lately, the social services department has arrived on the local government scene. A great deal has been written about how to structure this new department so that old problems can be tackled in new or different ways and prevention rather than palliative approaches can be a fundamental and practical aim.

To deliberate upon structure without considering its philosophical base suggests that the workers are in danger of slipping into ritualistic postures, if only as a defence against coping with strange and inordinate demands upon their meagre resources. If the social services department's primary concern is in the field of relationships and what was once termed Christian charity, then all the social and physical factors which prevent people from achieving a satisfactory way of life are within its scope. If, for instance, pollution contributes conditions which cause bronchitis and the elderly become infirm before their time, the objectives and resources of the department are affected; the Elderly Persons' Home becomes more like a hospital, or family situations are impaired, and the shape of community care consequently undergoes change.

It is therefore inappropriate for the social services department to concentrate upon established practice and classical casework method and to ignore the effects upon their charges of environmental factors which influence health or behaviour. To inform and to influence policy, to administer resources with flexibility, sensitivity and success means that good communication must be established both inside and outside the department. It is painfully obvious that problems are presenting themselves faster than solutions can be found. It is just as obvious that the department can never command the resources to match its ever-changing and increasingly complex responsibilities. The solution lies in deepening its involvement with the community, while at the same time participating with the people and their political counterparts in forms of service which release and redistribute resource, opportunity and choice and thereby emancipate the deprived from the dependence upon which they have been nurtured.

References

Amos, F. J. C. (1970) *Social Malaise in Liverpool.* Liverpool Corporation, Liverpool.

11 The relief function

François Lafitte

Social services are devices for enabling people to satisfy certain socially recognised needs. Some of those needs (food, clothing) are normally satisfied by individual purchase. In these instances the primary social service function is to provide the individual with money or its equivalent—*cash welfare*—when his own resources are, or are presumed to be, deficient. There are other needs (education, medical care) which people are no longer normally expected to satisfy by purchase. In these cases the primary social service function is to meet the need directly—*service welfare*—with the corollary that any financial impediment to use of the service (such as a charge) must be removed in case of hardship.

In a welfare state attention to people's financial needs is as evident in its taking away processes (the spreading of sacrifices) as in its handing out processes (the making of social payments). Differential income taxation, rating relief for a low-income household, the waiving of a school dinner or a denture charge are as much a part of cash welfare as are family allowances, family income supplements, student grants, rent allowances, pensions or free bus rides for old people.

Cash welfare

In the whole field of cash welfare the key policy issue is to settle the conditions on which members of the community agree to help one another financially. The answers the British people have evolved during the twentieth century hinge broadly on a distinction between what is appropriate when men are unable or not expected to support themselves by work and what is appropriate when they are earning but none the less possibly in hardship.

When the primary purpose is to supply income (or reduce costs) for people in non-work situations, we prefer the *benefit* approach—systems of payment (public or occupational) at fixed rates (flat or earnings-related) given on *presumption* of need as indicated by non-financial criteria (registered unemployment, retirement, support of children), with which we couple various charge exemptions (non-taxation of sickness benefit, excusal from N.I. contributions). When the primary purpose is income-enlargement or income-reduction among people who are normally at work and self-supporting, we prefer the *relief* approach—systems of payment, charging or taxing at variable rates after *ascertainment* of actual needs and resources. We tend to think it unreasonable to expect the neighbours of a man in full-time work to help him pay his rent, or to support his son in care or at a university, or to let him off part of his rates or income tax, unless he can in some sense show hardship.

We apply these preferences in no very consistent manner; and fashions fluctuate between emphasising the benefit or the relief approach, particularly in the matter of child-related adjustments of income. But, however far we may eventually pursue the benefit approach, it will not be possible wholly to dispense with a *relief function*, however residual, located somewhere in the pattern of social services.* And, however far we move in the direction of legally enforceable *rights* to relief, no hardship-relieving service can be fully effective without an element of discretion in the payments it makes.†

Cash and service welfare divorced

Should social work be dispersed among an array of specialised social services—medical, educational, housing, income-support—

* The British Association of Social Workers, no lover of means tests, concedes that 'no Bill concerned with the economics of housing only could remove the need for special help for those with inadequate incomes. We therefore welcome with reservations the Bill's proposals to extend rent rebates and introduce rent allowances' (B.A.S.W. 1972).

† 'The Supplementary Benefits scheme is a combination of specific entitlements and discretionary powers. There are some who argue that such powers are in themselves undesirable. I do not share this view nor do I understand how any social worker can uphold it. For the discretionary powers give the possibility of meeting unique and complex individual situations—they are a concrete proof of the acceptance of the need for individualisation' (Stevenson 1970).

each of which requires a welfare component to fulfil its main task, or should social work be divorced from them to become a specialised service in its own right, cohabiting with the other specialised services as an equal partner? Should cash welfare be similarly dispersed or should it be administratively divorced from service welfare? If divorced, should the divorce be complete? Should financial provisions based on the relief approach be managed together with or separately from those based on the benefit approach? Should relief functions be detached from service welfare functions? Should they be located in one service or in several? In central or in local government? What kind of people should exercise them, particularly when discretionary powers are involved—elected committees, clerks, administrators, teachers, doctors, health visitors, social workers? We have been debating these questions for some seventy years. When the debate began, elementary schooling apart, publicly provided cash welfare and service welfare were run together at a primitive level as a single set of local rate-financed Poor Law services, supplemented by grant-aided charities; and the protagonists in the Royal Commission on the Poor Laws, 1905–9, had no thought of separating cash from service, still less (save for employment and unemployment services) of removing either from local government.

The Commission's Socialist minority favoured a comprehensive system of municipal social services (education and child care, health, asylums, housing, welfare of the aged), each available to all citizens, each giving *both* cash payments and skilled service or special facilities. Many of these services would charge users according to their means, but the 'odious pecuniary inquiries' involved would be handled separately by a special local authority agency working through area offices. To all this the Commission's Conservative majority retorted (Royal Commission on the Poor Laws & Relief of Distress 1909, vol. 2, pp. 196–7):

> The question at issue is whether the work of maintaining those members of the community who have lost their economic independence can be safely entrusted to authorities whose primary duty is something quite distinct—such as that of Education or Sanitation. . . . We consider that the many and subtle problems associated with Public Assistance, especially when it is a family rather than an individual that requires rehabilitation, cannot be solved by the simple process of sending off each unit to a separate authority. . . . What is needed is a disinterested

> authority, practised in looking at all sides of a question, and able to call in skilled assistance. The specialist is apt to see only what interests him in the first instance and to disregard wider issues.

The language is different but the thought might have come straight from the Seebohm Report—with the difference that our new social services departments are shorn of the primary cash welfare functions which the majority of 1909 would have vested in them. For at the very time when Conservatives and Socialists sponsored their rival models for a local government welfare state, the Liberals in power initiated that process of nationalising key social service functions which has since been carried further by all political parties. The central government sector today comprises primary payments for the relief of poverty, virtually all (non-means-tested) benefit payments, employment services, the bulk of medical care, legal aid and advice. (It also bears a large share of the cost of social services which are provided by local government.)

For numerous reasons local government, social servants and social workers like this divorce of cash welfare from service welfare. It has shifted social payments from rates to taxes.* It encourages workers in health, education, housing, welfare and kindred services to concentrate on their special jobs—giving people advice, treatment, facilities, special kinds of care—in the belief that some other service will look after the incomes of any of their clients who happen to be in financial need. As to social workers, nearly all probably shared the view voiced by T. H. Marshall (1965, p. 84) on the final nationalisation of assistance in 1948:

> Relief in cash was shifted from the rates to the taxes. . . . The ancient tradition of the Western world that the relief of the poor was the affair of their neighbours was brought to an end. . . . Cash benefits were . . . sharply separated from personal services . . . The way was open for the development of modern welfare services, offered to all who needed them and free from any flavour of charity or taint of pauperism. But the taint remained obstinately clinging to the National Assistance Board. Should we say that it was sacrificed in order that the welfare services might be born free of original sin?

* One of the Greater London Council's objections to the Heath Government's rent assistance scheme is that a quarter of the cost will fall on the rates, whereas 'we consider that relief of poverty . . . is a matter for central rather than local Government' (GLC 1971).

An entirely new welfare service, the children's service, was created with virtually no relief functions at all, until in 1963 children authorities were empowered, if they thought fit, in certain circumstances to make 'provision for giving assistance in kind, or, in exceptional circumstances, in cash' (Children and Young Persons Act 1963). How strongly we are attached to preserving the divorce of cash from welfare is illustrated by a recent inquiry into the response of four children's departments to this new power. Heywood & Allen (1963) found:

(1) That 'many social workers and social administrators had no previous experience or theory to guide them about dispensing money'.
(2) That 'discussion of this whole subject was often painful', because 'many social workers believed that dealing in cash confused their role' or held 'that giving financial aid was not compatible with case work help'.
(3) But that, 'when money had to be refused, workers almost invariably offered some alternative help, such as referral to another agency'.

So policy is in a dilemma. As Olive Stevenson (1970) says, 'we have this split between "money giving" and social work and yet we know that individuals' financial, social and emotional problems are sometimes inseparable'. The central services which relieve poverty are well placed to discover needs which require something more than a cash payment and to undertake social work, but are virtually forbidden to do so.* The local welfare services are well placed to discover financial needs and problems which could be eased by money payments. But their money-awarding functions are limited. Many of their workers do not wish to have those functions extended, and would prefer other departments, not the social services department, to exercise the main relief functions which remain in local government.

The relief function in local government

Nationalisation of relief is far from complete. Of the 43 major means-testing systems in current use (Wilmott 1972), the majority

* In dealing with the Supplementary Benefits Commission's more difficult cases, say Heywood & Allen, 'there is invariably an element of social work diagnosis . . . as the SBC now recognises, "welfare" is not peripheral to its primary function of providing financial assistance to meet requirement but an integral part of the job of "getting the money right" ' (Heywood & Allen 1971).

are applied in local government services, and a majority of these probably by social services departments. Local government relief functions are being extended. Recent additions include assistance under Section 1 of the 1963 Children and Young Persons Act, rating relief on grounds of low income, remission of charges for contraceptive advice and supplies, various provisions of the Chronically Sick and Disabled Persons Act, 1970, and the new system of rent rebates and allowances. Local government cash welfare functions now include: (1) the granting of regular income or its equivalent (child fostering payments, free school dinners, support of pupils over 16 and of students, rent rebates and allowances); (2) the varying of charges according to means (rate rebates, children or old persons in residential homes, families in temporary accommodation, day nurseries, home help, mobile meals, chiropody); and (3) ad hoc grants (for school clothing, for keeping children out of public care, to help chronically sick or disabled persons).

So the local authority as a whole has a problem, seen at its simplest where the same council is responsible for housing as well as for personal services, education and (for the time being) some aspects of health: how best to organise its exercise of these relief functions? And its social services department has a problem: what should be its own contribution to the relief function? The relief function has five components:

(1) Determining standards of support or aid: what is the reasonable support standard for a child boarded out, kept at school beyond 16, studying at a university?

(2) Determining the level of charges for services not given free—price determination: what is the reasonable charge for a council dwelling, temporary accommodation, hostel residence, home help, a school meal?

(3) Determining standards of personal contribution: how much of the cost of support or of a charge should be borne by a family or person of a given type, with given resources and given needs or commitments?

(4) Investigating clients' financial resources and determining eligibility ('means-testing').

(5) Making the payments or collecting the charges.

The first three are policy functions. Policy enters into the fourth if discretion is allowed. Not all the policy decisions are within the council's own control. National rules govern mandatory student grants, the rate rebate scheme, and the main features of rent assistance and school dinner charging, while the 'fair rents' of council dwellings are fixed by independent quasi-judicial agencies.

But in other respects a local authority may settle its own policy. Thus in exercising its relief functions under the Education Act —providing aid 'for the purpose of enabling pupils to take advantage without hardship to themselves and their parents of any educational facilities available to them'—a council is (save for mandatory student grants) left free to decide for itself how it will define 'hardship'. The remarkable variation from place to place in the standards applied by different councils—especially in the matter of support for pupils above compulsory age—suggests that many local authorities do not think seriously about the notion of 'hardship'. In addition, there may be no consistency of thought about hardship between different departments of the same local authority. The same authority may apply inconsistent standards to aid to pupils under and over 16; to discretionary student grants; to foster payments; to charging for contraceptive services, home help, day nurseries, mobile meals, support of a child in care.

Should not a council have a consistent policy—common principles, standards, procedures—for all aspects of relief within its control? Will that come about so long as cash welfare policy and administration are largely parcelled out among the departments concerned with specific services, or shared between them and the treasurer's department and the finance committee? The expertise required in cash welfare is not specific to a health, an education, a housing or a treasurer's department. It is social. It is concerned with poverty, with relative deprivation, with minimum living standards and other aspects of social policy; and the experts in these matters are, or should be, in the social services department. Should not the council be looking to that department and its committee for advice and initiative in all such questions? If it wants to decide whether to modify (within the limits permitted) the Government's model scheme for rent allowances, would it expect its housing committee, or its finance committee, or its social services committee to argue an informed case, say, for more generous provision for single-parent families or one-person households? Is the education or the social services department better qualified to suggest standards for educational maintenance allowances or school clothing grants?

Is welfare divisible?

Relief administration is not altogether separable from responsibility for relief policy. Is administration of relief—financial assessment, deciding eligibility, exercising discretion—better handled by each department separately as an incidental function arising out of its main duties, or better vested in one department acting on behalf of all the council's services? As things are in many places, a family helped by the social services department may simultaneously, or within a short time, receive or deserve to receive attention from the treasurer's department (rate relief), housing department (rent allowance) and the education department (clothing grant, remission of school dinner charge)—not to mention several services outside local government. Would it not make sense to transfer administrative responsibility for some or all of these other local government relief functions to the social services department? If, as already in some places, that department can handle school welfare within the compulsory age range, could it not also handle educational maintenance allowances at the higher ages? Is it reasonable to expect workers in health, education and housing services to become experts in grant-awarding and charge-remitting for the relief of financial hardship?*

Can expertise in cash welfare be safely detached from social work? After prolonged trial of other methods, we have reached the conclusion that social work is indivisible. Now that we have in our social services departments (more perhaps in Scotland than in England) at least the prototype of a unified welfare service, deliberately intended to deal with *all* aspects of personal and family needs, is it not unrealistic to go on separating income-welfare from other welfare needs? Is not welfare, too, indivisible? It is at least arguable that a department whose prime duty is to think about

* The majority in 1909 thought not: 'The existing educational and sanitary authorities ought not . . . to be converted into agencies for the distribution of relief; and the less their functions are associated with the idea of relief, the better they will perform the public work for which they were specially called into existence' (Royal Commission 1909).

well-being and the removal of distress from all angles—in the 1909 majority's words, 'a disinterested authority, practised in looking at all sides of a question'—is much better placed than any other service to take those 'odious pecuniary inquiries' in its stride, handle them with skill and sensitivity, and use its powers constructively.

Leaving aside the extremely intricate question of the relationships between the social services and other local government departments on the one hand and the Supplementary Benefits Commission on the other,* there remains the more elementary question of how far social services departments consider they have a duty to inform their clients—and indeed the wider public—of their possible entitlement to various benefits and to take steps to help them claim what they may be entitled to.

Case records kept by the welfare services commonly have a space in which are entered some details of the client's income and other resources; rent, rates and certain other commitments; numbers of dependants, and the like. But this information usually seems to be recorded solely for the one issue of the moment: Shall she have free home help or chiropody? How much shall they pay for supporting their child in care? What shall we charge her for using our day nursery? What do they need to pay off their rent arrears? I have yet to see a case record† containing a benefit check list such as would encourage the social worker, in view of the resources, needs and commitments of the person or family concerned,

(a) to tick off benefits for which they may be eligible, e.g.:
supplementary benefit
family income supplement
free welfare milk
free school meals
school clothing grant
educational maintenance allowance
rate relief

* For thoughtful discussions see Stevenson (1970) and Heywood (1971).

† One of the few recent papers on the design of case records (Edmonds 1971) makes no reference to the possibility that it might be relevant to record the client's income and other financial circumstances.

rent allowance or rebate
attendance allowance
invalidity benefit
old person's pension
prescription 'season ticket'
remission of denture charges;

(b) to note any action to be taken in view of (a);
(c) to record the outcome of action taken under (b).

The future of the relief function

The foregoing reflections relate to the role of the social services department as it is, and is likely to be, in its initial years. Social workers dislike the relief function. The British Association of Social Workers has complained (1971) that 'social workers already spend far too much time investigating entitlement to means-tested benefits and helping with applications'. Can they—should they—be spared this work? The easy answer is to say that someone else should do it—meaning in practice people less well trained than social workers, less socially alert and critical, less far-sighted, quite possibly less wise and less humane.

The obvious way of passing the responsibility elsewhere is to complete the nationalisation of relief. The Supplementary Benefits Commission or other state agencies, not employing social workers, should be quite capable of administering (a) rating relief and rent asistance, and (b) all grants and charge remissions under the Education Act, from school dinner charges to student grants. Could state agencies (c) also administer charges for home help and day nurseries; payments for child fostering and charges for children in care; charges for people in temporary accommodation or hostels, for mobile meals and other services? Would it be in the best interest of people in need to complete the divorce of cash welfare from service welfare? If all local government relief functions were nationalised, especially those in (c), for how long would the associated services remain in local government? Is a social service, not staffed by social workers, confined to the single function of making a money contribution towards the removal of distress, ever likely to function constructively and preventively? Two decades' experience of nationalised assistance is hardly encouraging.

The less easy way out is to work for systematic reduction in the scope of the relief function. The big issues here, however, are beyond the compass of social services departments or of local government. They depend on national policies and involve sizeable increases in social spending—and probably in taxation—in some directions. Some simplification will certainly be achieved if the Government realise their ambition of 'using a single claim form for a wide range of benefits administered by both central government and local authorities' (Wilmott 1972). More could be achieved if more local authorities followed the example of the few which have already dropped all charges for family planning services, or considered whether, in their local circumstances, charging for a service like home help is still appropriate.*

But only Parliament can make the decisive changes. As examples:

(1) Age-related family allowances (as proposed by Beveridge), coupled with abolition of child tax reliefs and other tax reforms, and combined with free school meals, would (a) make most other child payments (including aid to pupils) unnecessary, and (b) greatly reduce the scope of the rent assistance scheme.

(2) If nearly all old people had pensions (state and/or occupational) sufficient for their subsistence needs, coupled perhaps with rent allowances, the SBC's caseload could be halved. Other measures to improve provision for single-handed mothers and the chronic sick, and a return to full employment, could halve its caseload again.

(3) Relieved of its mass means-testing function, scaled down to being an agency of last resort for exceptional minorities, the SBC would be in a far better position to work constructively for the welfare of its clients. But its deficiencies as an agency confined to cash relief would then become more evident. And with a caseload so reduced, there would be only 8,000 or 10,000 persons (and even fewer *cases*) needing regular payments at any one time in the area of the average British social services department after the impending local government reorganisation. In these circumstances, should they ever become attainable, the balance of advantage would lie with abolishing the SBC, denationalising assistance, vesting in social services departments undivided responsibility for the

* The medical officer of a London borough advised his council 'that the home help service should be given free. The saving on the cost of administrative time would approximately balance the income received from levying charges'. Was he talking sense? His council rejected his advice (Worpole 1972).

residual relief of financial hardship, and reverting (in Marshall's words) to 'the ancient tradition of the Western world'—still the current tradition of our European neighbours—'that the relief of the poor was the affair of their neighbours'.

References

British Association of Social Workers (1971) 'Statement on recent government decisions on social service expenditure, charges and exemptions', *Soc. Wk. Today*, 1, 12.

British Association of Social Workers (1972) 'Memorandum on Housing Finance Bill', *Soc. Wk. Today*, 2, 20.

Children and Young Persons Act (1963) Section 1. HMSO, London.

Edmonds, J. (1971) 'The case record', *Soc. Wk. Today*, 2, 14.

Greater London Council (1971) *Papers*, 14 December.

Heywood, J. S. & Allen, B. K. (1971) *Financial Help in Social Work.* Manchester University Press, Manchester.

Marshall, T. H. (1965) *Social Policy*. Hutchinson, London.

Royal Commission on the Poor Laws and Relief of Distress (1909) *Majority Report*, Cmnd. 4499. HMSO, London.

Stevenson, O. (1970) 'The problems of individual need and fair shares for all', *Soc. Wk. Today*, 1, 1.

Wilmott, P. (1972) 'Westminster Comment', *Soc. Wk. Today*, 2, 20.

Worpole, K. (1972) 'Why read on?' *New Soc.*, 16 March.

Conclusions

Malcolm J. Brown

It is not possible to go far in the examination of any social issue before becoming acutely aware that grossly unsatisfactory states exist in this country at the present time. Indeed, it would seem that in a number of issues immediately relevant to human welfare, there has been a deterioration in conditions over the years, despite central and local government intervention. While it is possible that our improved conceptualisation of problems and our greater sensitivity may account for a proportion of what appears to be marked deterioration, clearly welfare rights and welfare services offered to the community have not achieved the high hopes that a caring society originally had for them.

It seems that there are two main reasons for this. Firstly, many social problems are far more complex and intractable than had originally been supposed; and secondly, far more resources in the form of money and personnel need to be given to welfare services if there is to be any substantial change in the present position. Improvements need to take the form both of direct payments and of higher quality personal social services. This book has concentrated on social issues and seeing them primarily in relation to the implications for social services departments, and it has become most apparent that central government provision (or lack of it) vitally affects the functioning of these departments. It is necessary to pose the question, 'As a society, how do we want to treat our old people, our sick and disabled, our mentally disordered, our neglected, our foolish, our undeserving?' If the answer to these is 'niggardly' then we are right to carry on at our present level. If we want to be generous, however, if we want to show real concern, then there has to be a deep commitment to giving far more, as of right, by central government in pensions and allowances. Analysis of the circumstances of clients of the personal social services highlights all too clearly that the great proportion are impoverished and almost all of this group are totally dependent upon central government funds. Where these funds are inadequate (and where are they not), then this fact must seriously restrict the impact that the local authority can have; for it cannot, in any meaningful sense, top up central government provision to an adequate level. While it might and does appropriately give ad hoc services which are primarily financial, its provision of continuing services are not—nor should they be. One legitimate function, therefore, of the present social services is to spell out categorically the consequences of central government parsimony.

For the local authority services, the government's ten-year plan envisages that the expenditure is likely, in real terms, to double over the next ten years, and that there will also be a doubling in the number of local authority social workers. While half a loaf is invariably better than nothing at all, the great increase in the numbers of people coming forward or being referred for service does suggest that even this doubling of expenditure and the number of workers over the next ten years will still mean that we will be offering a very low level of service. It is simply not possible therefore to avoid the basic question, 'What quality service are we to give?' If we are striving for standards of excellence, then local authorities must be prepared to take things far more seriously than many are doing at present. Only when this matter has been settled can many other plans be legitimately developed.

Certainly, it is most central to the genericism/specialism concept. If we want to provide a mediocre service then it would seem that having nearly all social workers functioning generically would be the most economic way of achieving this. If we are concerned to have a quality service, however, then obviously specialist social workers are required; for it is nonsense to suppose seriously that workers can function at the highest level of skill in a wide range of types and services. And functioning at a high level of skill is a prerequisite for top quality service. It therefore becomes a matter not primarily of having the generic worker but of having a generic team, a team having within it both generic and specialist social workers with a mix appropriate to the needs of the area served. The generic period following unification is, however, contributing to defining some of the forms of specialisms likely to be needed.

Many authorities, aware of the certain difficulties to be experienced by workers moving into a generic role, retained specialist consultants. These were people experienced in one of the fields of child care, mental health, or the welfare of the elderly and disabled. In most cases the function of the consultant has been to advise inexperienced workers about the handling of specific cases. The consultant role has caused much confusion and frustration in practice. Often there has been uncertainty as to whether the consultants actually carry executive authority and therefore whether or not it is legitimate to ignore their advice, should one choose to do so. Senior social workers and area officers have tended to resent their workers getting advice from people other than themselves and have seen the presence of consultants as an adverse reflection upon their own skills and knowledge. Often consultants have been given fairly low-status positions in the department, and where this has been the case, the quality of their consultancy services has been questioned. Certainly they have been able to serve as a repository of knowledge which they can communicate to those who will listen to them, but while knowledge is an essential factor in social work, a quality service requires skill as well. This cannot easily be picked up from a few contacts with the consultant. The indications are that consultants are best used and find greater job satisfaction when their position is plugged in higher up the hierarchy, and where there is less involvement with the individual case but rather a concentration on the specialism. Indeed, to keep pace with developments in, say, alcoholism and drug addiction and to communicate appropriately to departmental staff on these subjects can be a full-time job.

It may be that the lower-grade consultant served a purpose in the early days of unification by imparting knowledge relevant to the individual client, but this role will undoubtedly fall away, and consultants remaining need to be based within the headquarter's team. While the original consultancy role closely followed the pre-unification lines, as with the specialist social workers, new ones are likely to emerge.

While experience of the generic social workers and the consultants have helped to clarify likely specialist needs, no definitive and comprehensive statements can be made at the moment, but specialisms in alcoholism and drug addictions, matrimonial and family relationships, mental health and MSW/PSW hybrids for medical general practice work would appear to be a few of a number worthy of serious consideration.

Much social work education is currently concentrated on the generic approach. This marked shift from the specific to the general came about with very little evidence to justify it and if a high quality education is to be offered to the field, certainly some specialisms will need to be introduced. The great difference for the specialisms of the future from those of the pre-unification era may well be that instead of offering a specialism within the basic training that generically trained workers will be given the opportunity of returning to the universities and polytechnics after a year or so's experience in the field. The opportunity to have done some 'across the board' work may assist workers to make a better choice when selecting a specialist training. Currently almost all social work teaching institutes are overwhelmed with applications for basic training. If, however, quality becomes the keynote of the day some resources must be given over to specialist work and therefore specialist training.

Neither should the enormous demands for social work training be allowed to prevent adequate social service management training from getting underway. Never before in local authority history have so many management roles so suddenly been created with so few opportunities to equip officers to fill them successfully. While a few social work education institutions have offered emergency courses for top and middle social services management, these have been far too short. It is folly to train thousands of social workers for service in hierarchical organisations yet do nothing by way of training to ensure that those rapidly promoted to manage them are enabled to do this. Yet at the time of writing this would appear to be the approach of both central government and the Central Council for Education and Training in Social Work.

Because people's problems do not fall neatly within departmental boundaries, the narrow 'hands off' attitude of some departments must be got to grips with. As was stated earlier, unification of the local authority personal social services is only one rational step. Health, housing, education and social work outside of the local authority are not automatically harmonised either with one another or with the personal social services. Yet clearly each, for good or for ill, will be much affected by the others and will itself affect them. While the concept of corporate management in the fullest sense remains very much an ideal in local authorities, it makes nothing but good sense to ensure that the policies of the department are at the very least not in conflict with one another, and that there is some sharing of information about what is going on. Corporate management lends itself to a 'going through the motions' process and if it becomes accepted local authority behaviour, energies will be consumed in putting up the pretence, while activities and relationships on all-important matters remain basically unchanged. Better by far to be less ambitious at least in the early stages and start with attempts at reasonable co-operation.

Outside the local authority, by far the most important area where full co-operation is vital is between the personal social services and the health authorities. Currently the quality of these relationships varies enormously from one part of the country to another. With the best will in the world, good relationships are not easy to achieve. The doctors are immersed in and preoccupied with their own reorganisation and the respective boundaries of health and social services will not always be conterminous. Often there is not the best will in the world; social services are cocky about their emergence and their newly found power. Rather like the adolescent cocking a snook at the authority of an adult, they are anxious to show medicine that they are not the docile subservient handmaids that they once were. Doctors have been so used to having others work for them and not with them that much resentment about the unified departments still exists. The strong likelihood that social workers in hospitals will become part of the local authority reorganisation does not in the short term help matters. Attempts to hold down social services emergence, however, are as futile as an angry parent attempting to stop his son from growing up. Yet some doctors seem to try to do this. Both doctors and social workers are deeply committed to the services of those in need, however, and once there is full realisation that patients and clients are suffering because of their animosities, they may succeed in working together.

In total, the human problems are so complex and so numerous, and developing and utilising relationships, with, say, health, housing and education so time-consuming that it is legitimate to wonder what else the social services department can do. It is all the more difficult if there is a real desire to raise the quality of service to a high level from the mediocrity that currently prevails. The Seebohm Committee saw the department reaching far beyond the discovery and rescue of social casualties, and the greatest possible number of individuals being enabled, through the department, to act reciprocally giving and receiving service 'for the well-being' of the whole community. These are rousing words which, like a call to arms, tend to evoke an uncritical response. Stopping to examine them, however, they do pose a number of points that require examination. The department is involved with only the smallest proportion of kindly acts that take place daily within a community. Neighbours are invited in for tea, children are minded, old folks given a meal, acquaintances driven to visit relatives in hospital, and limitless other informal means of helping one another take place, all without the knowledge of the department. This is the reciprocal giving and receiving of service within the community. Where needs cannot be met by these means, then it is often necessary for voluntary agencies to be involved, linking those requiring service with those having the time and desire to help. While many who give service are likely to require to help themselves later on in life, the likelihood of reciprocity in any restricted period of time is small. By and large at any time people either need a service or are able to give one. By the time we get to the social services department, the reciprocity notion is even more unlikely to be a valid one. The department employs professional staff to give a service to those who need it. Obviously the rewards of helping others are great, but the idea of helping one day and being helped yourself the next, on any significant scale, is unrealistic. Even if the department took upon itself the role of involving community members with one another and whipping-up good neighbourliness, true reciprocity would be unlikely to materialise. More important, it is perhaps questionable whether the department has a legitimate role in seeking to influence the community generally. A few local authorities, with heavy Home Office backing, have attempted some community development projects. They have all been confined to small, rather deprived areas and with only one or two exceptions, have all failed badly. Usually the social services departments have not been involved. To suggest that these ideas should be universally applied and that a blanket community development service should be given by departments is something that requires far more consideration than the Seebohm Committee gave to it. It is very doubtful whether departments have much to contribute to the community en bloc by way of setting guidelines for living and interacting; and the idea that they have is one that will be strongly resisted if serious attempts are made to act out this new and revolutionary concept.

To discover and rescue social casualties and to offer a comprehensive and top quality service to all in need of personal social services help is something currently far beyond the finances, staffing and skills of the present department (as the chapters in this book have shown) and will continue to be so well into the future. But this is the area of concentration to which all intermediate goals, plans and programmes must be directed. Any attempts to try and do something for everybody, apart from being ethically highly questionable, can only dilute these efforts and deflect departments from the vital tasks to which they have been assigned.

Index

(*Numbers in brackets indicate chapter reference lists*)

Index